Love, Groucho

Love, Groucho

Letters from Groucho Marx to His Daughter Miriam

Edited by Miriam Marx Allen

Faber and Faber

BOSTON • LONDON

Photographs from the collection of Miriam Marx Allen

Library of Congress Cataloging-in-Publication Data

Marx, Grouch, 1891–1977.
Love, Groucho : letters from Groucho Marx to his daughter Miriam /
edited by Miriam Marx Allen.
p.   cm.
ISBN 0-571-12915-3 (cloth)
1. Marx, Groucho, 1891–1977—Correspondence.   2. Allen, Miriam
Marx, 1927–   —Correspondence.   3. Comedians—United States—
Correspondence.   I. Allen, Miriam Marx, 1927–   . II. Title.
PN2287.M53A4   1992
792.7′028′092—dc20
[B]   91–44205
CIP

Cover design by Catherine Hopkins

Printed in the United States of America

Contents

❖   ❖   ❖

With love to my late father,
Groucho Marx

Foreword

*   *   *

Here is another side of Groucho.
    It's a dimension of this complex genius that you won't find
anywhere else, and a side of him many people will find surprising. Occasionally you hear admirers of his wit opine that he was probably a
cold man, perhaps because wit by itself can be a chilling thing. I can
honestly say that even before I got to know him I never shared this impression. Even at the relatively tender age at which I watched "You
Bet Your Life" (I caught up with the movies in later life), anyone who
didn't find him funny was off my list; and any witless boob who added,
"because he insults people," received the full blast of my teenage scorn.
It seemed clear to me that he was always good-natured and that only
those insulated against humor and devoid of perception could take
umbrage.
    This is not to suggest that these remarkable letters to Miriam, one
of his three offspring, abound in gushy sentimentality. But amidst the
abundant humor—which he adjusts appropriately as she grows
older—there emerges that age-old stock character, the Concerned Parent. And with all the usual appurtenances: hope for her happiness,
fears about her health both physical and mental and worry about her
boyfriends, driving, spending habits and all the other insomnia-
enhancing cares of a proud but fearful father.
    Groucho's need to be admired by his daughter leads him to con-
stantly inform her of upcoming appearances on radio with Dinah
Shore and others, and he is disappointed when she has not mentioned
them in her letters. And when she criticizes them, he accepts with dis-
arming grace.
    It is sometimes sadly clear that he is reminding her and himself that
he is wanted and employed. I am amazed at how frequently he was

out of work, how unappreciated he felt, and how much he had to, or at least did, worry about money. Later, when the game show comes along, he assumes it will be the last of his many failures in radio, and when the ratings go through the roof and he is the toast of the nation again, his spirits soar.

In a relatively early letter we see a man basking in the happiness of a tranquil home and good kids and a dog he loves and enough work to please him. Years later, when he asks for Miriam's understanding of the collapse of the second of his three failed marriages, the earlier scene becomes heartbreaking in retrospect. Detractors have said that he drove three wives to alcoholism, and whether he did or aggravated their problems we'll never know. But something in this highly sensitive man undid three attempts at the home and hearth existence that he so clearly craved.

If the ancient Greeks were right that the gods envy and punish the gifted, the brilliant and sensitive Julius Marx is prime evidence. But the loneliness and suffering that he endured are only hinted at here, and he is careful not to be sorry for himself in front of his daughter.

Of all the the arts, Groucho admired writing, and writers, the most and Miriam's talent for it makes him pleased and proud, showing her works to his brainy and illustrious writer friends and passing on their doubtless genuine praise. His own superb writing is hardly revealed here for the first time, but his mastery of the letter form is a thing to savor.

It's both revealing and surprising how many doubts and insecurities peep through the letters and how fearful he could be about his (of all things) ability to rise to the occasion when called on to speak extemporaneously. You want to shake him and say, "Good God, man, you're Groucho Marx!" His elation when the results are brilliant on such occasions is touching.

I doubt that many fans will read the letters straight through at one sitting as I did, but if there was ever a perfect bedside book, this is it. However the reader budgets his or her time, the perks are many: Groucho's opinions good and bad of contemporaries, his political views, his comments on writers, all are splendid stuff. An imaginary conversation with his beloved dog Duke and a six-line bit of dialogue with a soldier are worth the price of admission.

In one letter, he explains (so Miriam won't be jealous?) why he is putting his very small daughter Melinda on the quiz show. He feels that his roue image may need some tempering:

. . . since this can be a fairly disgusting character, I think the injection of a small innocent girl bleating the lyrics of Oscar Hammerstein may be helpful in letting the onlookers know that there is another side of this nauseating character . . . the father and stern parent, head of the household, bulwark of the American home, ready at a moment's notice to fight for Old Glory and the land he loves.

On this patriotic note, I will sign off, hoping you are the same.

Love and kisses.

And on that note, I commend to you what follows: these sweet, touching and hilarious letters from a man I assume you miss as much as I do.

Dick Cavett

Acknowledgments

✻   ✻   ✻

I want to thank all my associates and friends who have been so supportive and loving to me throughout my work on this book. I particularly want to mention my good friend Alexandra Garrett. Alexandra died unexpectedly just prior to the publication of this book and I am deeply indebted to her. She was a wonderful friend and I will miss her very much. Special thanks go to my friend and literary agent, Charlotte Gusay, who took the raw material I sent her and fashioned it into a book and then persevered until she found the right publishing house for it. I also want to thank my terrific editor, Betsy Uhrig, who has worked long and hard to make this book what it is and who had the vision to pursue it in the first place. And many thanks in particular to Frank Ferrante (who not only plays Groucho but at times is Groucho); to Paul Weslowski (a walking Groucho encyclopedia); Jane Fay, Jane Hart, Charlie Kochman, Lois Montgomery and Sandra Orchin. There are many other people who have helped me, too numerous to mention, but they know who they are. I want to thank them, one and all.

Introduction

"Someday this bitter ache will pass, my sweet . . .
Time wounds all heels."
—a Groucho Marx line from his 1940 film *Go West*

The remarkable life and seventy-two-year career of the great comedian Groucho Marx, his three wives, two daughters, one son and
a laugh a minute—I survived it all. Mine is the story of some fifty years
of unique moments and survival techniques with Groucho Marx, my
father. It is a fond remembrance of a cherished father-daughter relationship, with a few "bitter aches" and "wounded heels" thrown in to
keep it honest.

My father was a great deal of joy and fun, as well as a stern parent
during my growing up years, and I have nothing but good feelings
about him. There is one complaint I could make: quite possibly
Groucho made himself too important in my life. He was so interesting
and humorous that he made the boys and men I dated seem dull in
comparison. After all, what teenage boy could compete with a grown
man who was both famous and charming?

These letters were written to me by my father over a period of nearly thirty years from 1938 to 1967. During those years, whenever we
were apart, we wrote to each other, and I am glad to say I kept most
of this correspondence. I hope that Groucho's letters to me will be of
interest to his public because they show a side of Groucho Marx which
has not heretofore been publicized.

Groucho wrote letters to everyone: famous people, not so famous
people, to his family, to his friends, sometimes to his enemies. He was
a first-rate and prolific letter writer. Groucho's letters to me, however,
are different from the others. Groucho tended to let his hair down
quite a bit more in his letters to me. He told me things he would not
tell even some of his best friends. Padre's letters to me are full of his

creative intelligence, his angst, his anger, his love and above all that comic spirit which pervaded his life.

Groucho complained throughout the years that I did not write him often enough. Considering the enormous amount of correspondence he sent to me, I can understand why he thought I was writing him too infrequently. No one could have kept up with him. He scratched out handwritten letters when he was away from home, unless he was someplace where he had access to a typewriter. When he was home, he usually pounded out letters to me on his typewriter, and sometimes his letters were dictated to his secretary. (Groucho had two secretaries during the time these letters were written: Rachel Linden and Sara Roberts. Each made comments or sent affectionate footnotes on some of the letters.)

Padre was very interested in politics and the economic problems of the world, and he instilled this interest in me at a very early age. For this I will always be grateful. Unlike the parents of many of my friends and peers, Groucho never considered me "just a child" who should not be concerned with or discuss what was going on in the world. Politics, and his interest in them, is a theme that runs throughout his letters to me—in the best "liberal Democratic" tradition.

Reviewing the letters now I find them to reveal an intensely loving relationship between Groucho and me, between a famous father and his daughter. I am not going to tell you that my father and I never had our differences—what parents and offspring don't? For me these letters are evidence that we loved one another very much. I am proud of my father and happy to share these marvelous letters.

Groucho was a wonderful father—anger, humor, warts and all. I loved him very much and feel very fortunate to have been his daughter.

A Note on the Letters and Accompanying Text

This book contains most of the correspondence my father sent me with the exception of very short notes consisting mainly of travel or business details, telegrams and cards. Several postcards have been included. The letters are as close to chronological in presentation as I could make them. Many of the letters were not dated; dates appearing in brackets are postmark dates or approximate dates. A location appearing in brackets indicates that the letter was written on hotel stationery or a postcard.

Almost all of the letters appear here in their entirety. Occasional personal, business or travel details have been omitted and a few times whole pages were missing and had to be left out. I have noted where this happens. Groucho's secretaries often wrote notes at the end of his letters to me. These have been included where they contained something I felt would be of interest to the reader; otherwise they have been left out.

The spelling of names is as correct as possible, except in cases where I think a mispelling was intentional, or where I find it revealing. I have identified in my notes many people mentioned in the letters who may not be familiar to the reader and whose identities cannot be easily gleaned from the context of the letters themselves. I have also explained the circumstances in which certain letters were written in order to clarify what was being said. I have tried, however, to keep my notes to a minimum, allowing the letters to speak for themselves.

Love, Groucho

I was born in New York City on May 19, 1927. My father, Julius H. "Groucho" Marx, wrote his first letter to me when I was eleven years old. He was forty-eight years old and already a star then, having appeared with his brothers Chico, Harpo, Gummo and Zeppo (in various combinations) on stage, radio and in such films as Animal Crackers, Monkey Business, Horse Feathers *and* Duck Soup. *We lived in Beverly Hills with my mother, Ruth, and my brother, Arthur, who is six years older than I am.*

August 3, 1938

Dear Beautiful,
Sorry you were seasick and quite surprised — always had an idea you'd be a terrific sailor, but I guess you're just a landlubber, like your dad. We're very glad to know that you're homesick because if you weren't we'd feel that you were very happy away from us and this way, we know that you miss us. This is a very selfish viewpoint on our part but parents are frequently selfish, too, like children.

By a strange coincidence, the day after you wrote to Anne Graham, a letter came from her. I'm enclosing it along with this, so you'll get two letters for the price of one!

It's awfully quiet around here: the cat looks depressed and insulted; Shep peers around moodily and barks at the moon; there's no debris lying on the floor; the stairs don't shake and the whole household moves along without a sound. Believe me, we'll be glad when next week comes and the customary fighting, screaming and kicking between you and Arthur gets in full swing for the winter season. I took a swimming lesson yesterday from Tony at the club and I know it's a little late in life for that sort of thing, but it did me a lot of good. When you get back, I expect to race you the length of the pool. Around the club, I'm now known as the "Silver Streak." Betty Alexander keeps inquiring about you so perhaps you'll decide to stay in Catalina forever.

Love and kisses from your madre and padre and hurry home!
Groucho

This letter was written when I was in Catalina vacationing with our next door neighbors. My father got seasick whenever he went anywhere near the water.

3

Anne Graham was the girlfriend of playwright, producer, director and family friend Norman (sometimes called Kras) Krasna. Betty Alexander was the daughter of tennis player Fred Alexander. She and I didn't get along. We had called my father Padre ever since my brother had learned that it was Spanish for father.

August 4, 1939

Dear Mir;

Received your note this morning, from the length of it I wouldn't dignify it by calling it a letter; all I can gather from it is the feeling that you never want to come home. It's really not safe to allow a child away from home alone, because they get to realize too quickly that they don't need their parents.

I am sorry that you can't see the back lot now where we are shooting the circus stuff. It's full of circus clowns and elephants and you could realize your dream of riding on the elephant's back, and swinging from high trapezes. However, I imagine you are having a better time up at the ranch, and I guess it's just as well.

You can have a field day with the funnies when you return. I have piled up eight *New York Telegrams* and I can see you now on the floor blinking at Tillie the Toiler or whoever is in the funnies.

The house is terribly quiet now, with Arthur in Coronado and you away, and even Lillian admitted that she would be glad to clear up the mess you make when you get through with a fudge orgy, if you were only home. Duke has grown considerably and is beginning to resemble a water buffalo in size. His feet are plenty large and I think he has a good deal of growing to do before he is finished. The other day he ate half a ping-pong racket and he seemed to think it was pretty good. Some night if he is real good I may let him eat a baseball bat for dessert.

Well Darling, I must go to the studio now and be funny. (Oh yeah.) Have a good time. Lots of love and kisses, and hey—when are you coming home?

Your Da Da

The film he was shooting was At the Circus *(1939).*

[Book-Cadillac Hotel, Detroit] May 7, 1940

Dear Miriam:
You're a little louse, and probably by the time I get back—a big one.
I appreciate your position. I know you must be very busy and that you
have very little time for correspondence. Luckily, time hangs heavily
on my hands, and I practically have the whole day to myself except
for a few rehearsals and four or five performances. Anyway, it was
nice to hear from you and to know that you scored such a big success
with your new boyfriend. You have quite a staff now, and it must be
rather difficult for you to keep their various characteristics separated.

I dreamed of you the other night—all night in fact. I dreamed I was
taking you through the ghetto in New York City and showing you the
pushcarts and tenements and delicatessens, and you seemed quite interested. Some day I really want to show you this. Perhaps this year,
if I'm lucky.

We are leaving here Thursday night after the show and flying to
Chicago. I know you would like that. This saves us an all-night
pullman journey and getting up early in the morning.

I hope you are practicing the piano, although I doubt it. Without
Uncle Tom there to lash you on, I imagine that your practicing has become about as frequent as the visits of the eclipse.

I am very anxious to see your room, and I'll bet it looks beautiful.
If it does, it will just match you.

If you are not too busy, you might write me to the Chicago Theatre.
Love and kisses,
Groucho

[The Warwick Hotel, New York] October 26, 1941

Dear Darling;
Your mother keeps asking me every day, is there a letter from Miriam?
I keep saying "No" because you wrote in the letter you sent the piece
about Grandma, and asked me not to show it to your mother. In the
future, if you want to complain about her folks, you will have to write
two letters, one to her and one to me.

Well, Kras's show opened and it was a flop. It wasn't bad, but apparently the audiences are sick of plays about Nazis and their problems, and I think it will probably be off the boards in about another
week. It's too bad. This is a tough racket, and all the heartaches and
sleepless nights make it a pretty thankless profession, unless of course

you are one of the lucky few who put over a hit, and then everything looks different, and all the anxious moments are forgotten. Well, enough of this philosophizing.

How are you and my dog Duke? You apparently think Duke belongs to you, don't you? Well I had it out with Duke one day when we were together on the bike. I said, Duke, who do you belong to? Miriam or me? He looked up at me and winked. He said, I like Miriam, she is a nice kid and occasionally brushes my coat and throws me a bone, but to compare her to you is sheer folly. Why Groucho old boy, you are my man. That's the first time he had ever called me Groucho, and believe me I was thrilled to my fingertips. He usually calls me Julius, and to hear him saying Groucho affected me deeply. Well anyway, as he trotted along beside the bike he continued, you know I can never forget the hundreds of miles we've done together in rain and sunshine, the dogs I have fought and run from, the cats I have pursued up trees, I've lived my life with you and I can never be anyone's but yours.

Well, I miss him a lot and you too. I have never been attached to a dog like I am to this one, no, not even Shep. This is probably because I have been much closer to this one. If you see him around the house, kiss him for me.

I am so glad that Susie is out of danger and that she is on the way to recovery. I like Susie and be sure and give her my best and if you see her around the house, you can kiss her for me along with the dog.

I had a long letter from the Jerk Sisters. They managed to fill up seven or eight pages of trivia with what is going on around Westwood and its environs (in case you are puzzled, environs means neighborhood).

My plans are still uncertain, but they are close to the stage where I will certainly make a decision one way or another.

Had a letter from Irv Brecher. He has completed a play and is on the way East with it. I hope he has better luck than Sheekman and Kras had with their plays. It's a tough business this thing of being a playwright and takes a hell of a lot of skill. Kras is a little crushed, but you know Kras; he will bounce right up with something bigger and better.

I am glad you are back with George Englund if that's who it is. I think Pascal is a little on the mature side for you, and I would prefer you to go out with boys closer to your age.

Well my queen, I have to go now and do a million things. All my love to you and as many kisses as you will accept.

Your Pappy. Groucho, Julius, Padre, Shorty.

Did you hear me on "Information, Please"?

The Jerk Sisters (a term of affection) were Winnie and Frances, two friends of my father's who owned the Harper Method Beauty Salon in Westwood. My father and I went there to get our scalps massaged (by the "Harper Method") and our feet scratched. Irv Brecher was a screenwriter and director (he wrote At the Circus *and* Go West *[1940]). Sheekman (sometimes called Sheek) was the screenwriter and producer Arthur Sheekman who worked with the Marx Brothers on a number of projects and was a good friend of my father's. George Englund was the son of screenwriter Ken Englund and actress Mabel (Albertson) Englund. Pascal was Steve Pascal, the son of a family friend.*

[The Warwick Hotel, New York] November 1, 1941

Dear Orphan,

You must be very happy now with the whole house at your command and the flunkies under your thumb, but I imagine you'd rather be here in New York throwing nuts at the squirrels, or vice versa. Today Arthur and I were going to the Army-Notre Dame game with Salwyn Schufro providing lunch, transportation and tickets. Unfortunately, a small gale blew in from the northwest and deposited about five inches of rain on New York City. So I came to the conclusion that I'd better stick in my room at the Warwick, and not sit in the open Yankee Stadium and brave pneumonia.

I am not crazy about football, but I kind of would have liked to have seen this particular game. It's an extremely colorful game. The army boys march and drill, and go through all sorts of military maneuvers that I think would have been worth watching. Plus this: both teams are undefeated, and they always play each other a tough match. Tonight your brother and myself and the Ken Englunds (your future father- and mother-in-law) are going to see Norman Krasna's play, now named *The Man With Blond Hair*. I have seen it once, but it was such a curious audience, mostly shopgirls out of Macy's and Gimbel's, and it was pretty hard to determine what the actual values of the play are.

You would have loved that audience. They all spoke with that Bronx accent that you are so in love with. You know, like the shopgirls on the records from the "Pins and Needles" show. The Kalmar and Ruby show opened last night and went pretty well. The critics, however, didn't care much for it, and it is very uncertain what its future will be. It is terribly important for both Kalmar and Ruby that this play survives, for if it clicks they probably can get a job again in Hollywood, so when you say those long prayers of yours at night before you go to sleep (which I imagine now is around midnight), throw in an extra prayer for Bert and Harry.

About my own plans I am very indefinite, but I should know something in the next ten days or so. So study hard, drink lots of milk, bathe frequently, hang up all your clothes, keep your room tidy, pay particular attention to your homework, don't use any lip rouge, wear a raincoat and rubbers when it is raining, brush your teeth thoroughly, masticate your food slowly, eat very little candy, don't flirt with those big nasty boys at Beverly High, see that Duke is brushed and bathed daily, don't give the girls any backtalk and keep those big mitts off the Capehart. This long-winded preamble is just to tell you that I love you and wish you were here. Write soon, because I always get a belly-laugh out of your childish scrawl.

Your doting padre

Salwyn Shufro was my father's stockbroker. Groucho refers to the Englunds as my future in-laws here because I had such a crush on George. Kalmar and Ruby were screenwriter Bert Kalmar and composer/lyricist Harry Ruby, who collaborated on Duck Soup *(1933), among many other things. The Kalmar and Ruby show referred to here was probably* High Kickers. *The Capehart was a very expensive phonograph.*

November 14, 1941

Dear Pooch,

As you can well understand, things are a little confused, and will probably remain that way for some time. I'm leaving here and will arrive home on the twenty-eighth. That'll be two weeks from the day this letter is written. I would rather have come home sooner, but I have to play a benefit, called the Night of Stars, on the twenty-sixth, and will leave the day after. So you see, the whole thing comes out even.

Professionally, my plan is to begin almost immediately with Norman, rewriting our play, and should complete that by the first of January. If I do, I'll get drunk New Year's. From then in, my plans are up in the air. I probably won't do much of anything. Perhaps a few radio shots, if I can get them. If not, you know the usual routine. Duke and the bicycle, Winnie and Frances, Gilbert and Sullivan, and Armstrong and Schroeder.

Tonight we are going to the theatre with your prospective mother- and father-in-law. I guess you know I'm referring to the Ken Englunds. I imagine your mother will be coming home also around that time. There is very little left for me to see in the theatre, and those that I miss I'll see eventually as movies, made by RKO at a tremendous loss.

Arthur is very happy playing the role of business tycoon. He wears his hat on the back of his head now, smokes long, black cigars and pretty soon will be taking bicarbonate of soda. I have a lot to tell you when I see you—things that are hard to write in a letter, but they can wait. I had a long, seven-page letter from the Jerk Sisters. Luckily, the handwriting is so undecipherable that most of the letter couldn't be understood. The gist of the letter as I gathered was that you had accompanied them to Olvera Street, and then went home again. When a letter gets to this stage, the best thing to do is to close it.

Love and kisses from all of us, and take it from a man who's had many years' experience as a Don Juan, don't, under any circumstances, pursue George. It'll only ruin the whole set-up. Be sure he does the chasing.

Your padre

Armstrong and Schroeder's was a restaurant in Beverly Hills. It was during this trip to New York that my mother and father decided to split up. This is probably what he meant by "things that are hard to write in a letter."

[November 17, 1941]

Note: What's his name and address?

Dear Dick,
From your letter, you could be called "Poor Richard," because your letter, which Miriam read to me, was certainly a pessimistic one. I am a little surprised at the general tone of them. I haven't read all of them but Miriam has read two or three of them to me over a period of weeks and they contain a defeatist attitude that is extremely disquieting.

I am reluctant to advise you about your life. I doubt whether I am qualified to do that. I am constantly making mistakes of my own and I'm sure I'll continue to do so as long as I live. However, you must snap our of your dejection. You must also learn not to be surprised when you encounter anti-Semitism. This has, to my knowledge, existed for at least twenty centuries, but I'm sure that history will prove (despite the fact that it still flourishes all over the world) that it is definitely decreasing. Your case is not an isolated one. It exists, to a degree, in all the branches of the armed forces and in civilian life. It is bigotry based on ignorance and it will only be solved as the bigots become educated. Needless for me to tell you, though I intend to, it is up to you to comport yourself in such a manner that you will eventually gain their respect.

Offhand, I would say that this is pretty dull stuff—it is unquestionably bromidic and studded with cliches, but practically all sound advice that is dispersed is made up of these things. You must not let yourself become too despondent. Obviously, you haven't got the comforts and pleasures that you enjoyed as a civilian but your lot is far better than that of the hundred and seven thousand casualties—dead, wounded and missing. In order for you to be moderately happy, you will have to acquire a philosophy. You will have to learn to compare your lot with those who are less fortunate and, I assure you, there are hundreds of millions throughout the world who would gladly change places with you, even if this did not include the pleasure of knowing Miriam. So buck up, young fellow, and stop pitying yourself. You've got a job to do. It's not a particularly pleasant one but it can be a great thing for you. It's going to either make you or ruin you, but it's squarely up to you.

I hope you don't find this letter too pedestrian. I could write you a letter full of jokes and snappy sayings but, at the moment, I don't think that that is what you need. The receiver of a letter always has one great advantage over the sender. He can read it and destroy it much quicker than the sender can write it. I hope this doesn't put any ideas in your head. I haven't discussed this with Miriam but if you want to discuss it with her, you certainly have my permission.

In the meantime, relax and snap out of it.

Yours,
Groucho (Mr. Anthony) Marx

This is a letter my father wrote to my boyfriend Dick Comen, who was in boot camp in the Navy at the time. The letter was sent in care of me. "Groucho (Mr. Anthony) Marx" refers to a man called Mr. Anthony who used to give advice on the radio.

[Ambassador Hotel, Los Angeles, April 18, 1942]

Dear Miriam,
I'm here with Virginia O'Brien. Wish you were here to see us dancing
cheek to cheek.
                    Love,
                    Silent Cal Englund

*Virginia O'Brien was a singer I had a crush on. "Silent Cal" (after Silent Cal
Coolidge) was my father's private name for George Englund because he
claimed that George never talked either.*

[The Mayflower Hotel, Washington, D.C., April 29, 1942]

Tomorrow we are having tea at the White House. I hope they have
pumpernickel.
                    Love and kisses,
                    XXX Da Da XXX

*This card was addressed to "Ruth, Art, Miriam." Though my parents were
divorced when this was written, my mother continued to live with us for a
couple of years.*

April 20, 1943

Dear Miriam,
I was astonished to hear from you so soon. I had no idea you would
get the suitcase locked so quickly. I hope you have it open by this time.
If not, you can dig a hole through the top and go down a ladder to get
into it. There's a letter at home for you from Budgie, also two from
soldiers, one named Webber and the other named Gee. The day you
left—shortly after your departure—George and Patsy Englund
dropped around to see you. I don't know whether you regard this as
lucky or unlucky.
    Now for the business at hand: Tin Can Joe came around this morn-
ing and we went down and looked at the car, then we went to the Ford
place and I gave one of the mechanics there $2 to take a trial spin in
it. He said that if I could get it for $150, it would be worth buying.
He added that it would require at least $50 worth of essential repairs
and perhaps $25 worth of painting and top repairing, etc., etc. We
went back and offered the woman $150. She said she could get $185.
Tin Can and I then sat in his car out front and debated the whole situa-

11

tion in much the same manner, I'm sure, as Eisenhower and Patton mapped their African campaign. After due consideration, I sent Tin Can back and had him offer her $175. She is to let us know this evening. Then I journeyed home with Tin Can — a precarious trip, I might add, in that ancient ark — fed him a robust lunch and he is now guiding Duke around the block and I'm on my way to the insane asylum in Westwood.

Must quit as I am terribly short of time. Hope you are enjoying yourself. The house is terribly quiet without you, and Tin Can seems quite downcast.

Love and a few million kisses,
Your padre

This was written when I was in Palm Springs visiting my friend Janet Cantor, daughter of actor Eddie Cantor and comedian Ida Cantor. Patsy Englund was George's sister. Tin Can Joe was Groucho's name for Dick Comen, who drove a Model A Ford at the time. They were shopping for a car for me. The insane asylum was the Harper Method Beauty Salon.

[Roosevelt Hotel, New Orleans, July 5, 1944]

Dear Poochey — that's you, Mir,
Trip unbearably hot, finally ended. Gave a show in two hours, rushing to lunch. Hope you are well. Love and XXXXXX from your Padre.

[Hotel Jefferson, St. Louis, July 9, 1944]

Dear Pooch,
I have had one letter from you since my departure, eight days ago, but I guess that feeble mind of yours is unable to ad lib two pages of dialogue. I may cut you off without a nickel. I'll first wait and see how I fare the balance of this tour.

This is a sample of the dialogue on our tour:

A soldier (a healthy one) sidled up to me and said, "Mr. Marx, I'd like to ask you a question."

I said, "Yes, son, what is it?"

He said, "John Wayne was here last week."

I said, "Well," expecting more.

He said "John Wayne was here last week."

Realizing finally that that was the finish of the conversation, I said, "I'll think it over and let you know tomorrow."

Well, write and tell me all about the painting, and Duke, and your job, and how you are, and the scandal from the *Reporter,* which oddly enough I don't miss at all.

All I miss are you and Art and Ted, and Kay and Duke, and my mansion and those cool nights.

> Love and kisses and I'll be home soon,
> your loving Padre.

Groucho was on an army camp tour when these postcards were written. Kay was Catherine Marvis Gorcey, who became his second wife.

[Ward Hotel, Fort Smith, Arkansas, July 12, 1944]

Dear Mir,

If you can convince your mother that this is her war as well as mine and Arthur's you will be doing a good job.

It is 101 here today and we all look like dead cats. I have only taken four tablets in twelve days.

> Love and kisses to you from your
> Padre

The tablets he refers to here were sleeping pills. I used to worry about his sleeping pill consumption and must have told him so.

[Roosevelt Hotel, Fort Smith, Arkansas, July 12, 1944]

Dear Mir,

Our show went fine and the audience loved it. Raining today. Leaving the town today for Jackson, Miss. Have had no word from you, not at all. Surprised. Love and kisses, Padre.

[Beauclair Hotel, Okmulgee, Oklahoma, July 17, 1944]

Dear Gooch,

Sunday morning in Okmulgee. It is a hundred and four this morning and the only sounds are the buzzing of flies and the tolling of the church bells. I tried to take a walk down the main street, but there is no shade and after a block of aimless wandering past a few chain stores I ducked back to the comparative cool of the hotel.

I have had very little mail from you, three letters and a phone call.

13

I hope, by the way, that the phone call and the wire have cleared up whatever confusion you had in your mind about my attitude concerning your job.

I saw Donald O'Connor and a group of ancient actors that compose Universal's stock company teeter through a story that wasn't clear at any time but I did like him. I think he is going to be a fine light comic and prefer him by long odds to [Mickey] Rooney, who with his long hair is beginning to resemble a schnauzer with only two legs.

I have had an opportunity to do a little reading on this trip and finished two of Bemelman's books. The one is a sort of a travelogue and though interesting, too much of it becomes a bore. The other one, however, *Now I Lay Me Down to Sleep*, a book of the month, is merely wonderful, and I want you to read it when I return. I think you will find this a little over your head in spots (yes, I know you have read Santayana but some of his allusions you cannot understand), but it's a great book. He has a remarkable talent for description, not only of places but of people, and I think that he is one of the great writers of our time.

It's too hot to write more, and I may be home before this letter arrives next Saturday. I have a lot to tell you, and it's been an interesting trip in more ways than one. All my love to you and kisses and I am eager to see your beautiful but sulking face again.

Your Perspiring Padre

[Copley Plaza Hotel, Boston, December 3, 1944]

Dear Mir,

Just came back from a long walk down the Boston Commons, where the Minute Men were fired upon in 1776. The Minute Men are all dead, but most everything else is still the same.

The plane ride was uneventful until we got as far as Washington. From there to Boston, Ruby spent a good deal of the time throwing up in a small cardboard bucket that the airliners are conveniently equipped with.

We gave a show the day we arrived and played three hospital wards to boot.

Yesterday we motored to Newport, formerly the home of the idle rich, in a station wagon. It was bitter cold, and it felt good to get back in the hotel after that ride.

14

The show goes fine—the sailors yell for more, and it seems to get more blatant and obscene with each performance.

Friday night we will see Kras's show, as we play in town that day and will be through by eight o'clock.

This hotel is old, historic and rich in tradition. The beds are soft and the blankets warm.

Tomorrow we motor to Portsmouth, New Hampshire, I hope not in the station wagon, but in a regular warm automobile. It's two hundred miles round trip, and this is not the climate for station wagons.

There is not much to tell you as I just left. How was your party? Write me all about it. Be good—stroke Duke for me, and have you written me?

Love XXXXXXXXX
Padre

Dear Mir,

Never again will I crab about California. I've never been so cold in my life. If you have any old long underwear you're not using please send it to me.

The boys really like the show.

How did the play go? Be sure to write and tell me all about it.

Nothing more to say as your father said it all for me. Give my love to Janet, Sunny, Fay, Kellys, Duke.

Love,
Kay

Write.

[Copley Plaza Hotel, Boston, December 8, 1944]

Dear Mir,

Had one letter with no news. Kras's show is playing here and we will get a chance to view it Friday night, as that night we have an early hospital show.

Moss Hart is in town as he staged *Dear Ruth*, and yesterday he went with us to the hospitals and Red Cross Theatre. He was deeply impressed by the show we give and the audience response. Then we all had lobster at a fabulous restaurant in Boston that has been serving this dish for a hundred and thirty-five years.

The weather is temperate and pleasant.

I am on the air in an hour. Just a local broadcast for the U.S.O.

15

Yesterday I went to the Governor's mansion and had photos taken with [Leverett] Saltonstall. We hear he is regarded as presidential timber. Hope you and the play go well. Miss your glowering face a lot and love you and wish you were here.

Love and kisses,
Padre

Moss Hart was a playwright and screenwriter.

February 9, 1945

Dear Mir,

I have just returned from Yuma—Kay, Harry, Mitzi Mayfair and Ann Triola. The latter sings at the Bar of Music and murders the audience with her comedy songs—crazy ones. Mitzi Mayfair is a terrific dancer, formerly of the Ziegfeld Follies. We had a great show—an hour and forty minutes—and a steak dinner later with the CO. His name is Anderson. He's a stiff, pompous martinet. (In case you don't know, martinet means tyrant. This will save you the trouble of doing research work on it.) He's a good host but the men all hate him—they fear him. He's done a wonderful job with the camp. He's planted hundreds of palm trees and painted all the buildings white and it's really a garden spot in the desert. The trip was nine hours each way by army car and next time I intend flying or not going—it's too tough bouncing along in those little jalopies. Other than this there's very little to relate.

Kaufman wanted me for the new Gordon musical but they insisted that I sign up for two years which means that if the show clicked, I'd eventually wind up in Toledo, Chicago and those other whistle stops. That's all right when you're thirty but I just couldn't see it so they got Moore and Gaxton, I believe. I have no definite plans—I have a couple of hazy radio deals but there's nothing specific about them. The phone situation doesn't look too good but there's still a faint hope. I am now on the way to the house with Fay to clean out rubbish and do other odd jobs. This is good exercise and if I like it, I might handle Thayer Avenue for so much per house.

I haven't heard from you but I don't want you to spend all your time writing. Your mother phoned and told me that you were okay. I won eighty cents in the poker game last week and lost fifty dollars the preceding week. At this rate, I'll soon be a public charge. All I get out of it is a series of dirty stares from the other participants, none of which I remember the following day. I miss you very much and the house is strangely quiet without your breathless arrivals and even more silent departures in the middle of the night for Janet Cantor's. Give Janet my love and try not to lose your bank roll nor your heart to any of those city slickers. Regards to Irwin, too, and a million kisses to you.

Your padre

This letter was written to me in New York, where I was visiting my mother with Janet Cantor. Kaufman was Broadway playwright George Kaufman, who wrote the play on which the Marx Brothers film Animal Crackers *(1930) was based. Gordon was Max Gordon, a Broadway producer who had assisted on* Monkey Business *(1931) and* Horse Feathers *(1932). Fay was Fay Barrett, our maid.*

February 19, 1945

Dear Mir,

Happy to know that you're having such a good time even if the affaire Irwin Nathan had such a dismal climax. I think you are well rid of him and that he was hardly worthy of you. I received your wire today about the musical *Firebrand* and I suspect that it would need some goosing up for me. I hereby instruct you to borrow fifty dollars from Gordon, for which I'll reimburse him. The Chodorov play arrived to-day and it's pretty grim. It's all about Fascism and murder and death and destruction and it probably is extremely realistic but it's hardly the play for me. As a matter of fact, I hardly appear at all in the third act and the only one I can see in it is Sam Levine.

It was nice to hear your voice yesterday and to know that you are going to return to our little fifteen-room nest. I was also glad to hear the twins' voices and Katie. I am very fond of the twins and I've even been toying with the idea of marrying both of them. You see, combined, they are almost thirty-six and that would be a nice age for a girl for me to marry. As a matter of fact, I'll most probably marry one considerably younger but you might ask the twins about it and see if they are interested. I have a good deal of furniture and enough money to live on if they will pay for Duke's dog meat. Duke seems pretty lonesome for you and I think he just reflects my own attitude.

Kras threw a party last night—a farewell—he's going overseas by way of Washington. I told him about you and Irwin and he was elated. He said he didn't want to tell me but that Irwin had changed consider ably in the past year and, to put it bluntly, Kras described him as a cheap chiseler who would let nothing stand in his way.

This is pure lagnappe as I had promised not to write you again but I wanted you to know that I was disturbed by what you told me about your splitting with him and perhaps this letter will cheer you up even if only momentarily.

Give my love to George and Moss and even Salpeter — I might as well go whole hog — and when I say Salpeter, believe me, it's whole hog. All my love to you and as many kisses as you can reasonably take care of.

Your padre

P.S. Now you can really go out after Pierre. Personally, I like him much better.

> Chodorov was Jerry Chodorov, a playwright, director and screenwriter. The twins were Jane and Phyllis Murray, daughters of the famous dance instructors Arthur and Kathryn Murray. Salpeter was Max Gordon's real last name.

[Hotel Leamington, Oakland] Friday, [August] 24, 1945

Dear Mir,

Remember this hotel? It's where you and Kay raced down the halls? And the waffle parlor where you were afraid you would have to wash the dishes? And the lagoon where we went boating? And Arthur going away, and it was fun and kind of sad too.

The town is still the same, full of sailors and mildewed buildings.

And now it's all over, and perhaps Art will be back by Xmas?

The show was dreadful when we began, but it is beginning to take shape, and despite the arduousness of the tour, I must admit it was worth it. Most of Joe Fields' jokes were not jokes and had to be replaced by jokes of mine and Harris and Tulina's, and unless Mayo bungles it up too much (something he is quite capable of) we could have a pretty good picture.

Armistice Day was really something in San Diego. The police feared the inevitable riots and closed everything. The result was it was impossible to get anything to eat, and if it hadn't been for the popcorn that was sold in the movie theatres, the whole town would have starved to death.

I am glad you are having a good time. I miss that dour kisser of yours perusing the funnies in the library, but as Noel Coward put it, "I'll see you again."

All my love, and when I get home, I'll write you more in detail.
Padre 9XXXXXXXXX

This letter was written to me at Bennington College, Bennington, Vermont, where I was a freshman. Groucho had married Kay on July twenty-first. She was twenty-four; I was eighteen. Arthur had joined the Coast Guard. The show he talks about is A Night in Casablanca (1946), *which was rehearsed live on stage before being filmed.* Mayo *was Archie Mayo, who directed* A Night in Casablanca.

[September 9, 1945]

Sunday afternoon and a hot one.

Dear Mir,

I have been home since Friday night, and have only been out of the house twice, once to go to the drugstore and once to buy some gas without points. I didn't really need the gas, but it was such a wonderful sensation that I couldn't resist it.

I read two of your letters, one to Fay and one that you wrote to me. I also read an item in Edith Gwyn's column that you and Kay were fighting. How that got into her column I don't know. I know that you had told Lucy Kibbee all about it however, and from there it came back to Kay.

I am trying to make a go of this marriage and it is very difficult for many reasons: age, temperament, intellectual basis and so forth. The addition of a feud between you and Kay certainly doesn't help things any. I am going to be frank and say that I think you are far more at fault than Kay. Kay, I have seen, has tried to be friends with you but you fight her off. You yourself admitted that you have told Sunny all the details of my domestic life and I am sure that you also confided in Janet Cantor and Maxine and probably Susie and many others.

This I consider an unforgivable breach of confidence and conduct. You wrote Fay that you missed me but that you dreaded ever returning to the house and what it (to you) represents. I miss you too but I certainly don't want you to return unless you realize that I am married and are willing to help me to make this marriage succeed.

I remember when Arthur married Irene. One day he just left and moved over to the Kahn's. I felt hurt at first, but I gradually realized that he was married and that he had a right to do with his life as he pleased. You must let me do the same with mine. There are many details of this I could discuss, but there isn't much point to that. I pur-

19

posely am not pulling any punches, for it is important that you clearly understand how I feel. It isn't very good for my peace of mind to realize that half of Hollywood knows so much about my private life and I trust that this is the last of that. I am not specifically accusing you of giving these items to columnists, but you certainly haven't been secretive about my affairs.

If your frame of mind about returning is as dark as it is at present, I will arrange for you to live at a hotel both for your sake and mine, when you return for your vacation.

After reading this far you probably loathe me. I have been in bed many nights thinking this over, so don't think this letter is the immediate result of a bad lunch. I want to love you and be a good father to you but I don't think you have been a good daughter to me. I hope the school and its associations will help in knocking some of the cantankerousness out of you.

I am tired and don't feel like going any further with this. This wasn't an easy letter for me to write. It is always difficult to write unpleasantly, but I just had to clear up some misapprehensions you have been under.

Answer me soon and don't fly into a rage, just try and look at my side of this.

> All my love and kisses,
> Padre
> 9-XXXXXXXXXXX

Lucy Kibbee was the wife of screenwriter Roland Kibbee, who worked on A Night in Casablanca. *Maxine was my cousin Maxine Marx, Chico's daughter. Irene was my brother's wife, Irene C. Kahn (sometimes referred to as Ick), daughter of lyricist Gus Kahn and his wife Grace.*

September 11, 1945

Dear Mir,
Received your letter and I think we can now safely drop the whole discussion. I am sure (as I've said before) that the school will do many things for you. Getting along with people is such an important part of one's life that I just don't understand why it isn't a regular course in college, just as mathematics and other subjects are. Without that talent, everything is impossible. You know that if one is a bore, people are going to run, no matter if he's a wizard at mathematics, hieroglyphics or atomic energy.

I'll try to get your bike off tomorrow. I keep saying this and I do keep trying but there's so much for me to do that I just don't seem to get around to it. Fay left yesterday. She's a very good woman, honest and capable, but I'm glad to get rid of her. I became the servant and she became the boss. She got the jump on me during the war and she never relinquished it. At home I've led a hermit's existence because she was opposed to cooking for anyone but me and resented it deeply if I suggested that perhaps the following week I might have four people to dinner. I don't know why I'm telling you all this—you certainly know it as well as I do.

I just left Kay at home. She's dusting, straightening and cleaning and having a hell of a time. At two P.M. she's rushing to the eye doctor because she's slightly blind (this, as you know, accounts for our marriage—wait until she sees me with those new lenses!). Well, I won't worry about that now. After a joust with Dr. Fields, which, as you know, is at the Wilshire Medical Building, she shoots over to the Farmer's Market (I forgot to tell you, it's ninety-five today), picks up dinner, then rushes home to serve it. After dinner, Brecher and I are going to the ball park and Miss Dittig will be left in the kitchen, scraping off the dishes. I'll teach her to get married! We're getting along fine these days. She seems more sure of herself and certainly is trying hard to make me happy as well. You know I'm a peculiar individual and very trying so if she can please me, she will be doing quite a job.

Duke has suddenly gotten very old. He eats sparingly now—perhaps it's the heat—I don't know, but he doesn't seem happy any more. It may be the confinement of the small yard and the doctor's orders that he should have a minimum of exercise.

Do you get *The New Yorker* at school? If you don't, let me know and I'll have it sent to you. These days before the shooting of the picture are spent in fine-combing the script. Since our return from the vaudeville tour, it's considerably over length and the problem now is to clip twenty pages. Some of the clips won't be a great loss; the balance of the cutting, as always, will probably come in the love scenes. The lovers in our pictures make fleeting appearances—they're seen rarely and when they do meet, they usually have nothing to say that the audience is interested in. The popcorn situation in the balconies at the local theatres is steadily getting worse. It's the worst menace that has struck the amusement world in many years. If you have a solution, even if it's only a ten percent solution, send it on. I am growing desperate.

I love you very much and miss your dour kisser. Write soon and take care of yourself. Kay sends her best and lots of love from

Your Padre

September 18, 1945

Dear Mir,

I'm glad you miss me—I take it that this means we must have treated you pretty well at home. I'm glad you wrote to Kay and she is going to write to you as soon as she feels better.

I am working hard now—we start at eleven each morning, rehearsing scenes that weren't played on the road. Because of the strike, our schedule has been postponed—we were supposed to start on the seventeenth and now it looks like we won't get under way until the first of October—the day before my birthday. That's certainly a hell of a way to start one's birthday! The strike is pretty serious now. The studios are lined with pickets at all entrances and, being an old union man myself, I feel sort of guilty crossing them but this is such an outrageous strike, having nothing to do with wages or hours—it's just a jurisdictional fight for power—so I see no reason why I should not enter a studio. I hope it's settled soon though; I'm afraid there'll be bloodshed if it isn't. It's been on for seven months and pretty soon the fights will start. Stink bombs have even been thrown in various theatres around town and the whole thing is quite serious.

I'm sending a couple of pictures to you—they're not very good but at the moment they're all I have. I'll send others as soon as I have a chance to have them taken. It's not so easy to get a photographer to snap my face—it's easier for them to slap my face. Oh, well, forget it.

Irene received a cable from Arthur saying that he'll be home inside of a month—perhaps in two weeks. Even now he may be on his way. This doesn't necessarily mean that he'll be released—he may be assigned to a local Coast Guard Entertainment Unit—but I don't care about that—I'll settle for getting him back. It seems I can't get my two children together any more at one time.

Your lonesomeness, of course, is just a matter of routine. It was inevitable that you would get that way. Don't forget, you've never been away from home for any length of time. It sounds cruel, but this is going to do you a lot of good. I sent the bike and you should be getting it pretty soon—it's been on its way almost a week and I was told that it would take between ten days and two weeks. Rachel is taking care of the *New Yorker* subscription for you and if I can scrape up any recent copies around the house, I'll send them on.

This is a hastily written letter as Rachel has to leave the office. I'm just writing you so you won't get too lonesome. I miss you a lot and don't get too down in the mouth. All kids have to break away from home—I did it at the age of fifteen—and you'll find out in the long run that you won't consider these present days of yours such tragic ones.

Lots of love from Kay and myself and I'll try to write you more often.

> Your loving
> Padre

Rachel was my father's secretary, Rachel Linden.

[September 23, 1945]

Tuesday morning, I believe the twenty-third.

Dear Gooch,

There are certain high points in a man's life, I mean professionally of course. Last night was one of those. A night of satisfaction, like the opening night of *Animal Crackers,* etc. We gave a dinner to the Hollywood Ball Club. As you know if you read the papers, they wound up in last place, forty games behind the winners, and almost set a record for losing games. I had a notion that it would be a fine gesture if we gave a dinner for the team and presented them with gifts. This is usually done with a team that wins a Pennant and perhaps a World Series, but certainly never in the history of sports has a team that bordered frequently on the ludicrous been honored as these boys were.

My part in the proceedings was as follows. I suggested the idea originally, in a moment of bitterness, and it was immediately taken over by Gummo who undertook the physical end, such as collecting the money for the dinner and arranging for the dinner and all the other details that go with an undertaking of this kind.

Since I had suggested the dinner, I knew that I would have to make a speech. So I wrote and memorized one. Jessel was going to be master of ceremonies, at which as you know there is no one more expert. At eight-thirty he leaned over to me and whispered, "I have to leave here at nine o'clock, as they are running my picture at the studio." A cold chill ran over me, for I knew that I was destined for the job. Well, I did it and despite the fact that it was an audience of hard-boiled

23

characters, Brecher and Hecht and Krasna and Sheekman and Perrin and a huge crowd of writers and theatrical folk, I really slayed them. I had no idea that I could do it so well, and I may take it up as a career now that I have tasted blood.

As entertainers, we had George Burns and Jack Benny and [Jimmy] Durante and Joe Brown and Jessel and lots of others, and at the finale I made a little sentimental speech to Buck Faucett and the ball players, and all in all it was a most gratifying evening.

It's the old gag of the elephant: it's not that he does a toe dance well, but the fact that he can do it at all that is amazing. I am sorry that you are bored with the *New York Times*. This is certainly a quick switch of theme, but the *Times* is a little old for you. I should think the *Tribune* would be better, if you want *P.M.* and think that you have time for it, I will provide you with a subscription. I am also happy to know that your bike arrived in good repair. I don't know exactly what good repair means; I believe it is an English or New England expression. If you are interested, you can investigate it further.

When I came home from the ball park Sunday, the last day of the year for that, I was going to take a nap, as is my custom, but imagine my horror to walk into the library and behold your set sitting there, along with Mattie Swerling. Kay was washing her hair and there I was listening to that chatter, my eyes glazed from lack of sleep, and wishing they would leave. Kay finally appeared to rescue me and I made the customary lame apologies and staggered off to bed. I hope their feelings weren't hurt, but I just had to lie down.

I got pretty lonesome for you when I saw that gang. They told me, by the way, that is Sunny and Janet, that they contemplated leaving for the East in a few weeks or perhaps they said less. At any rate I am sure they keep you apprised of their moves.

I am sorry that I didn't let you know that I was on "The Dinah Shore Show" some weeks ago, but you are usually so bored with my air appearances that I didn't think it was worthwhile to even mention it to you. It was pretty good. As you know, I am not particularly proud of my radio appearances, and only do it to keep my hand in and make a little money, but it isn't anything that I would wire or phone anyone to particularly listen to.

By the way, I believe Fred Allen begins this week with a guest shot on the Bergen Show (Chase and Sanborn to you), and if you are near a radio, you might listen to it. I presume Alan Kent is working, for it seems he only phones me when he is out of work.

I must quit now, as I am doing [typing] this by hand, and the proper

24

method, I'll have you know, and my fingers are weary, in addition to not having any more to tell you. A word of caution: don't knock yourself out writing letters. You have a lot of work to do, and you should space your correspondence so that you don't have a huge backlog of letters facing you daily.

All my love to you from me, and Kay, and answer when you have the strength.

Your Padre

Jessel was George Jessel, actor, producer, author and "Toastmaster General of the United States." Hecht was author and screenwriter Ben Hecht. Perrin was Nat Perrin, a good friend of my father's who had written for many Marx Brothers movies. Alan Kent was an aspiring actor who became a screenwriter.

September 26, 1945

Dear Mir,
I wrote a long letter to you a day or two ago and this is just to be a note, principally to send your monthly check. You'll notice that there's a slight deduction—long distance phone calls and wires of yours to Washington, D.C., Stanford, Longridge, etc., etc., and they are your responsibility. As I told you before, I will not pay any long distance calls unless it's in an emergency or a crisis of some kind, and if you insist on making social long distance calls, you'll have to accept the expense.

Also enclosed are three small checks . . . and three pieces from the local sheets about our dinner for the Twinks. I don't know how funny you'll find these after seeing the deduction from your allowance.

Fay, as you know, is no longer with us and in her place we now have a character named Louise. She's approximately 4'6" and built like a jeep; she's an Ethiopian; her gross weight is about 150 and she seems to flourish on work, with which I'm sure we can provide her. It's certainly a relief to have someone in the house to whom you can give orders. We also have a new cleaning girl. Bernice did a good superficial cleaning job but actually cleaned very little. This girl started with the outside windows—something that's never been done in my time except by a professional window washer. I don't know how long this exceptional condition will continue but it's lovely at the moment. Now if we can get rid of most of the red points, housekeeping will become simple once again.

Last night we went to the [Humphrey] Bogarts' to dinner. They live high on a hilltop—a modernistic house. We had a pretty good time.

25

Bogey likes to drink—he wasn't drunk but he usually gets fairly well soaked during an evening and loves to talk and some of his talk doesn't quite make sense—but, after all, remember, he's an actor. She seems very nice—she's quite attractive and seems to be on the ball politically as well, far more than he is.

This is about all—you know, this started out as a note and I think I wrote you everything day before yesterday.

Your loving
Padre

The Twinks was another name for the Hollywood baseball team, the Hollywood Stars.

October 1, 1945

Dear Mir,

This letter is in answer to a letter written by you on September fifteenth. I've probably answered it before so if it's a repetition, attribute it to the fact that I can't think of anything to say.

Since this opening paragraph—written at the office—Kay called from the house and said that there was a letter there from you. She didn't read it to me but she said that in it you complained that there was very little mail coming to you. Last week I sent you two letters, your allowance, a blouse and some photographs. This is pretty good for a man of my age. I also deducted some money from your allowance, which is pretty bad for a man of my age.

Last week everyone began dragging out tweed suits, heavy underwear and Christmas ornaments. In the midst of this a monsoon blew in from the desert and for the past three days the temperature has been ninety-five, so yesterday and the day before I spent lolling on a public beach near Santa Monica. It's not very stylish but it's cool and the same ocean that the rich people with their beach and boat clubs enjoy. Going to the beach now is not much of a problem since gas rationing has been lifted; however, if the strikes increase, we may be back on gas rationing again before you can say Secretary of Labor Schwellenbach. Today is another blazer and I was planning on going to the beach when the phone rang and it was some character from the studio so now I have to journey to Las Palmas and Santa Monica Boulevard to get a medical examination. This is required by the insurance company before they'll insure the movie. I'm disappointed but I did have two days at the beach so I won't complain too much. We're starting

26

our picture day after tomorrow, October third, and tomorrow, the second, is my birthday. We and the Krasnas are having dinner downtown someplace and then going to Wrigley Field to see Satchel Paige, a great colored pitcher, play against Bob Feller, a great white pitcher. He's from Cleveland and is the best hurler since Walter Johnson, of whom you've never heard, I'm sure. I hope this clears up the baseball situation. Kay wanted to have a party at the house but just going to a restaurant and the ball park seemed so much simpler, I talked her into it.

I saw *Incendiary Blonde* last night and [Betty] Hutton is turning out to be quite a performer. It's not an accurate story of Texas Guinan's life but those things never are. She was in her middle fifties when she died and in the picture she died when she was around twenty-three, but it's nostalgic — has many scenes that bring back old memories — and I liked it quite well. The Rickenbacher picture was shown too. Generally, it got pretty poor notices. Many people are prejudiced because of his animosity toward labor but it seems to me that that's a silly way to judge a picture. That again dealt with the days with which I'm familiar — the 1920s or thereabouts — and I enjoyed it. I guess I'm just a fool about nostalgia and about you, too, now that I think of it.

I'll be on "The Dinah Shore Show" on October eleventh and I'm giving you fair warning. I don't know how it will be. You probably won't like it and I won't blame you much but, at any rate, don't say I didn't notify you. I believe it's at 8:30 in the East, NBC and I think WEAF. Now you have all the information, you know about it, even the jokes which I'm sure you've heard before. It's getting close to cop-circling time around my Cadillac — you know, the expert with the long stick with the chalk on the end? Kay gets citations about three times a week and she solves the problem very simply by just destroying the tickets. She says she's been doing this for years and it's the only way to outwit the police but she'll probably wind up in Tehachapi.

Goodbye for
   now
      and
         all
            my
               love
                  and
                     kisses
                        to
                           you—

```
                        well,
                    most
                of
            them,
                anyhow.
        I have to go now.
        "Your Ever Lovin' " — Padre Groucho
```

October 12, 1945

Dear Mir,

It was good to hear your voice again although it sounded so high-pitched and excited that I thought I was talking to Lily Pons. There was no particular point to the phone call except that I wanted to hear your voice; mine you can hear most any time on "The Dinah Shore Show" (the next time, November first).

I'm glad to know that you are satisfied with Bennington and that Bennington seems to be willing to put up with you. This morning I received a 64¢ collect telegram. The minute the boy said "Collect," I instantly knew that it was from your brother Arthur. However, it was worth 64¢, yea, even 74¢, to read that he was now quartered on the shores of Portland, that his unit contemplated descending on Seattle and that there was a strong likelihood that he would be down here in four or five days — perhaps even by the time you get this letter. I am and we all are very lucky to get him back in one piece and I am very thankful for that. So many parents didn't get their boys back at all and, as you know, hundreds of thousands who have returned won't ever be much good again.

I am delighted that your English prof, it that's who it was, thought so well of your last story for I am sure that those boys at college are pretty tough critics and if they think your effusion is good enough to send to *The New Yorker,* you must have tossed off a minor literary gem. How about sending a copy of it to me? I would be happy to read it. Alan Kent is still being given the run-around by the Morris Office and is still out of work. It's getting tougher now to break in — you see the armed forces are releasing dozens of former radio writers, many of whom are thoroughly experienced. I've sent some of his stuff to *The New Yorker* and perhaps that will be where the ray of light will come from.

The picture is running along uneventfully and may turn out surprisingly well. It's hard work but the vaudeville tour was of the utmost help because it gave us a chance to memorize most of the dialogue and memorizing dialogue becomes increasingly difficult as one gets older. We have scenes that I don't think Chico ever could have learned had we not played the stuff on the road. We have been getting along famously with Archie Mayo—he's no genius but he's far better than Buzzell. Buzzell tried to graft his own personality on us and it just didn't work. We have completed a week's shooting and now have only six more to go. We haven't been molested by the strikers. There are three pickets that aimlessly patrol up and down in front of General Service. It's a little humiliating to read in the papers that 20,000 pickets are patrolling Warner Brothers in Burbank and then to drive through the gates at our studio [MGM] and see but three pickets. I'm really ashamed and when people ask me about it, I lie and tell them we have eight pickets. The NLRB decision favored Sorrell who, I think, is on the right side. The whole strike was needless and I think the producers could have stopped it if they had so desired but they didn't want Sorrell's union—that was a little too liberal for them.

When Arthur gets down here, we'll call you some night and you can hear his rich baritone as in days of old.

I don't know whether you read in the public prints that Ida Cantor and two of her gin-rummy-playing cronies were side-swiped by a hay wagon when they were motoring to Palm Springs. They weren't hurt, just shaken up; anyway, Howard Harris said that this was truly an event—it was the first time Ida had been in the hay in ten years.

All my love to you and Kay's, too.

Your ever-loving padre,
Ronald Kornblow

P.S. Here's a check for 75¢ and I sent five portraits of you to you the other day. Kay seems to think that those are the only ones you left behind. I hope you're fine and seventeen letters in one day! Whoops, my dear, will you ever get them answered? If you were here, you'd have a grand time trotting down to the studio to watch the boys shoot—the sets are very colorful and they're using lots of extras. Too, they have their own dining room and an excellent cook—I've had lunch with them but once because I'm swamped in the office right now. Next week I hope to get down again. RL

> Lily Pons was a famous soprano. Buzzell was Eddie Buzzell, who directed At the Circus and Go West. Howard Harris was a radio scriptwriter. Ronald Kornblow (in the sign-off) was the name of Groucho's character in A Night in Casablanca.

29

October 18, 1945

Dear Mir,

I had dinner with your brother last night and he looks none the worse for wear; as a matter of fact, he looks precisely the same as he did four years ago when he lost to Richards in the first round at Long Beach. He's just as nice as ever though and you know I care for him in a big way. We all had dinner with the Kahns—an extremely bad dinner by the way—something unusual for that house. Their regular cook Anna abdicated and they have replaced her with a culinary queen who, I think, took on cooking as a profession probably three days ago. At any rate, despite this, it was nice seeing your brother's pan across the table. I understand that you spoke to him on the phone—that was before I got there. He isn't sure yet when he'll get out—it seems that he's with some kind of Coast Guard Band Unit and the scuttlebutt is that they'll use this group of journeyman musicians to thump the tub for the Victory Bond Drive. I don't care what he does—he has two arms and two legs and he's alive and that's good enough for me and probably for him, too.

The only reason you're receiving a letter from me today is because I haven't been shooting and, since I received a four-page narrative from you this morning, I thought I'd best answer it before the assistant calls from the studio to announce that I'm in the next shot. You wrote that I was pretty calm when you told me that you had tossed off a story that your school thought was almost good enough for *The New Yorker*. That's not quite true—I was very proud of you and told all my friends and relatives about it but, as you know, my enthusiasms don't run very high. This is only because my blood pressure is low and my enthusiasms correspond with that. Anyway, briefly, I am proud of you and I think you are doing a good job.

I read what you wrote about "The Dinah Shore Show" and I don't agree with you about the English sketch. I thought it was funny and so did a lot of other people who heard it. There were sections of the show that I thought were fairly dreary and, along with you, I don't care about jokes on Glendale and other surrounding territory. However, the temptation to insert these in a script is always overpowering to a radio writer for he knows that they are sure laughs in the immediate theatre where we're playing and, apparently, he doesn't give a damn about people in Vermont or even in New Hampshire. I am not particularly proud of my radio appearances. They are guest shots and I have very little control over the quality of the material. I don't have the advantage of [Fred] Allen or [Jack] Benny or any of the other ·

30

comics who are permanent fixtures and work their way all through a script and can rely on events that happened in their shows weeks previously for laughs. I have to go to bat from scratch each time I appear. You might explain this to those frosty friends of yours who sit apathetically through my seven-minute contribution. I am going on again November first and November twenty-ninth. My advice to you is not to listen; I'm sure I won't be any better. I have had a couple of offers for my own show but I am in no frame of mind emotionally or any other way to tackle that size job at the moment. I am only doing these radio shows because I foolishly signed up for them months ago. But I am not annoyed by your criticisms of the Dinah Shore shows, so lash out whenever you think they warrant it.

The picture work is extremely fatiguing and I am happy as a lark over this day's vacation, though most of it is being spent in writing letters. I am glad you are now smoking a pipe. I think since Arthur and I both smoke pipes you should also have the pleasure of puffing one. Perhaps I'll send a can of Blue Boar to you for Christmas.

You conclude by saying, "What do you think of the world's plight and what about the London Council?" A scientist by the name of Oppenheimer testified yesterday before Congress that it was conceivable that in the very near future forty million people could be exterminated with a series of atomic bombings. I agree with you that Attlee is not distinguishing himself but you must realize that he inherited a tough problem from Churchill. Churchill is certainly lucky that he got out from under. Here's a nation that has been ravaged and semi-pauperized by this last war, a small island whose resources alongside of ours are minute—I don't think anyone could have done much better. The Labor Party after the last war inherited the same giant headache and they were finally thrown out by the Conservatives. This may well happen again.

Now I have some sad news for you. Duke was put to sleep today by the doctor. We've had him in the hospital for the past ten days. He had a cancerous growth and he was nothing but skin and bones and it was much too cruel to permit him to live in that condition. I hate to write this to you but you know it happens to everyone, even animals, and he just couldn't be saved. I feel sad about it and I know you do too, but there was no choice in the matter. He would have died shortly anyway and this way at least his suffering is over. I am sorry I have to conclude this letter on such a sad note but I had to tell you this.

Lots and lots of love to you and I hope your vacation was a happy

31

one. We are all well and there's even a chance that the strike may be settled one of these days. Write soon.

Your padre

October 26, 1945

Dear Mir,

I haven't heard from you in almost two weeks. I don't want to become a Mildred Pierce—I don't know whether you've seen *Mildred Pierce* but it's about a mother who's so wrapped up in her child that she finally ruins not only her own life but the child's. The picture was produced by Warner Brothers and is playing at Warners' Hollywood. There's also a Looney Tune on the bill—a very bad one—with Abbott and Costello mice when they should be playing rats. Zachary Scott is the heel who's apparently in love with Mildred Pierce and is only using her and playing around with her daughter—that would be you, if you were lucky enough, as Zachary Scott is a very fine-looking fellow; at any rate, I haven't heard from you in almost two weeks and, not that I want to be a Mildred Pierce, which is playing at Warners' Hollywood, it seems to me that you could write a letter at least once a week even if you only say, "I'm having a lousy time, wish you were here instead."

I have been shooting steadily and regularly every morning at nine—I'm in practically every shot—and am living the life of a hunted animal. No matter where I am, the unit manager calls and says, "Nine o'clock for you." It's like labor pains, making movies—you forget the misery between films and/or children, but while doing it, it's not much of a life. The rushes look very good, surprisingly so. It's a good thing we followed Harpo's advice and took it on the road for we could have had some terrible stuff.

I was supposed to go on "The Dinah Shore Show" on the first of November but persuaded them to postpone it until the eighth. I'm giving you fair warning and this time you don't have to listen to it. I suppose you heard about Bea Kaufman because I understand that newspapers are delivered in Vermont. Speaking of mail, we've had a little difficulty with our mailman. He got fresh with Kay the other day—just as he attempted to do with you. This enraged me and I wrote a note to him. I said: "Dear Mailman (a fine beginning), My wife has complained to me that you have annoyed her repeatedly. If this occurs again, it will be necessary for me to report you to both the police and the postal authorities." In return for this, he left thirty-one bills for me yesterday and not a letter that any self-respecting burgher could read. I think the man is slightly mad—not that I don't think you and Kay are worth making a play for—but apparently he fancies himself as a house-to-house Romeo. You'd think he'd be satisfied with that one bag he carries on his shoulder and leave the others alone. This gives you an idea of life in Westwood—I never had that trouble in Beverly.

It's certainly nice having Arthur back. I don't see much of him—a couple of times a week—but at least I know he's safe. He now smokes cigars, pipes and cigarettes and I don't think he'd reject an offer of marijuana. He expects to be out inside of a month. He's not complaining at the moment for he gets $75 a month; $25 for Irene and $5 a day sustenance, which gives him nearly $300 a month and is probably far more than he'll make in civilian life. One of these days I expect to receive a phone call that Kay is about to become a grandmother but so far they deny any trend in that direction. However, I don't trust them for it seems to me that they spend a good deal of time in the hay or thereabouts.

I presume you saw the picture of your gang, Maxine, Sunny and Janet, picketing Warner Brothers. I meant to send one to you but I had an early edition paper and it wasn't in it but I am sure one of the three sent this photograph to you. I am certainly happy that the strike is over. I always felt kind of squeamish driving through the line of pickets at our gate. Whether right or wrong, they all looked rather pathetic pacing up and down with those signs. They only make a living and not a particularly luxurious one, and some day, both sides—Capital and Labor—are going to have to sit down and work out a more sensible formula for labor problems than any they have yet devised. Don't forget, the big industrialists are always rich and the little guy is fighting for a few extra bucks so, despite the fact that occasionally he is in the wrong, and admitting that there are labor abuses in the union that should be remedied, I am still for them. None of them die with twenty-eight million dollars in the bank or have yachts in Sheepshead Bay. I don't know why I tell you this since I know you know how I feel about it but it helps fill up paper and, despite the apparent scarcity of it, there seems to be a hell of a lot of it around this office.

So the picture opens with Mildred Pierce loving her daughter and hating this man—well, you can see it and, in the future, a letter once a week, old girl, or I'll cut your allowance in half. Speaking of money, which I planned on doing all through this letter, there's an honorarium coming from a Miss Murray, who, I understand, is a daughter of Arthur Murray of dance fame. Also, I sent a blouse to you. When one sends a blouse to a louse, one expects an acknowledgment for blouses do not grow on trees. If they do, what was I doing in that dress shop?

Lots of love and kisses and I think of you a lot.

Your padre,
Dr. Hackenbush

Bea Kaufman was George Kaufman's wife, who had just died. Dr. Hugo Z. Hackenbush was the name of Groucho's character in A Day at the Races *(1937).*

October 30, 1945

Dear Schmere,

"At long last," as the King of England said when he abdicated, I got a letter from you and a pretty short one, too. I'm sorry you didn't have a better time in New York but you see, the East has mice and cockroaches just the same as the West. I am sorry, too, that you got the impression that there was something wrong with my home life. There isn't—Kay and I get along fine and she's a good wife. As a matter of fact, she resents going out any night and if she thinks I'm tired, we stay home. I have been home almost every night since the shooting began. I can give you my routine—I arrive home at 6:30; Kay fixes an old fashioned for me; I then read the *Reporter* and the *Daily News*; at seven, Miss Five-by-five, our ebony jewel, waddles in from the kitchen to announce in a quaint Poll Tax tone that dinner is served; at eight, I turn on KFAC, light an expensive stogy, read the *New York Times* and all the other contemporary magazines around; at ten, I take a pine-needle bath and knock myself out. I have taken three sleeping tablets in six weeks so I don't imagine they will do me any harm.

This is a rainy afternoon; I shot all morning; Irene and Art came to lunch; this afternoon I'm free and from here I'm going home, read awhile; pluck the guitar; look for a letter from you, which I know won't arrive for another week; take a nap and hope I don't get an early morning call. I am in good health, free, white and 101. I've lost five pounds and my old Benham suits from 1939 are beginning to fit me again.

This isn't really a letter—I just wanted to reassure you that I am in fine fettle, whatever that means. (Fettle is probably a word; I wish you would look it up as I'm very busy. I use it all the time—I'm crazy about it—and some day I'm going to find out what it means.)

Your allowance is enclosed, not that I think you need it, for I imagine you are well-heeled. I read somewhere that you're the richest girl in Vermont or maybe it was one of the smaller states.

I love you very much and have a good time—a better time than you apparently had from your last letter.

Your padre,
Groucho

November 5, 1945

Dear Mir,

I was pleasantly surprised to get a letter from you today. I read your midterm report and, briefly, my analysis of it is that your intelligence is higher than your concentration. However, I won't regard this too seriously until the term expires and then we can sit down and talk it over man to Andy Hardy.

The mailman situation has abated so I think you can again send your letters to my home. I don't see the mailman any more—he hurriedly shoves the bills into my box and scampers off. I'm sorry I had to be so stern with him but you know him and I decided that was the cleaner and more effective way of stopping this nonsense.

Last night I saw the Gershwin picture and enjoyed it a lot. For a man of my years, it has much to recommend it. It's full of names and actors that I am familiar with, and [Al] Jolson at the age of sixty-two still evidences what a great talent is his. Obviously, it isn't an accurate story of the Gershwins but they play a lot of his music and beautifully and I had a good time. I guess it's too much to expect any studio to do the story of anyone's life the way it was actually lived but one did get the impression that Gershwin was an extremely egocentric character and that his brother is a nice fellow. [Oscar] Levant was a little tough for me to take for I don't care for the gent in any form. You can have his comedy too as far as I am concerned. He has a brittle hardness and rudeness that just irritates me; however, the seats were comfortable, I had chewing gum and two cigars and the music was beautiful. If you expect to see a great story, duck it. If you are interested in two hours of Gershwin music, don't miss it.

Kay is writing to you today and will tell you about the party we had Saturday night. I missed having you there. It was for Arthur and Irene and I'm going to repeat it in about three weeks for another group. I now have to give my shindigs in sections as my house is too small for those Scheherezades I used to throw.

All my love and write soon.

Your padre,
Groucho

The Gershwin picture was Rhapsody in Blue.

November 10, 1945

Dear Mir,

I was pleasantly surprised to get a letter from you today. I wish you wouldn't send them to the office, for Kay might get the feeling that there's collusion between us and that we're attempting to conceal something from her. In addition to that, this letter, for example, I would have received this morning from the mailman. As it was, I had to come to town to my office to get it.

I note what you say about being able to get a good car for $150. If it's still there, you can have it for your Christmas present. However, I would like you to think carefully about this, for if you are going to New York in December for three months, you would find the car of no use there and quite a burden, in addition to being a heavy financial anchor. A car cannot be garaged in New York under $40 per month, so think about it.

I'm glad you now enjoy the *New York Times*. It's a great paper, not one of the outstanding liberal ones but it's not reactionary and they do give you the news and let you decide for yourself—something that the local papers don't do.

I won't make this a long letter for this is Rachel's half-day off and I don't want her typing all afternoon. I'm sending two pictures to you and they're self-explanatory, except that the camel's name is Martha and she's fifty-two years old. We gave her a small birthday party on the set and I brought a bag of peanuts with three candles in it.

Yes, life does change and will continue to. You say that things will never be the same again. They will be as far as we're concerned. The fact that Fay is gone and, by the way, she's now working in Beverly for some other slave-driven family, and that Duke is gone, isn't too important. I miss Duke but these are all the non-essentials of my existence. You and Art and Kay are the ones that count. I mean deeply, personally. There are others who count, but not in the same way. This is pretty involved but it's Saturday afternoon—see paragraph above—and I'll write you a lengthier letter next week. Kay wants to know why you don't answer her letter. Please send my letters to the house. Think the car problem over carefully before you make a decision.

Love and kisses,
Your padre

November 16, 1945

Dear Mir;

I have only a few minutes—it seems that I always start my letters off in this vein—but it's the truth, so help me.

I'll try to answer all your questions briefly and quickly. To begin with, I received the story and I liked it moderately well. Frankly, I'm a little weary of the subject matter. Mrs. Delano has now been profiled by Arthur Marx, Alan Kent and yourself. There must be other subjects in this wide world that could be of more interest either from an amusement standpoint or a dramatic one. It's always difficult for a father to appraise the efforts of his children. Of course, if they are athletic, it's comparatively simple, for if you have a boy who runs the one hundred yards in 9.6, there it is—you've got to concede that he's a swift runner. The literary field, however, is such a nebulous one—what I consider good, someone else might find mediocre and vice versa. Then there's always the danger of trying to be too fair as a parent and criticizing a piece with more savagery than it deserves. Of course, there is the other parent who is certain that his child can do nothing that isn't super and he is just as foolish and wrong. Therefore, I feel that any criticism I can give you is worthless. In addition to that, I don't feel qualified to judge a literary work. I think you write better than you did a year ago. We had better just forget about it though, for there can be no critical relationship between two people where there is an emotional element involved so I won't waste your time by commenting any further.

In answer to your letter of November thirteenth, the offer of the Christmas present still goes. Be sure that the tires are in good condition lest you blow yourself up on the road and have someone examine the car for its mechanical condition, for when it comes to that sort of thing, you're indeed a babe in the woods. I'm glad you have transportation now.

I presume that your girlfriends have arrived by this time and that you are ecstatically happy. It would be very interesting to be at the keyhole and listen to what goes on between you three. I imagine it would be pretty revealing, too.

I'm on "The Dinah Shore Show" next week—Thanksgiving night. Apparently you didn't like my last "Dinah Shore" appearance for I see no mention of it in your letter. Even if you don't like them, it might be advisable to tell me and tell me why—or is this just as difficult for you as it is for me with your written pieces?

I have to go now. I'm glad that you're happy and having a good time.

My love to you and a million kisses.

Your Padre,
Groucho

P.S. RL wants you to know that she sent a large package to you today. Cookies and candied nuts from your mother, and be sure to find the small package enclosed from me—take them according to directions. And I understand that Maxine is to be on the "Sherlock Holmes" broadcast, November nineteenth—Monday—you might want to listen in.

Mrs. Delano was my mother's mother, Josephine Delano, of whom I was not very fond. She was a very vocal bigot.

[November 24, 1945]

Dear Pooch;

This is Sunday afternoon the twenty-fourth of November. Kay is hacking away at the piano, and all else is quiet and serene. I am attempting to write you a letter as next week is a particularly hard one. It's the week of the process shots, and it involves physical hard work, climbing and crawling and wind machines blowing on me to give the appearance of a plane in flight. There will be plenty of errors in this letter, for my typing is not the kind that won Billy Rose the championship as the fastest typist in the Unitik States, to steal a pronunciation from a girl who once lived in my house.

We were all shocked deeply by Benchley's death. He was loved by everyone who was lucky enough to have known him, and like Broun and Woolcott, there is no one around that is going to take his place. Bob as you know was a terrifically heavy drinker. He had been warned against this by all his friends and doctors, but he didn't care much, he was tired of living, and I think he is glad it is all over with. I am not morbid about Bob's passing (as the Scientists have it) but it is too bad it couldn't be Gerald Smith, or Franco or someone like that.

I heard through Rachel Linden that you have been laid up with a cold, and that you were incarcerated in the local infirmary? I think she got the info from your mother, and I can only hope that you have fully recovered by this time.

We had a big party last night, but Kay can tell you all about it; she will give you the woman's angle, always more interesting than the man's.

Next week is the last week of the shooting and don't think I am not looking forward to it with great anticipation and pleasure. People always say, "Why don't you fellows make more pictures, you can shoot one in eight weeks." That's true, but from the time we started planning the story, through the rehearsals for the stage tour, through the rewriting, the shooting, the dubbing, the previews and the re-takes, it will be exactly one year from the time we started last January.

I want a rest when I complete this. I want to sit down and read, and sleep and listen to music and go to the movies and arise when I please, not at the whim of some stupid bastard known as a unit manager, who apparently gets a sadistic delight on summoning actors to the set six hours before they are needed. Well, it will soon be over and some day it will all seem like a bad or a good dream, depending on whether it is a good picture or not.

I am glad you liked "The Dinah Shore Show" of a few weeks ago. Did you listen to the one I did Thanksgiving? It was even better than the one you heard. I am on again on the sixth of December. We will try and do a little story again like we did on the last two.

I am sorry that you were disappointed in Janet and Sunny, but that is only natural. Friendships require not only constant repair, but constant adjustments. Your writing has improved enormously, and it is as much evident in your letters as in your writing. You are learning about life the right way through personal experience, the only knowledge that is important and vital. You are learning things that can't be told to you by a parent, and things that you can't learn out of books. The changed relationship with Janet and Sunny is the result of a part of a new and different life that you are experiencing firsthand.

This is a pretty screwed up analysis. I can only hope that it is clear to you.

I can't write any more as I am sleepy and jumpy and want to lie down for a while and contemplate my duties for tomorrow, which consist of swinging on a ladder from a moving truck onto a plane that apparently is going two hundred miles an hour.

In closing I want to report that yesterday I saw seven reels of *Adventure in Casablanca* strung loosely together, and it looked as if it might

39

be good. All my love to you and I hope you are better, and that you are happy. Excuse all the errors, for I am a miserable typist and seem constantly to get worse instead of better.

> Your ever lovin'
> Padre
> XXXXXXXXXXX
> Kay sends her love

Benchley was Robert Benchley, author and humorist. Broun and Woolcott were Heywood Broun and Alexander Woolcott, also writers. Gerald Smith was Gerald L. K. Smith, a right-wing political leader who ran for president in 1944.

November 29, 1945

Dear Mir,

This is the maid's day off and my morning. It's raining intermittently and frequently—in fact, it's raining right now. We expected to be through shooting last Saturday but now it looks like we'll run until December fourth, which will be Tuesday. I am on "The Dinah Shore Show" Thursday. I'm glad you liked the last performance and the preceding one—a little story does help, doesn't it? I am head over heels in hogwash (mail, to you)—it's an accumulation of many weeks' debris and I am so conscientious about correspondence that I suppose on my first free day, I'll spend most of it knocking my brains out.

I am glad to hear you are out of the infirmary. Kay started a siege at the dentist's yesterday and it's going to be a WPA project really. She's neglected her mouth—I guess all girls do until they hook a husband. She told me she wanted to get her teeth fixed years ago but that Leo wouldn't pay for it and since she had no money, there was nothing she could do. Anyway, it was quite a day. I got home from the studio about the time she arrived from the dentist's. The dentist was having dinner with us, along with Irene and Arthur, and then we were all going to a movie. What happened was that Kay's pain grew increasingly worse, she had two drinks and was plastered and was staggering around the library like a chicken with its head chopped off. This, I know, is a well-worn simile but it precisely fits this particular case. Anyhow, after dinner, I had to take Kay back to the dentist's. He phoned his nurse, who met us there, and we spent the whole evening on the fifth floor of a theatrical office building while Kay alternately groaned and wept as this fiend the dentist, her dinner guest, plowed deeper and deeper. This is a grisly tale but that's life. While I think of

40

it, if you have any teeth that need repair, try to wait until you get married. I'm inclined to believe that most girls would remain single were it not for their teeth.

Anyhow, I am fairly happy today—the picture is almost over and I think it's going to be good. Kibbee thinks it's going to be our best. That I don't agree with but I think it will be a whole lot better than the last three we made at MGM.

I've thought it over and if you require a heavier coat, buy one. I wrote you last Sunday in my own inimitable style. There's not much new to tell you. Arthur is still kind of bouncing around, not sure yet what he will or can do, but there are millions of other boys in the same frame of mind. Alan is working for Parkyakarkus. He has a twelve-week guarantee at $100 a week. It came in the nick of time for I had lent him $70. He's all right, though, and will pay it back as soon as he gets some money. He, too, has to find himself and hasn't yet. In Irene, I detect a faint yearning for her old work—cutting film at the studio. I think she found that far more exciting and satisfying than being the wife of an ex-serviceman who's looking for a job.

It isn't quite clear to me about your forthcoming New York sojourn. Does the school obtain a job for you or do you have to scout around on your own? Too, what kind of work does the school expect you to do? The whole thing is very shady and I wish you would explain it to me in detail.

Must run now. A million kisses and lots and lots of love.

Your padre,
Groucho

Leo was Leo Gorcey from the Dead End Kids film series. He appeared as a regular with Groucho on the radio show "Blue Ribbon Town" in 1943 and was Kay's ex-husband. Parkyakarkus (Harry Einstein) was a comic who appeared on radio and film.

December 8, 1945

Dear Mir,

I received your letter and am glad to know you're all right again. This is being written hastily as you probably suspected from the opening. I'm meeting your brother in eight minutes at which time we're rushing down to the L.A. Tennis Club to see Budge, Perry, Tilden and Riggs play the semi-finals. It's apparently attracting a lot of interest for I'm finding it very difficult to buy any seats for Sunday—that's tomorrow, I mean, suh. That's a joke, son—er-r, I mean daughter.

I saw the picture yesterday. It ran two hours. It seems pretty smooth and the story is quite interesting—whether it's funny or not, I can't tell. The general feeling is that it's going to be good. Audiences laughed a lot at the stuff on the stage so I'm sure they will when they see the picture. The last reel is a wild chase, apparently a basic requisite for a comedy. I think it's quite ingenious and pretty exciting.

I didn't like "The Dinah Shore Show" I did last Thursday so you don't have to write about it, you can wait until I go on again and then tell me you didn't like that. I'll be on the Ginny Simms show next Friday and I predict it'll be even worse. I'm gradually talking myself off the air and into semi-seclusion in my small hovel in Westwood.

Your plans are very vague. Are you spending the next three months in New York? If so, have you an occupation or are you just going to walk the streets—a profession, by the way, that at times has been a very lucrative one. Please write me a long, comprehensive letter. I don't know just when I'll get to New York. I don't imagine it'll be too early—as a matter of fact, I'd prefer coming in March but a good deal depends on what plans crystallize here in the next few weeks.

This is, fortunately for you, a brief letter. I'll write you a nice one the first part of the week. From here in I'll have nothing but leisure. I'm glad you enjoy the snow—you can have it. This letter could be longer—your brother and Irene are sitting here glowering at me with that hungry look that wolves acquire when they are pursuing their prey. Your letters are pretty infrequent these days. You'll have to do something about it.

Love from all.

Your padre,
Hackenbush

Monday morning. December sixteenth, 1945

I missed your presence today when I went to buy the tree. We always had an argument about it: you always wanted a real tall one, while I, with one eye on price and one on practicality, always favored a small one. As I remember it, you always won out, and as I also remember it, that was usually the last time you looked at the tree.

Kay dressed it and did a fine job. It is loaded with balls, spangles and bulbs, plus eighteen candy canes that we were shrewd enough to gobble up at Martha Smith's before the usual looting begins a few days before Xmas. I am sure that we bought the whole supply, making it virtually impossible for any other child in Beverly to have a candy cane this year. This is the real Xmas spirit, and we are very proud of ourselves.

I am glad you liked the Dinah Shore show that you wrote me about. Did you hear the one I did with Ginny Simms, who is the poor man's Dinah Shore? The agency liked it a lot and they want me back soon, so you see I am becoming the boy who sneaked back into radio and is making good without Dick Mack or even Warwick, Legler or Morris. Brecher's show, "The Life of Riley," which cost exactly half as much as the Danny Kaye show, is a fifteen Hopper and Kaye has a ten. "The Dinah Shore Show," which also is far less expensive than the Kaye show, also has a fifteen. I don't care about Kaye flopping, but I am happy to see Warwick and Legler be over their heads in worry. I am really a jerk. I remember once comparing Warwick to Sam Harris, not even the Sam Harris that was in *Yankee Doodle Dandy*.

I hope you are enjoying yourself in New York. Also that you are looking around for some occupation. In mentioning Danny Kaye before, it made me think of Janet Cantor. Is she still in the East with Sunny, and do you see them? They dropped out of your correspondence after you mentioned them the first time and I wondered whether you have adjusted yourselves or whether that is all over like the baseball season.

You have never told me whether you have made any new friends in school, or who they are. Or are you a lone wolverine roaming the hills of Vermont on your own? As a matter of fact, you have told me very little about your activities up there in New England, and now that the press of school is off your shoulders, it might be a good idea for you to open up and give me a child's eye view of life in a small Eastern school.

Today I am going to Schaindt. Nothing serious, I hope, just the six months customary probing around with that long steel hook that he is so fond of using. I am lucky, for in the past few years I have had practically nothing done by him that I couldn't have done myself, so I am not complaining.

Then later in the week comes the eye doctor, and also stills for the picture. I believe that I prefer the eye and tooth examinations. Next Thursday, that's this one a week, I am on the Shore show again, and after that the preview, and then who knows, maybe New York. At any rate, by the first of the year I will know much better what my plans are for the coming season.

Kay, not Danny, is going to add a few words to this, so at this point I will sign off, with my love and kisses.

Groucho Padre

Dearest Mir,

If you never speak to me again, I wouldn't blame you; it has been over a month since you have heard from me. But honest, Mir, I have a good excuse. I have been going to the dentist every day for three weeks, and I mean every day, one day I was in his clutches for five hours and then passed right out on the floor. I'll never go that long again. I'm having all my teeth fixed. I've neglected them for so long that now they are a major project. When you see me next, I will have teeth like yours, whose teeth I have always envied. So please forgive me for not writing to you for so long.

Yesterday I received the lovely scarf you sent me for Christmas. It's beautiful, Mir, and something I always hesitate to buy for myself. Hope you have a prosperous Christmas, and a drunken New Year (me too).

Love and Kisses,
Kay

P.S. Say hello to your mother for me, and I'll write you all the news soon.

Excuse errors.

I was living with my mother in the Gramercy Park Hotel in New York at this time, working for a publisher during my first winter break from college. Dick Mack wrote and directed "Blue Ribbon Town." Warwick, Legler and Morris were also radio writers.

[December 18, 1945]

Dear Pooch;

I don't start off this way when I dictate to Rachel, for it's a little embarrassing for a man of my age to say that to an elderly steno with graying hair. Anyway, Dear Pooch, and your letter of December seventh received. It is ten in the morning and all through the house hardly anyone stirs, therefore this letter.

Alan as you may know is working for Parkyakarkas, the Jewish Greek, and apparently doing well, for I haven't heard from him in two weeks. As a rule he only phones me when he is jobless and destitute. I don't mind for he rarely ever discusses anything but his job when I see him. Anyway I am glad he is working, for there is nothing sadder than a writer with nothing to write.

I went to the tennis matches with Arthur and Irene and saw Bobby Riggs play tennis that was not far from perfection, and polish off Don Budge after dropping the first set to Don, eleven-nine. Apparently that was all Budge had to offer, for after that opening he faded and it wasn't long after that he was decisively trounced and whipped; Budge claimed a cramp in his right arm in the third set, but he was cleaned up long before then. Curiously enough I felt terribly depressed by his defeat; it seemed like something personal. On thinking about it now, I guess it was just the shattering of another idol, and incidentally my emotions may have been raked by the fact that I had ten dollars bet on Don.

Anyway the tennis was excellent, the crowds were tremendous and the weather balmy and fair. It seemed like one of the most pleasant days of my life, having Arthur back, the war over and the picture about finished. I saw the picture last week. It ran two hours and everyone seems to think it's good. I can't tell, and I won't venture an opinion until I see it in an audience and get their reaction. Archie Mayo says it's one of the best pictures he has ever seen, but oh boy, can Mayo be wrong. Anyway, it's through except for little minor touches like scoring (by Werner Janssen), looping by your correspondent and other little touches.

According to Hoffman in the *Reporter*, Fields and Chodorov labored and brought forth a louse. I am sorry for Chodorov's sake, I don't care much about the other character. Well, perhaps it isn't true, and maybe the New York critics will come out and acclaim it the play of the year, but with the customary exceptions, when Hoffman comes out with an obituary review he is usually right.

I hope you have a good time in New York and that you occupy yourself with something that will be of help to you. I am also glad that you like the place so much and I am sure that I will consent to your going back next year, unless something alarming happens to your grades in the coming months.

Oh, it's so wonderful not to rise at seven in the morning for the shooting. It isn't that I care so much about rising early in the morning, but you know me. As soon as I know that I have to get up early, I just tighten up at night and cannot get to sleep. Well that's in back of me now.

The Victory committee asked me yesterday if Kay and I would fly to Honolulu for five days of hospital stuff around the holidays, but I want a little rest before I make any further plans. I am on the Ginny Simms show Friday and up to date the script stinks. If it doesn't improve by Thursday I will try and bow out and give the job to someone who needs it more than I do.

This about completes the news to date. Have a good time, write soon and remember I love you. Kay too sends her love, and regards to your mother.

Your handsome and fascinating Padre,
Padre XXXXXXXXXXXXX

Fields was Joe Fields, Jerry Chodorov's collaborator on several plays and musicals. The "louse" referred to here was probably The French Touch.

December 20, 1945

Dear Mir,
This won't be much of a letter. I received the Steig cartoon book this morning and read it with avidity. (Avidity is an Armenian neighbor of mine who lives across the street and he always drops over whenever I have a book of Steig's cartoons.)

As Mrs. Delano would say, your letters are as scarce as hen's teeth — or probably as scarce as Mrs. Delano's. In spite of this I am enclosing a check for $50 for you. This can be spent for champagne, a platinum bra or six suits of heavy underwear. This is a kind of supplemental present as I'm still willing to go through with that car deal sometime after the winter snows have melted. (Gosh, he writes exactly like Walt Whitman.)

Saturday night we are going to the Sheekmans'. They are having a preliminary Christmas party. Christmas Eve we're going to the Gershwins'; Christmas noon we're throwing a luncheon for Kay's group of gorillas and Christmas night we're going to the Kahns'. Saturday, a week, the twenty-ninth, we're again going to the Sheekmans'. They are giving two parties within an interval of a week. Gloria, who is really the Mad Hatter, explains this by saying that she is so popular, it can't all be swung in one night. Sheekman's complexion turns a glassy green at the thought of this. New Year's Eve, we are going to Harpo's — that is, provided he'll let Arthur and Irene come. If he doesn't I'll drop out as I want to be with them that night. Since it is a twelve o'clock supper and not a dinner, I don't imagine he will object. He's not having a big crowd.

This has developed into a pretty lengthy letter for a man who was just bent on sending you a check.

All my love to you and have a Merry Christmas and, for the love of Gerald K. Smith, take that typewriter that was bought with my money and use it in the direction of California.

Your padre,
Groucho

[December 25, 1945]

Dear Pooch;

While Kay is upstairs putting the finishing touches to her face, we are on our way to the Kahns' for a quiet family dinner. It was nice to hear your eager voice on the phone yesterday, although it was too bad to hear that you had a cold. I called you that day because I knew how impossible it would be to connect with you on Xmas, or even the day before.

Well it's Xmas today, and your present arrived, and it's lovely (as the girls would put it). I am sorry that you squandered such a large piece of your allowance on it, but it's your own fault, you shouldn't have parents. Kay gave me a wonderful Dunhill lighter, a fine bathrobe and a box of expensive cigars. I gave her some teeth (twelve hundred bucks), something that she wanted above all else. It would have been far cheaper to have bought her something romantic, but in the long run I know that she would be happier and more grateful for that, in fact she is now, as she wanted that above all else. I also gave her a waist and a hand sewn slip, a bathrobe and slippers. I got a baseball glove from the Sheekmans, and a ball to match. Some perfume from someone else, a silver dish to Kay and me from Art and Ick and something that looks like wine from the Rubys.

All in all, I had a very fine Xmas. I even got a frozen turkey from my sponsor, and what is more important, seven weeks on "The Dinah Shore Show," me to pick the times I want to go on. I am a pretty lucky fellow, and I am very thankful for all I have. My marriage is turning out fine, my kids are too, I am working, I have my health, a house, a car, a Capehart and we are keeping Gerald K. Smith in check.

Last night I went to the Gershwins' to a Xmas Eve party, and I had a long talk with Dotty Parker and she asked about you, and she was so happy that you are becoming so hep politically, and she asked me to be sure and arrange for her to meet you when she goes back to New

York in about another month or so. She always asks about you and I also told her how you admired her. I hope you get the job you want and that you work hard at it.

December 28

The preceding paragraphs were written on the twenty-fifth. It is now the twenty-eight, and I am firing up the incinerator to take care of the refuse that accumulated over the holiday. Since I began this letter I have appeared on "The Dinah Shore Show"; if you heard it, the re-broadcast was better, if you didn't hear it, the Eastern show was the best. I am not sure that the story idea holds up on a show that involves four songs by Dinah and a hell of a long commercial by Von Zell, so my next time on, sometime in January, I may go back to the customary sketch that I formerly did on the show. (Editor's note: there was a short intermission at this point as the author was forced to return to the incinerator to remove the surplus ashes. Now go on with the story.)

The maid was stricken today. I believe with the flu, and I am hoping that we aren't laid low in the next few days. Kay is doing the housework and the dinner and the dishes. I volunteered to take her to a restaurant, but she has an allergy to eating out that is astounding, considering the fact that she is a female (of that I am certain).

We had a nice dinner at the Kahns', turkey for the fourth day. It's always pleasant over there. Grace is an amiable host, and seems never happier than when surrounded with a lot of people. We even had champagne, domestic, Cooks, far better than the imported, and far cheaper, and when you return if ever, I will kill the fatted calf and open up bottles of Cooks.

I am going to Harpo's New Year's Eve, a small select party composed mostly I imagine of comics, and they are certainly the best ones to be around on a night that to me always seems exceedingly sad. Anyway I will drink a toast to you (in Cooks) and I will be thinking of you. The notion of phoning you is out of the question that day above all others.

Tonight, on your recommendation, I am going to see Pride of the Marines at the Uclan—if Kay is up to it—and tomorrow night I am supposed to go to a party, but our plan at present is to duck it and stay home and read.

So a Happy New Year to you and all our love and hope you get the job you're after, or some other job, and take vitamin A for the pill that will ward off colds (Dr. Henstell, 1945).

Your loving Padre

P.S. Bennet Cerf is reprinting my Hoffman piece in the S. *Review of Literature* December twenty-second.

Von Zell was Harry Von Zell, a radio announcer.

December 31, 1945

Dear Mir,
I had a letter from you this morning and I'm glad to hear that you're still working. It's unfortunate that you have such a dull job and I think you should keep your ears cocked for something where you can use your mind instead of your legs. Money can be made with your legs but that's a different business. You might call up Morris Ernst (incidentally, he's quite a wolf). He has vast connections, particularly in Manhattan, and he might be able to get you better situated; also Max Schuster of Simon and Schuster. If you think it'd help, I'll write a letter to Schuster, not that a letter from me would be an open sesame but it might enable you to get your feet inside the door.

Last night we went to the Brechers'. By we, I mean the two of us and Art and Ick. Brecher has invested in a movie machine (16mm) and we saw *Mr. Deeds Goes to Town.* It's a Capra-Bob Riskin oldie of about seven or eight years ago. Cooper is comparatively young in this film and does a fine job. Anyway, it's a very pleasant way to see a movie except that Mrs. Brecher insisted on embellishing the Riskin dialogue with her own observations. I didn't tell her, but they were not nearly as good.

I'm glad to hear that you have acquired such interesting and fascinating female accomplices at Bennington, and the changed relationship you tell me about with Janet and Sunny is quite normal. As you go through life (this is the old man clearing his throat and putting on his pontifical outfit) you will find that your relationships never remain static—this occurs with your parents and it also occurs with everyone else that you meet, have met and have mitten. (This is Pennsylvania Dutch and perhaps can be found in Mencken's *Treatise on the American Language.*)

There isn't much to write you for it's only been a couple of days since I slipped one of my own badly typed missiles (not missives) in the mail. There are still remnants of the war hovering over Beverly—

sailors and soldiers on bicycles, no butter in the stores and not much of anything else. However, after reading a detailed report of conditions in the various European countries, I'd better keep my big mouth shut, as Doris Samuels would put it. By the way, I had a short letter in the *New York Times* last Sunday, December twenty-third. If you have a copy around, look at it, but it isn't good enough to warrant any research work.

Anyway, a Happy New Year to you and your mother and all my love and sometime in the next few months I'll be seeing you—probably in all the old familiar places. I look at your picture every day in my bedroom, or does that sound like an old maudlin beer song? At any rate, you're not a bad looking girl. Would you like to exchange photos?

Your padre,
Groucho

January 8, 1946

Dear Mir,

After our phone conversation on Sunday, I sent a letter to you at 153 West 73 Street. This is where you told me you were going to live. You might check on that letter. There's no money in it but there's a vast amount of windy information.

I received your special this morning and it's unfortunate that the situation is as it is. In case you didn't get the other letter, I received a letter from Shufro interceding or attempting to but I wrote him that you were almost nineteen and if your life was unpleasant with your mother that you had to make your own decision. It's too bad that nothing can be done about this. As you know, during the latter years of our married life, I attempted to get her off the stuff but it all fell on deaf ears. It is a sickness and, as I wrote you, perhaps if you could take her to Dr. Richard Hoffman, she could be given a series of treatments that might help her. Max Gordon can give you his phone number and address. I feel terribly sad about this—perhaps living with me so many years drove her to it and I feel sorry that you have to battle this alone but I don't know what else to suggest—psychiatry, Christian Science? I'm even toying with the idea of having Arthur write.

Anyhow, I thoroughly approve of your leaving *Time* magazine and going with the *Herald Tribune* and I'll send you the difference. I agree with you that to get $20 a week in a job at which you won't learn anything is worse than a job without pay where you have a chance to use your mind. So let me know when you want to start on the other job and I'll send you an additional $80 a month. I'll also drop a line to Morris Ernst and, by the pink note enclosed in your letter, I see that you also have a boyfriend whose first name is Hudson. I am happy to know that you at least have a boyfriend. There are not many office boys who have a boyfriend. Does he know that all you do is clean out receptacles and fill water bottles or does he think you're related to Luce? Well, enough of this unfunny stuff. Do all you can to help your mother. See if you can't shake her out of this alcoholic daze. She needs someone strong to rely on. Don't worry too much and remember, I love you.

Your padre,
Hackenbush

P.S. What exactly is your new address? Please clearly print it, including zone number.

> *On New Year's Day, 1946, I had moved out of my mother's hotel room because she was drinking heavily and we were not getting along. Morris Ernst was a famous attorney. Henry Luce Enterprises (Life magazine) was the name of the company I was working for.*

[January 14, 1946]

Dear Miriam,
I didn't sleep so well last night, thinking about you and the phone call. Things being as they are, the best thing was to get out, but it is too bad that you now have to live alone. I suppose, as they say, in the long run it will do you good, but it's a big town and one can be very lonely in a big town. I was surprised to hear that you assumed I was going to leave you penniless just because school had folded for three months. I realize that you need money, even though school is suspended, and your allowance will appear just as XXXXXXXXXXXXXXX (the last word I typed was so misspelled that I decided to abandon the whole thing and begin over again) miraculously as though you rubbed a lamp and a genie appeared, except in this case it will be a jewnie (that's a joke, daughter).

I am glad to hear that your job isn't as bad as you originally thought, and you had better stick it out if only for the money. The one thing I don't like about your living alone is that if you are ill you have no one to look after you. What about all those girls from Bennington?

Isn't there one among them that you could room with? What about Sunny and Janet? Can't you tie up with them in some way? As to your mother, I think it's possible that Dr. Hoffman could straighten her out. He is pretty good at that sort of thing, and perhaps if she had someone to confide in and tell her problems to, she could be convinced that the solution for her is not to pour booze down her throat.

It is bitter cold today, and feels like Boston during the football weather. We are taking Art and Ick to the Beachcomber, a place where I haven't been in months, and then home and to bed. Harpo is in bed with a cold, and the epidemic has practically decimated the town. I have been flirting with it for a few days, and am watching it carefully.

I am going on the Shore show next week instead of Sinatra. He is sick and instead of going on the seventeenth I am going on the tenth. I had planned on going to Frisco for the Camp Shows, but will go the week following, health permitting.

You might also call up Schuster of Simon and Schuster about a job. I suppose one of the reasons it is difficult to get a decent job is the unwillingness of a concern breaking in anyone for three months and then having them walk out and back to school again.

There isn't much news to tell you, as you probably realize by the time you reach this point in this letter. These publicity men we have engaged are jerks—no worse jerks than the run of the mill publicity men, but their ideas of what constitute stunts are fantastic, in addition to being unfunny. For example, they hatched a scheme that involved me in full makeup and a spyglass in the lobby of the Chinese Theatre. I told them quickly and firmly that those days were over, and that I had no intention at my age of making a public spectacle of myself. They countered with the worn out plea that "it was for the good of the picture and that it would increase the receipts enormously." I said perhaps, but that I would not do it for the picture or anyone else.

Last night we saw *They Were Expendable* and I was confused from the first reel to the finale. It's part of that director's theory in this that if it's dark and obscure on the screen, it must be good. Well my mind isn't that bright and sharp and I have trouble with real simple pictures; the complicated ones like Hitchcock's throw me into a deep fuddle. Some of the shots I must admit were vivid and lifelike, but I never did find out whether the Americans were leaving Bataan or just arriving. It was shot by John Ford, who made *The Informer,* so I am convinced that I am a dull-witted lout and should stay at home and re-read Hans Christian Andersen.

Must close now as it's late. Write soon, and don't worry too much. Yesterday I sang for eleven blind kids from the hospital (Army). That's real trouble. As long as you have arms and legs and eyes, and a fair amount of health, and some money, you're a lucky gal. Pretty soon perhaps I can get a job on the air as the old philosopher? God knows I'm old enough.

Good-bye and lots of love to you from the both of us and write soon.

Your loving Padre,
Padre—XXXXXXXXXXXXX
Take good care of yourself.

Miriam, this is the letter your dad sent to the wrong address. It's pretty ancient but you should have it and here it is. Lots of luck and remember your mother, the only one you'll ever have. RL

[January 14, 1946]

Dear Miriam;
I received two letters this morning from New York, one a letter from you and one a letter I sent you to an[other] address . . . Apparently you gave me this address in one of your wilder moments, for the following letter from you gave me the other address.

I am happy to hear that the man you are going with at the moment is not a fairy; I should have known this—I am sure that no one on the Luce Publications is anything but virile.

I am sorry that you found out through a newspaper that you may become a sister to a small boy or girl. We are not sure of it ourselves, and tomorrow Kay is journeying downtown with Helen Perrin to find out from a doctor if it is so. If it is, I will see that you are informed promptly and with the proper amount of ceremony. I was embarrassed when it appeared in the local *Times*. It came through Gloria Sheekman and then Frank Finch on the local paper, who is Gloria's brother. This last sentence doesn't quite make sense, but I think you understand.

Now to the business at hand. We previewed the picture last Friday night at Huntington Park, and it ran an hour and fifty-three minutes. It was a semi juvenile audience, the kind that all the theatres seem to get on Friday nights. At any rate, they laughed a bit, but mostly at Harpo. Either they didn't understand my stuff or they weren't amused. We are taking twenty minutes of dead stuff out of it (there seems to

53

be plenty of that) and previewing this Wednesday night again, at some other town, I hope. Dave Loew agrees with us that Mayo turned in an extremely inept piece of directing, but that's over now and can't be remedied. There may be a lot of re-shooting after this preview but we can't do anything about it until we show it again, considerably condensed.

I was terribly depressed at the preview. We had worked so long and hard on this, and thought we had it so solid and tight, and then to see reams of it emasculated by that fat idiot (Mayo), well it was heart rending.

I am not going to worry about it too much. It's done now. I am sure that it will be better than *The Big Store,* but it will never be another *Night at the Opera.*

I wish you wouldn't apologize for not hearing me on "The Dinah Shore Show." I don't expect you to hear it. If you are near a radio and can conveniently flick the dial, fine, if not, forget about it. I am sure you have enough problems in New York without that responsibility facing you. The show, by the way, was pretty good, my next appearance being the thirtieth of January.

Arthur, that's your brother, just called me, as excited as a stage mother, to inform me that a piece I didn't care for had been sold to *Esquire* for sixty dollars. This will give the postal authorities another reason for attempting to bar *Esquire* from the mails. I presume he told you that he is working on a scenario, for which he is getting paid. He got the job through Larry Bachman, who I predict will end up his days as the head of MGM.

I can't write any more today, I am in a hurry. This incidentally is the first letter I have had from you in a week, so if you expect the additional allowance, you had better get hot with that machine.

> Love and lots of it from Kay and your
> Padre,
> XXXXXXX Padre

Dave Loew produced A Night in Casablanca. *Larry Bachman was a screenwriter.*

January 21, 1946

Dear Miriam,
I was deeply disappointed when your lover the mailman arrived today without a letter from you in his sack. Apparently our correspondence

only blooms when you need something (like money, for example). Anyway, I heard from another source—a note relayed from Morris Ernst—that you are now involved in confusing Harper Brothers in their publishing business and I hope you are getting a princely or queenly salary and that you are enjoying the job.

Since last I wrote you, I have purchased a new home; that is, I have paid a deposit on it and unless the house collapses from termites or the negotiations hit a clinker somewhere along the line, I'll be living at 1277 Sunset Plaza Drive about the first of April. Thus, already prospective buyers are trampling through my little nest in Westwood, peering in closets, peeking in bedrooms and generally making a nuisance of themselves. The thought of moving again appalls me. I won't write you any of the details as that's a woman's work and Kay promised to attend to that herself—so one of these days you'll get a long wind-blown letter from her full of inaccuracies and badly misspelled. In this, she'll tell all.

Between the Granets and the Brechers, I'm gradually seeing all the old films. Last night we saw *The Awful Truth*. This is eight years old and just as wonderful as it was when it was first released. The writing is beautiful and the players are superb. It's regrettable there isn't a theatre out here that constantly plays the old features.

We previewed again last week and although the picture has some good stuff in it, it still needs a world of fixing with perhaps some reshooting. Mayo's directorial work was just hideous. He has managed to take some of the best scenes we did on the stage and wring them dry. David Loew, who originally was so strong for him, after the second preview sadly confessed that he had made a mistake and that Mayo's direction was shockingly old-fashioned. We are now running it in the projection room, clipping and cutting and pasting together, and it may eventually be all right but it's going to take a lot of work. Some of the damage is irreparable.

I had a letter from Alan Kent and he also sent a copy of his play to me. It has some pretty good stuff in it and certainly there are definite indications of talent. He is in Santa Barbara. How he is living, I don't know—he probably has snared some millionaire to subsidize him—to put it nicely. . . .

The Granets were friends Bert and Charlotte Granet. Bert was a Hollywood producer. The last page of this letter is missing.

55

February 1, 1946

Dear Miriam,

Your writing is more frequent lately and it's probably due to the job with that big desk and those pleasant surroundings—I guess you just can't resist punching the machine.

I spent a very pleasant evening the other night at the Cantors: [George] Burns and [Gracie] Allen, the Cantors, Jessel, Abel Green of *Variety* and us. Cantor was very pleasant and refrained from that too-confident manner that he customarily uses. He made a few glancing remarks about *Nellie Bly* and, all in all, was quite charming. I guess an occasional failure is good for one—it's so deflating. We had a good dinner and, fortunately, as soon as that was over the women wiggled out into the next room and played cards and an evening with Jessel and Burns is always fun. I meant to ask about Janet but it completely slipped my mind. I've also asked you about Janet and Sunny but you refuse to open up.

We previewed again Wednesday night—in Inglewood—and it went quite well. It's far better than it was, but it will never be a first-rate picture, thanks to the producing, directing and the choice of Werner Janssen to score the picture. The music sounds as though it fitted *Spellbound* and since none of the three of us is a Gregory Peck, it doesn't quite fit. The picture will no doubt make money but, as far as my ego is concerned, I get no kick out of it at all. It's quite a disappointment. We labored long and hard on this, and with some intelligence contributed by the others it could have been a very good picture. As it is, it's a kind of a *Duck Soup* plus. Large hunks of the story have been scissored but the audience laughed and I suppose they'll buy tickets but the critics won't throw their hats in the air. If they throw anything, it'll probably be their dinner. Well, enough of my griping. It's done and there's not much that can be done about it without a great deal of re-shooting, which David Loew isn't too eager for. I'll say that with the way he spends money, he should be able to retain his forty millions indefinitely. He's a curious combination of incompetence and miserliness.

Kay is reading a book called *How to Raise a Baby* and she predicts that hers will begin kicking next week. She's very excited and in her spare moments knits all kinds of strange-looking objects that I am sure won't fit anything.

Lena Horne told me that she had dinner with you in New York or vice versa and that she was tremendously impressed with you, so you see you're probably turning out better than you ever anticipated.

I sold the Westwood house to a Pontiac dealer. I didn't get as much as I asked for it but more than I paid. When I think of moving again I begin to reel a little but everything passes and someday I suppose I'll be complaining about the new house.

My plans are still in the air. I received a play, if I didn't tell you, from Max Shulman and it's god-awful. Tomorrow I am getting the Mary Chase play and will let you know what I think of it.

Take care of yourself and write soon. All my love and be a good girl—but not too good.

Your padre,
Hackenbush

Abel Green was the editor of Variety. *He also hosted the "Radio Hall of Fame" show, which Groucho guested on, and appeared in* Copacabana *(1947). Max Shulman was a playwright, novelist and later the creator of the television series "Dobie Gillis." Mary Chase was a playwright who won a Pulitzer Prize for her play* Harvey *in 1944.*

February 5, 1946

Dear Mir,

This won't be much of a letter, just something that I apparently forgot to explain the last time I wrote. Unfortunately I can't come to New York now and this would be the best time for me. To begin with, you are in New York and we are not yet in the active throes of moving, but because of Kay's previous experiences with trying to have a child, the doctor has forbidden her to leave until she is five months along. This will be around the first of April and just about when we're in the new house. Even then the doctor doesn't want her to take the train; he suggests that she fly—in a plane, of course. Unfortunately, you will be back at college by that time and I'd only see you on weekends. I know there are many people who would prefer that to seeing you daily, but I guess because I'm your father, I have a soft spot for you—I think it's my head. At any rate, we'll just have to wait a few weeks and see how things progress.

I was at the Zelinkas' eleventh anniversary the other night. (An eleventh anniversary actually means that the wife hasn't caught the husband yet.) Saul Chaplin and his wife were there. They are very nice people and spoke highly of you. She even said she had had a letter from you recently. We whanged away the evening, singing old and new songs. The younger generation sang the new ones and I sang the old ones.

I am fooling around again with the radio notion and if we can work out a deal with Kibbee where his demands are not too exorbitant, one of these spring days I'll be waxing a show, as they say in radio. I saw Dick Mack yesterday at Brittingham's and he was astonished, he said, when he read that I was to become a father. He said he was pretty proud of his own achievement until he read about mine, so I smirked appropriately and promised to call him up.

The picture is completed. David Loew, who is a very nice fellow, with the brand of wisdom that has characterized this entire production, has already committed it to the exchanges for release some time late in April. This brilliant stroke makes it impossible for us to do any re-takes, something the picture desperately needs. He keeps saying that it will do a big business, and it probably will, but had we had a first-class producer who would have given us more help with photography, music, direction and cast, we could have had a very fine picture—one that might have compared favorably with *A Night at the Opera*. The hell with it—it's water over the dam and I'm squaring my shoulders for the critical attacks I feel sure we'll get. Ironically enough, the best scene in the picture is one we didn't play on the road. I don't know what that proves but if I'm ever caught again in a cellar dressing room in a vaudeville theatre in San Diego, I hope someone who loves me will whip out a gat and plug me.

So good-bye for now, all my love and write soon.

Your padre,
Dr. Hackenbush

The Zelinkas were radio writer Sid Zelinka and his wife. Saul Chaplin was a composer, songwriter and musical arranger.

Saturday afternoon three-thirty [February 11, 1946]

Dear Poochy Gooch:

I usually write you on Sunday but it seems that a group of local schlamiels masquerading in Hollywood baseball suits are playing an exhibition game tomorrow afternoon so I will hammer out a few words today. All is quiet in the house. Kay is at the market turning on the charm so that she can get more butter than we deserve, and Louise is down in the bathroom dolling up for a colored lover who is squiring her tonight to some joint on Central Avenue. There is no dinner here tonight, for Krasna is throwing a party and we are attending, along with (unseen, just guessing) Eddie Buzzel, Rene Claires, Jerry

Walds, a man named Teitelbaum, an architect and perhaps Ronnie Reagan and his wife. It's not a bad life, and I am not complaining, except that my electric blanket is acting queerly lately and it looks like a long trip downtown to have it repaired. Everything of any importance is downtown here in this village, and it's a long, tedious trip.

Your check left here long ago, and I presume it reached you some time ago, unless the mailman grabbed it off for himself. I have been seeing a lot of old movies lately at the Bert Granets' across the road. I don't know whether you ever met them, but they are very nice people and also know where we can get butter. They have a projection machine, sixteen millimeter, and they run about three nights a week. Most of the movie colony now has this equipment, and the drawback is that most of the films on that size film are old stuff, so old that you forget that you had seen them and you don't remember it until the picture is almost over, and then you conclude that you would have been better off had you gone to the local theatre and seen a new picture. I did see a new picture the other night at the Carthay. It's called *Marriage* or something like that, and it had Robert Donat. It's an English picture and it is wonderful, and I want to see it again. It is so adult, not in content, particularly, but in dialogue, they never write down. Apparently they write pictures assuming that the audience is composed of grown-ups who have been partly educated. Well anyhow, if you get a chance to see it, remember Donat is in it, and it was made in England.

I spent a distasteful afternoon yesterday at the Harpo Marxes. It seems that the press agent on the picture conceived the idea of having us keep house in what is regarded as typically Marx Brothers fashion. So we donned aprons and posed in the kitchen washing dishes, dusting and sweeping in the other rooms, vacuuming the rugs and then out in the garden tilling the soil, climbing trees and all the other harebrained and foolish antics that a jerky public has been led to expect from us.

I hate to talk about the picture anymore. Loew did a dreadful job on it, as I am sure I have told you before. The scoring is bad, the direction is putrid and the photography (maybe that's all for the best) is dark. I am fond of Loew, for he is really a nice man, but God is he stupid when it comes to making a comedy. He keeps saying, "Don't worry, it will make money." Of course it will, what the hell wouldn't in these times, but as Norman pointed out, it would make even more had it been a great picture. Well, live and learn. But unfortunately I never do. I will be just as stupid the next time.

I am glad you liked the last radio show I did. It seemed to be pretty generally liked, but as you know, guest shots are always a gamble. They are retaining Zulinks [Zelinka] and Harris and have assuaged the sponsor by hiring an additional writer, so at the moment all is peaceful at Young and Rubicom. I wish I could sing a song each time I appeared on the show but unfortunately there aren't enough songs to go around and I always wind up doing the same songs.

I was happy to read that the knockwurst reminded you of me, but I am not really that fat. I am trying desperately to take off ten pounds. It has all lodged around my stomach, but it's tougher as one gets older, and I have almost despaired of ever getting rid of it. Kay is thrilled about the impending child and is determined not to lose it this time. It's a strange world and strange things keep happening. I didn't believe that someday I would again be going through the throes of father-hood, and I hope I am up to it.

About the play. It has some good stuff in it. But it would need a tremendous amount of rewriting before I would be interested in it. It is full of comedy parts and one is almost as good as another. I am not sure that they would be willing to do that much work on spec. I am writing Chase Monday.

Well Honey Gal, this is forty for today. It used to be thirty but remember we now have inflation, despite Truman's speeches. All my love to you, and Kay too, and kisses and I'll be glad when I can see you again. Your lovin' Padre. Last night I dreamed of you. Good-bye for now.

Padre

Jerry Wald was a movie producer.

[February 18, 1946]

Dear Miriam,
Sunday afternoon, and people are prowling through the house with that look in their eye that all prospective buyers have when prowling. It is a very domestic scene. Kay is knitting and whining that the stitches don't match. I don't know what she is trying to say, so to play safe I throw in an occasional grunt.

By this time you have received a letter from Kay describing all the details of the new dwelling, so I won't embellish that with any more words. I will try and answer your question first. My present plan is for us to come East the first part of April. This however will depend on her physical condition and the status of the new house. When do

60

you plan on returning to the Coast? Also, how long do you plan on staying? Also, what happened to Janet and Sunny? Do you see them at all? Or is your sole companion now Margot Stevenson? Speaking of Janet reminds me that we are going to dinner tomorrow night at the Cantors', just what the occasion is I don't know. I am sure that it has nothing to do with *Nellie Bly*. I presume it is a big shindig, for the invitation came about a week ago.

The day after tomorrow we are throwing a Chinese dinner cooked by an Oriental who labors at the Farmer's Market at his leisure. He was dug up by Gloria Sheekman, who has a flair for the bizarre unequalled since the early days of Mrs. Basil Rathbone.

Your dream girl Dorothy Parker will be there, and I told her all about you. As a matter of fact, I never speak to her that she doesn't inquire about you. I told her about your attending a Communist meeting in the big City (New York, according to Lardner) and that seemed to make her very happy. I don't want you to be a Communist; all I expect you to be is a good liberal American, and I am sure that you have enough sense for that. I certainly have no objection to your attending any kind of a meeting that interests you, and I think that is the only way you can decide what you want to be.

This is a busy week for me. Tonight a surprise party for Ruby on his birthday. I don't know how old he is. When one gets to our age, one doesn't discuss anything as depressing as that. Tomorrow night the Cantors'. Tuesday we are having our party. Wednesday night we are previewing, and Thursday night I am on "The Dinah Shore Show." I don't know how long that racket is going to last. For I think they are dissatisfied with Harris and Zelinka, and the sweeping out of them may mean that they have also had enough of me, and they may ask me to look for other fields for my talents once they have cleaned them out. . . .

I have relayed your message to Lucy Kibbee and I wouldn't be surprised if one of these days you received a letter from her. Had a letter from Gordon enclosing all the notices from his new hit and it must be a big hit, for after *Hollywood Pinafore* I didn't get any of the notices from Max, just a curt note explaining that it was all a mistake. Also had a letter from Jerry Chodorov in which he intimated that all was over between Joe Fields and himself, and that he was a lone playwright who planned on staying in New York and the only thing that would bring him to Hollywood would be a dwindling bankroll.

Harpo is leaving next week for Miami where he will join Lou Holtz, that outstanding Jewish scholar. I am sending you a piece from the *Times* that you may find interesting if you haven't read it. It's 1929 repeating itself, and it's all too disquieting.

Well, I think this covers everything up to date. I hope you are well and enjoying the winter weather that you always longed for. Kay sends her love and so do I and write soon. Love and kisses.

Your Padre,
Padre

Part of this letter had to be left out as it was illegible. Margot Stevenson was an actress and a good friend of mine. Gordon's new hit was probably Born Yesterday. *Lou Holtz was a radio performer who hosted "The Lou Holtz Show" in 1942.*

[February 23, 1946]

Dear Mir,

This has been quite a week. Kay came down with what we thought was just a cold, and perhaps it was, but from there it segued into what Dr. Henstell pronounced as bronchitis and this is the eighth day Kay has been in bed. With luck, Henstell says, she may be able to get up Monday. That will make a nice ten days in bed. She has been very good about it, and she certainly has far more patience than I have. I caught a cold about four days ago and still have it, although I believe it has abated somewhat. At any rate there is quite a run on our dwindling supply of wipies and Kleenex.

Yesterday was the maid's day off and I cooked breakfast, dinner and lunch. Also did the dishes and all the other odd jobs that women usually fall heir to in a home. Any woman who has the choice between a job and housework is mad if she doesn't grab the job. Man was pretty foxy to foist housework on the female. It's not that it's such hard work, but Christ, it sure is monotonous and dull. And the people you see: milkmen, garbage men, mailmen, electricians, plumbers and carpenters. In flush times, perhaps an occasional Hoover salesman, or Holeproof sock vendor. The only advantage it can possibly have for a woman is that it eliminates the necessity of wearing high heels.

Well, today Ethel the maid is back and things are more or less serene around here again. I did "The Dinah Shore Show" Thursday with a new pair of writers, and I am interested to hear what you thought of it, assuming that you heard it? I had a bad cold all through the day, and it was just the broadcast that I sang a song, my voice had all the musical charm of a frog in his death throes but perhaps you were lucky enough to have missed it.

I was glad to read that you have newer and more luxurious diggings again and I can imagine how happy you are. There is nothing like a little hardship to make one realize the advantages of a soft and velvety life, and I am sure those weeks at that dingy rooming house have done that for you.

Next week is the anniversary of Ick and Art's marriage and Grace is throwing a small shindig for them. If we are able we will attend and throw the customary small and useless present at their feet. I think if the millions of useless presents could be eliminated from the national life, there could conceivably be a fifty-billion-dollar hack in the federal budget in ten years or less. However, at the moment Truman is cruising somewhere on the Potomac with a few of his jerk cronies, planning what piece of major legislation he can next screw up. I think that the Pauley appointment is a disgrace and although I hate to see the Democrats get a slap like that, I think it would be a good thing to have the Senate reject him and chuck him back in the President's kisser.

Well I am off to do the shopping now and it's Saturday and the stores are so crowded, what with Washington's Birthday anniversary yesterday, and Sunday tomorrow, so I have to take my little basket and toddle off to the markets. The new vegetables, meaning the spring vegetables, are coming in now and it is really thrilling to see them all nestling together in their baskets. So have a good time and write soon, and love to you from the both of us, and I do mean Kay and I and me and Groucho.

Padre
XXXXXXX

February 26, 1946

Dear Schmier,
It was nice to hear your cast-iron voice on the phone Sunday and even nicer to hear that you were charging the whole thing to your mother's hotel bill. That's the right way to phone and remember it in the future. I'm glad that you're back in such elegant quarters and that you're on the way to having a new stepfather. It's about time we had an Irishman in our group, anyway. By the way, Leo McCarey was arrested for drunk driving the other day. I just throw this in to keep you informed of things on the west coast.

Kay is slowly recovering from eleven days of bronchitis. She had quite a siege — including a penicillin tank and lots of other expensive paraphernalia. I still have a slight cold but I'll eventually shake it off.

Tomorrow night we are going to the Kahns' — it's Irene's and Art's anniversary — and I'll buy a cheap trinket to present to them. Thursday night, I am going to Arthur Schwartz's. He is throwing a party for George Kaufman who has just arrived to do a play with Nunnally Johnson, Schwartz and Ira Gershwin. I'm working on a radio script with Kibbee and we plan on auditioning it in a couple of weeks. Tomorrow night, too, I'm doing "Mail Call" for the government. Despite the fact that the war has been over for quite some time, the need for entertainment (if you can call mine entertainment) is still great for the thousands of boys overseas.

I read with considerable interest that you have retired from the Communist party and that the mantle of Emma Goldman is flung from your shoulders and that you are no longer warmed by the heat from the Stalin candle. As you know, I am in complete accord with you in this and have at times made myself extremely unpopular with certain groups out here with whom you are familiar. To them, Stalinites can do no wrong. Despite the fact that they are gobbling up half of Europe and a good hunk of Asia, they are just as stoutly defended by these fanatics as though it were a small kingdom in the Balkans completely surrounded by enemies. You know that I have never tried to persuade you one way or another because I knew that your common sense would convince you that there is only one way — and that's the American way — for us. This sounds trite but I can't help it — these kind of phrases are grabbed upon by charlatans and used for their own purposes. Well, enough of this.

The trip to New York seems vaguer and vaguer. I have so much to do here that I just don't see how I can swing it. The process of moving is beginning already and I'm appalled at the thought of it: shopping for carpets and other things and trying to dispose of some of the stuff we have, while like labor pains — something, by the way, I've never had — all will be forgotten and life will begin anew at 1277 Sunset Plaza Drive around the first of April. (Peddlers use rear door.)

This, I am sure, brings you up to date.

When, specifically, do you plan on returning to the coast? Your room will be ready for you and you'll get a warm welcome both climatically and emotionally.

All my love to you, and Kay's, too.

Your padre,
Dr. Hackenbush

Leo McCarey directed Duck Soup. *Arthur Schwartz was a composer and producer.*

March 8, 1946

Dear Mir,

Your letter sent me into tears. It was one of the most pitiful stories I've ever heard. I saw *Bloomer Girl* only once and would have left after the first half but I kept thinking that the second half would be better and besides that, I had paid so much for the seats. I feel terribly sorry for you—it's really quite a problem. You know, if your mother marries Geraghty, there's a strong likelihood that you'll have to see *Bloomer Girl* once a week for the rest of your life. You should explain this to her—I don't think any woman's love can be that strong.

Anyway, your pathetic letter worked $25 out of me. Last night, lying in bed and full of aspirin, high hopes and apprehensions, I thought to myself, "How can I get this young girl out of the clutches of *Bloomer Girl*? Around eight o'clock this morning, just as all the neighbors' cars were shooting madly up and down Thayer Avenue and all honking their horns to rout the kiddies out for their daily tussle with an education, the whole thing came to me, so I'm enclosing a check for $25. This is an Easter present; actually it isn't—there'll be no Easter present—but I think that with $25 you can see at least eight shows at $3 a crack, leaving you a surplus dollar for popcorn and gumdrops.

This is quite a day for me—it's Friday, the day when I usually meet with Bunker, Harris and Zelinka to plan how best we can stink up the next week's radio show. At nine this morning, Kay was getting a metabolism from Dr. Henstell; at eleven, she has to see the baby doctor; at twelve, we're meeting the builder at the new house to discuss repairs and painting; then I have to shoot Kay to Hollywood where, at 2:30, she gets a set of new teeth installed. I had no idea that she was without teeth until she hooked me. But now that I think of it, it always did seem strange to me that even when she bit me, she never bit me. After that I have to rush back to Westwood to meet the writers.

I note what you say about the money for the school and it will be attended to in time so that you won't be barred at the front gate when you return to Vermont.

I met Sunny's mother—quite by accident, I assure you—in the Beverly-Wilshire dining room yesterday and she told me that you had told Sunny that you were terribly homesick, but she said that Sunny loved it in the East and had no desire to come back. We are doing the

65

best we can with your room. It will have nice wallpaper and a nice bed, we hope, and you will have your own bathroom. This is all providing the builder gets through within a reasonable length of time. If he doesn't, you can sleep with Kay or maybe by that time Greer Garson will have relinquished Gable and you can pick up where you left off.

In closing, you wrote that yours was a dull letter, which (a) was not true. It was a very amusing letter and I've shown it to two or three people who laughed heartily at your concern with prostitution; and (b) as I've told you before, no letter written by a child to his parent is ever dull. Parents are funny that way even if they are not always funny on the radio.

All my love to you and it doesn't look like there's a chance of our getting to New York now but I would have liked to have seen you and also the shows. The shows I'll have to forget about, but I'll be seeing you soon anyway and I'm looking forward to it.

Your padre,
Dr. Hackenbush

Geraghty was Jack Garrity, my mother's second husband. My father seemed to spell his name differently every time he wrote it. Jack Garrity's father was the stage manager for the play Bloomer Girl.

March 15, 1946

Dear Mir,
I'm enclosing a piece from the Hoffman column and also a hunk from the *New York Times* in case you haven't seen them.

I received a letter from you on blue paper and, yesterday, one on white paper. The one on blue paper was a pretty depressing letter for a young girl to write and I think you should snap out of it. Perhaps it's the excess weight that you've put on that's responsible for your pessimism. I've always been under the impression that fat people are happy — maybe you're just an exception. At any rate, there's not going to be any war — I think the American people are on to Churchill. He was repudiated by his own Labor Party in England, he's been an imperialist all his life and he has no standing today in war politics. He was a wonderful aid to England during the war. He keeps yowling about Russia but you notice that he never mentions India or all the British territory that they controlled throughout the war. As you know, I am not anti-English or anti-Russian, I'm trying to be an American and the only thing I'm interested in is what is good for America. Well, enough of this!

The other night I saw a newsreel and instead of its being full of the football games, which bore me all through the winter, it was devoted entirely to bestowing red hats on the cardinals in Rome. The cardinals were all dressed in flowing robes—they looked like pregnant midwives—and when the Pope entered, they all prostrated themselves on their fat stomachs and groveled. When they finally reached the Pope's pulpit, they kissed his feet. I think it was one of the most sickening sights I've ever seen and I don't think it's good for the Catholic Church. The Pope, incidentally, looks like Chico and has the same kind of dialect. Imagine kissing Chico's feet!

I've decided against the car at this time. Your junket east has been pretty expensive and I think it's something that you can do without. We can discuss it for the future when you come home. Your mother last year got $23,600 in alimony, she's also getting $40,000 for a piece of our property in San Fernando. Why don't you put the bee on her? Our relationship has been very good since you left. Let's try to keep it that way and not allow an old convertible Chevrolet to come between us.

As for your getting fat, I'm surprised that you let yourself do this. Why don't you use a little will power—you'll find that you can do it if you apply yourself to it rigorously. The most important thing for you at this time is a slim body and what goes with it. You are very intelligent—I know you are aware of this—so get some iron in your soul and vow that you are going to knock off that unwanted blubber.

I can't write any more as I have to go up to the new house now—there are so many things to do up there.

Love and kisses and I hope there's nothing in this note that offends you. If there is, you can cut it out.

Your padre

March 18, 1946

. . . going to like it a lot. The wallpaper is on and it's not at all chi chi and fancy, it's quite subdued and the room looks like one of those rooms in a New England cottage. The room has another advantage that I didn't mention: it has a door leading to the outside so that you can sneak in and out without being seen if you care for that sort of thing. Plus this: it has a closet that is going to hold all the liquor I have stored up, and at night while the rest of the house sleeps—that's me—and Kay is scrubbing the bathroom floor, you can quietly get plastered.

There was a slight interruption here as I answered the phone to accept an invitation to a stag birthday party given by Cantor at Chasen's for Georgie Jessel. Tonight is the official opening of the baseball season, but at the moment it is raining and it looks like it will be postponed until tomorrow. Well, that's life and baseball. I am auditioning the radio show that I wrote with Kibbee sometime next week, and if I am lucky enough I may get a sponsor before the New Year arrives.

Had a letter from Jerry Chodorov and I hear the play he has written about Barnaby turned out very well and I would love to seen him knock out a hit show without having that crook Fields participate. Gordon wrote me that he is arriving in town around the middle of April, and a number of people I know who have gotten wind of it are planning to leave for Guatemala and points even farther South.

Well, I believe I have told you everything, and if I haven't I will in my next letter. Write soon and all my love and Kay's too and what more could any girl want except Gable and perhaps Gregory Peck. 9###############

Your padre

[P.S.] You were very lucky about the guitar, as I was on the verge of giving it away. However, I will send it on as soon as possible. The music will have to wait until we get into the other house as it has all been packed by those demon packers, and I don't mean the Green Bay Packers. Love and kisses.

The first page of this letter is missing.

[March 20, 1946]

Dear Mir;

This will probably be loaded with errors as this is the first time I have laid my gifted fingers on this machine for two weeks. I have been so busy with a number of things that I can't find time for it. Then again, I had to see *The Dolly Sisters,* a classic produced by George Jessel. It was at the Village Theatre in Westwood and as you know one can smoke in the balcony. I had a good cigar and a pouch full of very fine tobacco, but it just wasn't enough. I am beginning to conclude that smoking in the balcony has caused me more discomfort than it is worth. I only like to go to theatres where I can smoke with the result that I pick out those places regardless of the attraction. Well, smoking couldn't help this one, and Jessel ought to be ashamed of himself and of Zanuck, or they both ought to shoot themselves and I am not sure that Lois Andrews didn't divorce George because one night when they were in their boudoir together, he explained the plot of *The Dolly Sisters* to her.

The people finally moved out of the house and now the work begins, painting and cleaning and repairing, and it's constant trips to the house and back again and shopping around. Yesterday for example I bought a crib. If someone had told me a few years back that at my age I would be out shopping for a crib, I would have had them charged with lunacy. In between there are constant calls to Gummo about the show we are planning to audition next week, and an occasional shot for Dinah Shore and the card game every week; well, it's a lot for one man. In between I try to write a funny piece for someone. Last night at the card game I won fifty-four dollars, enough to pay for the crib, so that helps; if I can keep that up I can have a kid every year.

Harpo just called up. He was in Florida and had a fine time fishing and sunning. He said the people down there are just horrible, mostly black-marketeers and assorted thugs and gamblers, and that it resembled Coney Island at its worst. He said he was with Moss Hart down there, and it looks like he will marry Kitty Carlisle, who is getting twenty-five hundred a week singing in some cafe, but that is not the reason, for Moss is loaded, but it's just that he is lonely and that he likes her.

Kaufman is here at the Garden of Allah and apparently in good spirits. He played cards last night with us and lost steadily to seven of the worst poker players in the Unikid States. I told him he ought to write a sketch called "If Men Played Cards Like We Do."

Whatever concern you may have had about Kay not having a baby you can now dispense with. She is getting fat and will soon equal you except that you are not having a baby, I don't think. Did you read about the heiress in the middle West that ran away with a truck driver who had in addition to his truck, a wife and two kids?

I guess love is something that takes place all over the world. Even in the middle West. This is the goddamndest letter I have ever written. At the moment the phone is ringing, and [the maid] is winging herself through the lower floors with a vacuum that is twice as noisy as the new Constellation, and all hell has broken loose. There's an expression I never did understand: all hell broke loose; what the hell can that mean? It's eleven in the morning and I haven't shaved or bathed or dressed yet and the new house, which in reality is an old house that is being painted, is calling me, so I must quit now and get started, and don't forget to see *The Dolly Sisters*—it is two hours of the worst garbage that even Zanuck has ever put together for the American public.

Love and kisses and we'll give you a hot welcome when you return and maybe even a cake and ice cream or caviar, now that the war is over and hasn't begun yet with Russia.

###################### these symbols are supposed to represent kisses from Your Padre and Kay Marvis from the El Hardeen

Zanuck was Darryl F. Zanuck, screenwriter, producer and studio executive who headed Twentieth Century-Fox. Kitty Carlisle was an actress who had appeared in A Night at the Opera *with the Marx Brothers in 1936. The "El Hardeen" refers to the El Jardin, an apartment house in Hollywood where Kay had lived before marrying my father.*

22 March 1946

Dear Mir:

With your brother at the keys, I will save Miss Linden the trouble of rapping out a letter. For some curious reason, I've had very little mail from you (me too. Art) since I wrote you that I thought it was advisable to forget about the car. I regard this merely as a coincidence, however, and I'm willing to assume that you have been too busy for anything as mundane (and Tuesdane) as writing to your old man. As Gershwin once put it, a father is a sometimes thing. As a matter of fact, I'm kind of relieved that I haven't heard much from you recently. I'm head over my heels in different projects and hardly have time to get to the Marquis. There is not much new to write you. The fact of the matter is, I doubt if I would have written you at all if I weren't using it as a device. Kay and I were having dinner here with your brother and Ick. At the conclusion of the meal, swept by a fit of madness, I stupidly offered to help with the dishes. I have done this before, at which point Irene always says, "Nonsense. I'll do them tomorrow." Tonight, to my horror, she accepted my offer and told me I could dry. The next thing I knew, I was sitting on a big couch, Arthur was typing, and the girls were in the kitchen scraping grease off the china.

Maxine and her boyfriend were over the house to dinner the other night, along with Lois and Don. Maxine's lover seems like a very nice chap, although at the moment he is not working (who is?), and appears to have no funds whatsoever. This I don't believe disturbs Maxine much, as she has been around Chico for many years, whose

70

financial condition is quite similar to Maxine's inamorata (boyfriend, to you). They seem to be madly in love, and I wouldn't be surprised if some day they got married. I think the only thing that is holding it up at the moment is Maxine's inability to get a steady job. Don is also out of work and so am I, so the three men sat and discussed the unemployment problem from all sides.

We spent quite some time at the new house today. Most of the top floor has been papered and painted, and there are carpenters and workmen of all kinds in various rooms, reading their union books of rules. It's amazing what paper and paint can do to a place, and I think you will be charmed when you see the baronial sweep of its halls and the narrow closet for your clothes. What did you do with the twenty-five bucks I sent you? Did you invest it in eight sterling Broadway plays, as I suggested, or womanlike did you squander it on something useless like heavy underwear or brassieres? I sent you this money to improve your cultural outlook. I know just how you felt about *Bloomer Girl*. I writhed through it once with great difficulty, and the thought of seeing it three times would have sent me to the river. That's a very precarious life you're about to embark on. Suppose, for example, your mother marries Mr. Garrety, and next year he becomes company manager of a revival of *Abe's Irish Rose*? Maybe you had better stay in Vermont, where the snows are thick and the shows are few.

They are giving a big dinner the evening of the thirty-first of March for Norman Corwin. Norman, in case you don't know, has just won the Wendell Wilkie award, and he is about to embark on a tour of the world, in the interests of world peace. They wanted me to be one of the speakers, and I would have accepted, but it's the night before our moving and it was just too much to have come all together. I regretted refusing him, for I am a great admirer of Corwin's. They have an imposing list of speakers, and I would like to have attended, but I couldn't make it.

Well, dear, the dishes are just about done. I can hear the last closet door being shut in the kitchen, and now I can, with safety, bring this letter to a close.

Love from all of us, and write soon, but not for money.

Padre

Dear Mir:

I thought maybe you were dead, but it seems from this letter that you're not? What's the matter? Don't you answer my letters anymore? Aren't I good enough for you? Or is it that you don't want to have anything to do with anyone out of a job? Don't forget, you'll be out of a job in a few days, too, so don't be so damn cocky.

Love,
Arturo

Dear Mir;

This is your stupid stepmother, who at the moment resembles a cow, wanting to know why the hell you don't answer my last letter? That's about all for today so take care of yourself and write soon.

Love and kisses,
Kay

Lois and Don were Lois and Donald Kahn. Donald was Irene's brother. Lois eventually married my brother after he and Irene broke up. Norman Corwin was a well known writer. Groucho starred in his radio play, "The Undecided Molecule," which was part of his show, "Columbia Presents Norman Corwin," which ran from 1944 to 1945.

March 28, 1946

Dear Miriam,

I don't know why I should write you again. This is the third letter and no mail from you since that bombshell of no car descended. Are you angry with me, disappointed, or are you just too busy to pound out a few words? At any rate, I'm enclosing your check for April. For a few days, I seriously toyed with the idea of not sending you any more money but the picture of your being arrested for vagrancy in the swamps of Vermont melted my stony heart; hence the check.

It was nice knowing you and if you ever find time and are desperately in need of money, you might drop me a line.

Your padre,
Dr. Hackenbush

P.S. I'm to be on the Dinah Shore program next week and on Monday, April first, we move to 1277 Sunset Plaza Drive, Los Angeles 46, California.

[March 30, 1946]

Friday afternoon

My Dear Miriam;
I just got through with the radio writers, working out the plot of the sketch that I will do on the sixth of April on the Shore show. Downstairs the movers are packing books and records and kitchen utensils and all in all it's quite a mess. We were going to move Monday the third, but when I went over to the new house this morning and saw the condition of it, I decided we had better wait a few days more until we move in. Kay was opposed to this as she is so eager to get in, but the smell of paint pervades the house (the lead in the paint is bad for a woman pregnant) and lumber is all over the rooms and carpenters are hammering and will be doing that for a week or two so Wednesday is the fatal date.

I was worried about you, not getting a letter in such a long while and I thought it was because I changed my mind about the car. But today I got a letter and now I feel better. You say it's a hundred and fifty dollars. Miriam, I don't want you to ride in such a vehicle, a car that can be bought today for that sum wouldn't be safe to ride in and I would worry too much about it. Wait till you come back for the summer and we'll discuss it. By that time the car situation will have eased somewhat, and perhaps then we can work it out.

I was depressed by the news that your mother was drunk again. I hoped now that she had a new love life she would quit it, but it looks as though she is going to become a chronic drunk. I think her worry is needless about the clause I asked for, I don't intend to get divorced again, but I think I am entitled to some protection if such a situation should materialize. I think she is acting very foolish about this. If she were any kind of a woman, she wouldn't even want to extort any money from me and be married to another man. What she is asking me is to support her married to someone else. It's pretty shabby, but it's obvious that her ethics aren't nearly as high as her greed.

I don't know why I tell you all this; I am sure that you couldn't explain it to her — she would just curse and tell you what a bounder I am, and when I say bounder, I mean bastard.

I sent you a piece from the *Reporter* about my Uncle Julius. Did you get it and if you did why didn't you tell me about it? . . .

The last page of this letter is missing.

73

April 6, 1946

Dear Mir,

Your letter of April second received and next week, weather permitting, I'll ship a guitar to you. I could ship "Two Guitars" but that's the name of a song and, anyway, the second would be surplus since you can hardly play one.

Well, we have finally moved and I spend the days dropping paper and other debris into the incinerator, tripping over shavings in the living room and stumbling over as miscellaneous a group of Percy Kilbrides as ever appeared in *George Washington Slept Here.* We are moving in gradually. There is no living room at present but it adjoins my bedroom and at eight in the morning, two very well set up carpenters begin pounding on my walls with giant stone hammers so, regardless of what time I retired, I get up at eight each morning. Termites have been found in the library floor so that will have to be ripped up. The dining room has to be carpeted; the hall cannot be painted until the living room is finished, so all through the house are huge barrels filled with sawdust, crockery, furniture, books—God, I never knew we had so much stuff. We seemed to have so little at Westwood and suddenly this has all blossomed into enough to outfit a fifty-room house—or so it seems. Anyway, everything comes to an end and some day we will be rid of all the noise, clutter and sawdust and I can revert back to my former sedentary existence.

Next week we are rehearsing the radio show on Wednesday and waxing on Friday; then Gummo and George Gruskin will each take a replica of this performance, tuck it under one arm and go out through the highways and byways looking for soft money—sponsor, to you. I think the show is pretty good, at least the script is; however, it might not come off, we may get a bum audience, it may be badly played—but if we don't like it, we'll make another waxing. This is frequently done because many things can go berserk on a solo show. I have no hopes of selling this. Naturally, I hope we do—I think it can be good, but it's a pretty expensive show. Also, all the good spots are taken. There are two ducky spots coming up, I understand, and if we could get either one, it would be fine. One is the Abe Burrows spot—CBS, Friday, six P.M. It's a bad show. I've heard it a number of times and I hear that the sponsor, Phillip Morris, doesn't like it. The other spot is the Rudy Vallee time—7:30 Thursday night, NBC. However, I understand that that sponsor would prefer more of a glamour show since their products run in that direction and, although I regard myself as extremely glamourous and romantic, I doubt whether they would.

I'm glad you're back at Bennington where you are so happy, and keep dieting—remember, you still have to catch a man. It's enough that Kay's getting fat—you try to get the other way.

Love,
Your padre
Doc Hackenbush

P.S. When do you get home?

Percy Kilbride was an actor, best known for playing Pa Kettle in the Ma and Pa Kettle films. The radio show they were rehearsing was the unsold "Beverly-Groucho Hotel."

[April 11, 1946]

Dear Mir;

Max Gordon arrives on the Coast in about two weeks, and in return for that Sheekman including Gloria and George Kaufman leave for New York. This is hardly a fair exchange but that's the way it is and I guess that's the way it will always be.

At any rate it's hot as a young groom today and it makes for a very nice evening at the ball park. Last night I took Brecher and we had a lot of laughs. When we get together we try to top each other and though it's a little wearying on both of us it makes for a very gay evening, as your mother would put it. Hollywood had a lead of nine to nothing when the sixth inning rolled around and then went on to lose twelve to eleven. It was a riotous game and terribly exciting. Shufro also arrives here in two weeks and I will have to yield my room and sleep with Kay until he leaves. The maid's room is still being hammered into shape, but it looks the same every day. They work steadily but the results never seem to change.

I received a one-page letter from you today, and as you say it isn't important how much you write; just to keep hammering away at the machine to make a letter longer seems kind of futile, and hardly worth the effort.

Speaking of Krasna, he is going to New York I believe this Sunday to defend a few lawsuits on two different properties, *Dear Ruth* and some other one. If I find out where he is going to stop and you want to see him let me know and I will send it on. I mean the address, with apologies to Claghorn. I agree with you about the senator becoming repetitious, but that's inevitable with that line of dialogue. He will have to get a whole new slant I believe for the fall. At any rate, it is so far superior to the rest of the radio characters, both in conception and in satirical quality, that we should be grateful for him, and not complain.

I am going to wax our record next Tuesday the sixteenth, and I think it has a chance of being good. Kibbee sold a story to MGM for twenty-five thousand and it has changed him considerably. He has become quite cocky and it's interesting to see what a little success can do to change people. I don't mean by this that we are unfriendly, but it's just a confidence and belligerence that he has acquired, and it's the difference between having twenty-five grand and not having it.

Incidentally, as soon as I discover where the Sheekmans are living I will give you their address, for they want to see you. Arthur Sheek is interested in you and always asks what progress you are making, so I usually show him your letters. He thinks that your writing has improved enormously, and as you know he is a pretty good judge of that sort of thing.

At the moment your brother is at the depot to welcome your mother back to the Coast. He is going to enter the Beverly Hills Club tournament that takes place next week. You know the cast by heart: Gilbert Roland, and Fotre, and Larry Bachman. Other than that he works steadily at his work, and plays very little of anything. He is a fine lad (as they say in Irish plays) and you can be mighty proud of him, as they say in New England plays.

I have to leave now, so much to do and so little time (good title for a play), so be good, all our love, and Kay will write you soon.

Your Padre,
Padre XXXXXXXXXXX

Claghorn was the demagogic southern Senator Claghorn, a recurring character on Fred Allen's radio show, "Allen's Alley."

April 17, 1946

Dear Mir,
The "Beverly-Groucho Hotel" was waxed last night. The audience seemed to like it and the Wm. Morris people who put up a great deal of the money for it seemed to think that eventually we would get somebody to buy the show. This was a difficult test—the rehearsal was kind of haphazard since many of the people we wanted work on other radio shows and we had to adjust our time to suit theirs. But, despite this and playing to an audience of average radio goers, sans servicemen

76

(who are much bigger and louder laughers than civilians), the show seemed to please. Well, all I can do now is wait and hope that the Morris office is successful in nailing a sponsor. A radio actor without a sponsor is a good deal like an automobile without a motor—it may look good but it doesn't get anywhere. It may take some time before we get anyone to buy the show but I'm not in any great hurry. I would like to go on this fall but we are going to be choosy—no beer sponsor and, if possible, no cigarette, although I'm not going to be adamant about the latter. I am also going to be picky about the time I go on and the radio chain. Unless you have a decent time and station and sponsor, it's practically hopeless. Even Allen, as good as he is, jumped five points when they placed him following Bergen. He never could get better than a fifteen and now he has a twenty. I'm slightly exhausted today—there's always a letdown after a thing like this, particularly when you're the star of a show and so much depends on you.

Things are progressing slowly at the house. The hammers are still driving nails into my bedroom wall. It's a strange thing—it seems to get quiet around two o'clock in the afternoon and even at eleven in the morning but at eight it sounds like a battlefield. Everything ends and I suppose this will someday.

Tonight we are going to the Krasnas' to dinner and then to a rally of the American Veterans Committee at your old high school—Beverly. The speakers will be Doug Fairbanks—Jr., of course; Tyrone Power; Gene Markey; Frank Loesser; Bill Rogers—Jr., of course; and Ellia Patterson. It's a kind of liberal offshoot of the American Legion and it promises to be an interesting evening. I'm not a veteran of this war—I could be a veteran of the Civil War, but those boys aren't meeting anymore except at Forest Lawn and Sawtelle.

The picture was reviewed in the *Reporter* and *Variety* and both of them were quite good, astonishingly so to me because I don't think much of it. I had a note from Abel Green, the editor of *Variety,* saying, "Saw *Casablanca* and it's okay for B.O. [box office]," which, to my mind, means that personally he doesn't think much of it but that it will do good business. I'm so incensed with David Loew and the people who surrounded him because it could have been an awfully good picture had not so many stupid mistakes been made; however, that's water over the tinker's dam and let the tinker worry about it.

You certainly are having erudite meetings these days. You will be so intellectual when you return that we won't understand a word you're talking about. For this, I send you to college? (Oh boy, page Mrs. Nussbaum.)

By the way, the guitar thing isn't practicable—it requires crating and a lot of stuff that I'm not up to; however, when you go back in the autumn, you can tuck it under your arm. In the meantime, you can practice on a wash line.

Oh, yes, I'll be on "The Dinah Shore Show" next week—April twenty-fifth.

All my love and Kay's, too—and write soon.

Your padre,
Hackenbush

Mrs. Nussbaum was another character on "Allen's Alley"—a Jewish housewife.

[April 29, 1946]

Saturday morning around ten o'clock, five after to be precise.

Dear Mir,

I have been pretty busy this week, and had no time to write you, so now while the mechanics and artisans, such as they are, are gone this letter will be sent to you. As you know, I was on the Shore show last Thursday, did you hear it and how did you like it? I thought it was pretty good and far better than they have had recently. It was written by Harris and Zelinka and your correspondent.

Last night the press previewed [*A Night in Casablanca*] at the Fox Wilshire along with a Maria Montez picture, a natural combination by the way. I didn't go as it does something to me, but Harpo, who is far sturdier than I am, reported to me this morning that it went well and that the audience liked it. I will wait until it arrives at the Marquis and view it there from a smoke filled balcony.

So at the moment I haven't much to do. I have one more shot with Dinah, who at the moment is laid low with a throat infection in the Valley of San Fernando, and after that the probability's I will never work again. I always get that feeling after I do anything and someday it will come through.

I am trying to do a little matchmaking so I had Shirley Mitchell and Eddie North at the house to dinner. She I believe needs a man, and he is kind of a lonesome fellow who could use a girl, I think. This is all conjecture on my part, neither of them has ever said a word to me to that effect. I think it is just the natural reaction of one who is married and is curious to see how many others he can euchre into the same fix.

Anyway, she just called and told me what a good time she had last night and that she liked him a lot and that he asked her out again so that may be the beginning of a romance for which, in years to come, neither party will forgive me.

Now that I think of it, it may have all been a mistake in strategy — perhaps I should keep North for you. Don't worry, he may be still around by the time you return. While I think of it, you can come back on the Constellation, and while on the subject, I wouldn't worry too much about it, for yesterday there was a train wreck on the Burlington that killed about eighty people, and the Constellation only holds forty, so you see you are pretty lucky.

According to your last letter you certainly have enough work to keep you out of mischief, and you will be the most brilliant girl on Sunset Plaza Drive by the time school is over. I had a ride in your old jalopy last week. Mrs. Zelinka came to the broadcast and we went to a restaurant in the little fellow, along with Mr. Zelinka. She had a new top put on it, and though it wheezes along the same way it always did, with the new top it looks almost like a Rolls Royce. Anyway, she loves it, but that isn't what I wanted to tell you, what I meant to tell you was that Mrs. Zelinka had lunch with Betty Kelly and all she did was speak about you and what a wonderful girl you are.

Well, that certainly was a long way around to compliment you, but a compliment is a rare thing these days and if there is one around it should be delivered even if it does consume more space than it warrants. From the errors in this letter you can discern that I am slightly out of practice, and hardly the typist I used to be. It's like the old days at the club. The Beverly Hills Tennis Club, that is. They are playing a tournament there and Arthur is batting hell out of the opponents and yesterday he called one in a match he was a linesman on, and it was against Gilbert Roland, and he blew up and wouldn't talk to anybody, and it's all so trivial and small, and I only mention this to show you that at the tennis club things are back where they were some years ago. Yesterday I met Betty Alexander on the street, speaking of tennis, and she has lost her looks completely. It's shocking. I know you never liked her, but I think even you will concede that at one time she was beautiful, but now she looks exactly like her mother, and you know that's a dreadful thing to write about anyone.

Two wrinkled octogenarians are appearing here in a few minutes to hang drapes in my bedroom, so before they nail me with their chatter, I am beating it out of here and to the village to meet Ruby, who looks just the same as he always has.

79

Love and kisses and the Sheekmans are at the Waldorf, give them a buzz, they want to see you. I will let you know if and when Kras arrives.

Your Padre,
Padre

May 8, 1946

Dear Mir,

I have notified the Sheekmans that you are in Bennington, Vermont. They are at the Plaza Hotel—that is, if they haven't been thrown out by now for non-payment of rent. They are a shifty couple, these two—and they'll skin a hotel as quick as Cornelia Otis Skinner.

I enjoyed the part in your letter about Von Zell. He is indeed a fat slob. I suppose it is partly his fault that he gets so coy on the air but if the producer of the show knew anything, he wouldn't tolerate it. At any rate, they're not picking up "The Dinah Shore Show" for the ensuing year, which means that I am again out of work. Pretty soon I'll be known in radio circles as the "kiss of death." The reason the show was so confused the week you heard it was that Bunker had left town and the whole thing was in the hands of one of those giant agency minds. Right before we were to go on the air, he announced that we were four minutes over. This was a bombshell and in the next hour we had to hurriedly cut four minutes. This is about two pages and is quite a chore. At any rate, Thursday a week is my last fling unless I am lucky enough to hoodwink a sponsor with my new show.

They finally gave Danny Kaye the air. While he was on, they were secretly negotiating with Cantor, America's leading double-crosser. Warwick and Legler engineered the whole thing. I question whether Cantor will do as well Friday night on a beer program as he did Wednesday with a physic, although I must say there's not a great deal of difference between the two products.

I showed your letter to Krasna and Bert Granet and they both think you write very well and that you have a good chance of being a successful writer.

My life is fairly uneventful these days. I spend the afternoons trying to buy a loaf of bread. After visiting six stores yesterday, I finally smuggled half a loaf out of a delicatessen. In the evenings, I go to the ball park, so it's bread in the afternoon and baseball at night—not a bad life.

The Shufros are still here. They are an odd couple, although very nice. She is a liberal and he is reactionary. He still thinks Hoover was a great president. It's amazing to me that they remain together. It shows how tolerant two people can be. Well, what can you expect from a guy in Wall Street?

I just completed reading a book called *Sixty Families*. This is the most devastating and revealing book on America that I have ever read. I know I am quite emotional politically so after I had finished it, I lent it to Krasna, who is stone cold about such things. He was tremendously impressed with it. When you come home, you can read it. It's not a new book—it was published in 1937. I had been planning on reading it for many years but just got around to it. I am now going to try to get Ferdinand Lundberg, the author, to see if he can persuade his publishers to put this out in a two-bit (25¢, to you) edition.

I could write lots more but I have so much to do and I'm not as young as I used to be. All our love and let us know when you're coming home so that we can try to make a Constellation reservation for you. This shows you how things change. Fifty years ago if you had said to someone, "I'll make a Constellation reservation for you," they would have thought that you were embarking on a trip to the moon.

Take care of yourself, write soon and stop worrying.

Your padre,
Doc Hackenbush

Cornelia Otis Skinner was an author and actress.

[May, 1946]

Monday Night

Dear Mir;
The Shufros have left and all is quiet again in the house. Not that they were noisy or troublesome, but two extra people in the house in these days of temperamental servants are an additional burden. In the meantime Kay came down with a bronchial condition and at the moment is in bed, under Hentsell's care. She is in no danger, but she isn't too strong, and has to watch herself.

I have just completed fifteen hundred words that I hope some magazine is going to find funny enough to buy for a niggardly sum. It isn't the money particularly that I write for, it is just that I am a restless soul and when I am not working I get too introspective, and that only leads

81

to unhappiness. I am afraid I will always have to have some work to keep me from thinking too much about myself and the state of the Union and the World. I have just finished reading a book called *Sixty Families,* I may have mentioned it to you in a previous letter. Anyway, I lent it to Shufro to read on the train East and after he arrives there, he will send it to you, per my instructions, as they say in business communications. Read it carefully—I think you will get a tremendous boot out of it.

The radio business with which I am remotely connected is going through the dithers. Whether it is because of the changing tax conditions, or the scarcity of production, they are lopping off many radio shows that we have come to accept as fixtures. Among the casualties mentioned so far are the Shore show, the Bob Burns opus, "Baby Snooks" and even the Joan Davis show is up for cancellation. It is hardly the most propitious time for me to have waxed a show for a sponsor, but I am not going to worry about it, if that doesn't come through there will be other things. In the meantime, the house and its improvements progress slowly and laboriously. Each day there is a considerable amount of painting and hammering (usually around eight in the morning) but when the day's work is examined, there doesn't seem to have been a great deal of progress made.

Most of our furniture is still in storage, and we are getting a little weary of both sitting in the same chair.

Yesterday Art and Ick and I went to the matches and saw Jack Kramer polish off Frank Parker in straight sets. Parker as you no doubt know is no pushover for anybody, but he was clay in Kramer's hands and Jack looked like the first top flight player I have seen since Budge and Riggs were on their way up. He is being sent to Wimbledon and if he doesn't get stage fright, I think he has a good chance of winning that prize. Anyway it was fun, the weather was nice and it is particularly restful watching tennis when your son, I mean my son, isn't involved.

We don't get much mail from you these days, but I presume you are busy and that you have a lot of correspondence to take care of.

Gordon, the demon producer, was here for a whirlwind visit. He breathlessly told us all about his plans for the coming season, under the impression that there is no other subject that is of any interest to anyone. Also the old familiar tale about his money, and that he is all set come what may, and what a great man Churchill is, not was, but is, so I had to call him on that, and then he left town, still infatuated with himself and his little world.

82

He isn't really a bad guy and he surely is a shrewd businessman, but in many ways he is such a square.

There isn't much else to write. I realize that you are going to be nineteen in a few days, and that will be your last visit in the teens, now come the twenties. God, that seems young. I remember when I used to think thirty was doddering age; now I realize that life begins at sixty, what a horrible thought. I found a lovely mountain walk that goes right past our house and up the hill, and if you are in any kind of physical shape when you come back, I will lead you there. It is only a few minutes from here, but it seems like hundreds of miles from Hollywood. It has that kind of mountain smell that you get at Tahoe and other places where dentists congregate.

Well I think I have told you everything I know. That didn't take long. All our love to you and write soon and Happy Birthday from all of us.

Yours,
Padre and Kay
9 XXXXXXXXXXXX

May 17, 1946

Dear Miriam,
Rachel has phoned for your Constellation reservations both ways and we expect to have some word for you soon. If they don't come through, you can always come by pogo stick. Of course, I realize that by pogo stick it's much slower and it gets cool at night but at least it's steady and you don't have to talk to a lot of strangers. If you plan on coming by pogo stick, be sure to pack a lunch, though I suppose you could stop off for food at various places. It would save me a lot of money if you traveled this way. I was pricing pogo sticks only yesterday and I can pick up a good one second-hand. It's one that was used by the Finnish army but it's in very good condition and I'm sure it would give you a lot of good service. If you don't trust it, I could buy two and you could carry one on your back with the lunch. Don't reject this idea without giving it a lot of thought. I figured it up and if you made fifty miles a day (that is, traveling night and day) you could do the whole thing in a year. In that way, you wouldn't have to go back to Bennington at all and I would save a veritable fortune.

Our new maid arrived yesterday. She's about sixty, 5' 7" with phony teeth, and though it's too early to judge her, my guess is that she'll be a flop. Kay told me that she wears booties in bed and a nightcap. God help the burglar that breaks into her room — he'll be in for the ride of his life. The old one left last week, taking a few sheets and a smoked tongue that I had bought for Sunday's lunch. I can just see her walking on Central Avenue with my tongue hanging out — smoked, no less.

Did you hear "The Dinah Shore Show" yesterday? It was my fare-well appearance and everybody thought it was good. Dinah has only two more weeks to go for General Foods but she is in big demand so I imagine that she has something lined up already for the new season. I heard a rumor that she may go with the Ford Company. Anyway, the panic is on in radio and many of the big, expensive shows are going to be dropped. Whether or not this will help me, I don't know. I'm not going to worry about it, though; if I don't do radio, I'll do something else — if not, there's always the *New York Times*.

You make a mistake when you write that I'm probably not interest-ed in what you are doing at college. I have written this to you before but I'll repeat it again — parents are always interested in what their children are doing and it's just as important to me for you to write a story that is well received by your associates as it would be for me to write one that I've sold to a magazine. I don't talk about it, but don't you think I'm worried when I see that Arthur isn't placed yet in some reliable job? After all, Arthur isn't eighteen any more — he'll soon be twenty-five — and I know he worries about it, too, but he's such a nice boy that he doesn't bother me with it. I'm trying to help him and I'm pulling strings here and there but it's awfully difficult for a novice to break in unless he either has extraordinary talent or extraordinary relatives. Everyone dishes out the same excuse — let's see something you've written or what credits have you? Obviously, it's pretty hard to have credits unless you're working, so, as Pierre Laval would say, "It's a Vichy circle." Anyway, he's plugging away on a musical book with Don Kahn. I think Don is pretty smart and maybe a miracle will happen and they'll knock out a good one. But don't ever refrain from writing me about yourself and the details of your machinations.

Lots of love, happy birthday and write soon.

Your padre,
Hackenbush

May 27, 1946

Dear Schmear,

Rachel's already phoned for a reservation on the Constellation with you for your schoolmate and it continues up to San Francisco after its stop here. WHAT'S HER NAME? We have to let the ticket office know.

I've just returned from a flying trip to San Diego. I went down there to speak on the platform with Kenny, Rogers, Patterson and Lucille Gleason. My speech got more laughs from the politicians on the stage than it did from the audience. It was a piece I had written for a magazine, slightly condensed, of course, and converted for speaking purposes, but there's a big difference between reading something and talking it. One cannot be quite as leisurely with an audience—the jokes have to be more frequent and shorter. I'll know better next time. I was supposed to leave San Diego last night after the rally but the 11:19 plane from Dallas that I was to catch was three and a half hours late so I stayed over, sans pajamas, toothbrush or anything. I slept in a Porisknit undershirt, and though El Cortez is a nice hotel, it's a fairly ancient one and the windows rattled like a Boris Karloff residence. Every hour I'd get up and stick blotting paper in the windows. I finally ran out of blotting paper around four in the morning and fell into a troubled sleep, dreaming of Patterson, Kenny and Rogers, so today I am really bushed.

We finally got our furniture and now have more than one chair in the house. The place isn't very orderly but the sound of hammer crashing against nail has ceased and it's a godsend. Your room looks nice and I think you will be happy in it. If you're not, you can always come downstairs and see how the other half lives. I've put your volumes of *The Call of the Wild* and *The Sea Wolf* back in your room so if you get a literary craving during the night, you can always hop out of bed and peruse Jack London.

We have a new girl now. Her name, believe it or not, is Brunetta. It sounds like the name of a colored girl for a radio show. She is very nice looking and neat. I don't think she can cook but I'm so accustomed to poor fare that I won't notice it. The preceding one, Ada, lasted one day. She came in the morning, gave me my breakfast dressed in a dirty, buttoned sweater, left the dishes in the sink and went to her room. At four o'clock I pounded on her door and she reluctantly came out shouting belligerently that she had to have her rest, so I told her that she could have a good rest by getting out right then. So that was the finish of Ada who now is probably back in Decatur.

85

The streetcar strike is gradually being settled. It hasn't been much of a hardship for people with cars but those who had to use streetcars for getting to work surely have had a horrible time. I won't attempt to analyze the various strikes for I don't know the solution nor does anyone else, including the administration.

I'd better quit now or I'll fall asleep while I dictate.

Lots of love and will see you pretty soon now.

Your padre,
Hackenbush

June 3, 1946

Dear Mir,

Naturally, we're all very happy over the acceptance of your story. Incidentally, it might be a good idea to send us a copy so that we can read it and find out the type of literature that flourishes in Vermont. I also received a mysterious, cryptic and noncommittal telegram requesting the cancellation of the Constellation reservation for your girlfriend. It has been taken care of and that's that.

At the moment, I am reading *The Hucksters*. It's all about the radio business and the advertising agencies of New York and Hollywood and, for my money, superb is the word for it. I forget the name of the boy who wrote it but it's been taken up by the Book-of-the-Month Club, which means a guaranteed circulation of 350,000 copies, so I should say in round figures at least a million people will learn a little about the bastards who control America's advertising. I haven't finished it yet—I still have about a hundred pages to go—but it's one of the few books I've read in recent years that I'm eager to get back to, and that's my only way of knowing whether I like a book. You can read it when you come home. This chap has written a previous book called *Shore Leave* which, I understand, is even better than this one.

Krasna is in New York and Ruth is leaving Friday. They will be there in about two weeks. He's in the East on business. He promised to call you at Bennington so if you hear a high-pitched, rapid-fire, nervous voice screeching in your ear, that's Krasna. He always asks about you and so does she.

The house is gradually taking shape which is more than I can say for Kay. She is beginning to resemble a small bungalow, but she doesn't mind. She's terribly excited about the house, spends all day cleaning and polishing and hanging up rules for the servants, with broccoli spelled "brockerly." I asked her if that wasn't a town in Long Island. Anyway, she's much excited about the baby's arrival and the house. After all, what two more important things can happen to a woman? She's very nice and we get along fine. Anybody who can get along with me must be nice. Luckily for me, I have my own room and can hide away for hours at a time.

Budge Patty phoned the other day. He's going to England to play at Wimbledon. He's stopping over in New York and said he would phone you. I presume this is the last you'll hear of this because, although he's a nice boy, he's a little dizzy, but he always asks about you.

I've asked you this before: what about a boyfriend—do you have anyone or are you reduced to just going around with women? You don't say much about this side of your life so you are either hiding a dark secret or Mr. Right, as Lardner used to call them, hasn't come along yet.

Well, I will have to close this for there is a stack of stuff facing me here. The primaries are tomorrow and I'm curious to see what will happen.

All my love and write soon.

Your padre,
Hackenbush

My story had been accepted in the Bennington magazine, the Silo.

[June 15, 1946]

Friday afternoon.

Dear Mir.
I don't know why I should waste my time writing letters to a worthless daughter, when her poor old gray-haired father is sitting home waiting at the window for a letter and hoping the mailman will soon deliver the missive that will restore his sanity again. But as some character says in one of Shakespeare's plays, "How sharper than a serpent's tooth is a thankless child." If this means that your old man is a snake, why the hell with him, and he can go to blazes and let some other wretch ruin his eyes reading all that balderdash written in olde English so that a man can't understand it. I always say that it is better to see him performed than to read him, for they are plays and need the touch that the theatre gives them, and anyway I don't understand it when I

see it. It is really better to stay home and let [Walter] Kiernan explain it on "Information, Please," and besides, it is so difficult to get railroad accommodations and the hotels are so crowded in New York, and it's all right to go to but I wouldn't want to live there if you gave me a farm on Times Square, and can you catch anyone giving anyone a farm in the middle of Broadway, and where would the cows graze? So you see the idea is ridiculous, and the sooner forgotten the better for all of us.

I don't know whether I wrote you that I had a wire from the Guild, Theatre Guild that is, offering me the title role in *Volpone* for the ensuing season but I rejected it for it meant going on the road too, and when I think of Detroit and Chicago and the rest of those towns, why I just get a little squeasy inside.

Anyway, I just bought a lot of porch furniture and who is going to sit in those chairs and look at the hills if I am not here? If I ever do work I would like a job that I could take care of in my bedroom. As a matter of fact I had such a job and in about six weeks or less I expect you to be the sister of an infant, sex unknown.

How did you like the *Sixty Families*? Or haven't you gotten around to it. I hope you read it carefully for it is important that you know about the American grab, and how little the people have to say about the conduct of the nation, despite all the speeches on July Fourth and Decoration Day.

I am flying for Seattle Wednesday to appear at a monster political rally, along with Jimmy Roosevelt and Olivia de Havilland, whom *Time* magazine this week refers to as "swimming pool pinks." I am getting to dislike *Time* more each week and their attempts to appear as a liberal magazine steadily become more ludicrous. When I say it is a monster rally, that doesn't mean that everyone there will be a monster—actually the only one I am sure of is me. I will be gone three days, and it's a good thing that the Stars aren't home during that time, otherwise I don't think I would have consented. Anyway I haven't been to Seattle since I appeared there at the Orpheum Theatre some twenty years ago and I am going over to the theatre and see if the same audience is sitting there.

I have to close now as I'm going to the Perrins' for dinner and then to the ball grounds, so I will close this and hope someday there will be a letter from you explaining all. My wife, the former Miss Dittig of the Newark Dittigs, joins me in sending her love to you and anticipating your homecoming with a considerable amount of relish, which we have a lot of in the kitchen pantry. Love and kisses and all that sort of thing.

Padre

June 19, 1946

Dear Mir,

I'm just dictating a few lines to Rachel over the phone. I wanted to write you a regular letter today but I just can't get around to it—I'm leaving this afternoon for Seattle and there are too many things to do.

I had a letter from you yesterday and my inquiry about your love life was based on nothing but curiosity. Glad you had such a nice time with the Krasnas. I haven't heard a word from them but you know the Krasnas—out of sight, out of this world.

Thanks for your Father's Day telegram. It's nice to know that I am your father. Many parents are not so sure of that. So take care of yourself; Arthur told me he wrote you four days ago; Kay promises to write but you know Kay's promises.

Love and kisses, see you soon and good-bye.

Your padre,
Hackenbush

June 27, 1946

Dear Mir,

I presume you are very busy; otherwise, you have a hell of a nerve for writing so rarely. It's an excuse for me, as I am old and feeble, whereas you are young and feeble.

As you know, I have just returned from Seattle where I had a very successful tour. I spoke twice—once at a banquet and once at the ice rink. When I spoke there, the people weren't skating, they just sat and listened. I even wore a black mustache and did a speech as a sort of political Rankin or Bilbo. I was quite nervous at first, never having done this kind of thing, but it wasn't long before I had the audience laughing heartily and then I became my superb self. The point of my going up there, which may have puzzled you, was the following: you see, there's a group of Congressmen in Southern California—Holafield, Healy, Patterson, Helen Gahagan, Izac—who all think alike politically and therefore vote en bloc. In the state of Washington, there's Congressman De Lacey and two others who have always voted in collaboration with these California congressmen—because of this, there is usually a group of eight or ten liberal congressmen from the west coast whose voice and votes can be felt in the hall of Congress. You'd be surprised if you saw the newspapers up there—in one, I was labeled a "swimming pool pink." Imagine me, a disciple of Wall Street, being classed with Stalin. It's such an easy smear—anytime you're for the slightest liberalism of our present laws, you're instantly charged with being a Commie. Fortunately, the public sees through a good deal of this, and if Roosevelt was any criterion, they don't pay too much attention to red-baiters.

We're about through fixing up the patio and it looks quite nice. It's an awful temptation to just sit in the backyard and read the *New York Times* and tell the world to go to hell but, fortunately or unfortunately, I can't do that. I'm going to wield as big a stick as I can as long as I can.

The butcher shops here are empty; that is, the counters are empty; the stores are crowded but all they have to sell is pig's feet, yesterday's fish and some shriveled squabs; even the black markets don't seem to have much. As somebody once said, "There's scarcity of everything but money."

Tomorrow, I am speaking at a charity bazaar at the home of Jay Paley. I can never remember whether he's the cigar impresario or one of the owners of CBS, but I seem to remember vaguely that his wife mispronounces all her words and never wears a hat that costs under a hundred bucks.

While I think of it, Olivia de Havilland went up north with me. She's very nice and a hard worker and quite bright but she'd better watch her weight. She's about ten pounds over now and she's kind of tiny. Ten more pounds of fat and she can get a job as a medicine ball at a bathing beach!

I'm off now to do the shopping.

Let's hear from you—it's 1277 Sunset Plaza Drive and a stamped envelope will reach me there. If it doesn't, I'll go to the mailbox and pick it up myself.

Lots of love and kisses.

Your padre,
Hackenbush

Jay Paley was the president of CBS.

July 5, 1946

Dear Mir,

Don't worry about your arrival. I am meeting you sans mother. You don't arrive until a quarter to twelve midnight; by that time, though, the plane will be four hours late and you'll probably fly in around four A.M. At any rate, I'll be at the airport with a fat lady—unless she has the baby in the meantime—to greet you and escort you to your dungeon on Sunset Plaza Drive.

I am throwing the first of a series of brilliant social events Monday night. Ruth Gordon and Garson Kanin, better known as Mr. and Mrs. Kanin, are coming, along with the Sheekmans, the Epstein twins, the Krasnas and a group of others. I'm sorry you won't be here because it's a group I think you would enjoy having around. I'll try to have some kind of a party for you after you arrive, provided you pay for the ice cream and pickles. Moss was coming but he's leaving the day before for New York. He came out here to cast his play, which is only half written. Kras read what Moss has written and he thinks it's wonderful. Last week I read Norman's new play, *William and Mary*. It could be called *The Further Adventures of Dear Ruth*. It's not similar in plot but it's about the same kind of people. I enjoyed it enormously and I think he'll have another hit. Moss is reading it this week and if he likes it, he'll stage it Incidentally, I read *The Middle Ages* this morning, the play I wrote with Norman some years ago. We may try to do a rewrite on it and I may appear in it if it works out. I told Norman I wouldn't consider two years in it but, if it were good, I'd play a year in New York if necessary. Of course, if the show flops, there wouldn't be any problem at all.

I saw *Awake and Sing* the other night. It's a Clifford Odets play that was written in 1939. Some of it is still good but since he wrote it there have been so many revues with sketches in them kidding the Odets style and the misery he piles on all his characters that, to me, parts of it seem kind of burlesque now. I took Irene and Art and they weren't too crazy about it either. I'm going to see *Henry V* next week with the Sheekmans. It's Shakespeare and I doubt whether I'll understand much of it; however, the reviews have been so overwhelmingly ecstatic that I'll have to sit through it even if it is all muddled. I did see an English picture the other night at the Oriental—no smoking in the theatre except surreptitiously. It's called *The Way Ahead* with David Niven—he has such charm—and it's so quiet and unpretentious. It's a war picture with very little of that in it—it shows the conversion of a British civilian into a soldier and it's beautifully written and underplayed. I bet it won't gross $300 in America.

Well, I think when one gets around to discussing pictures in a letter, it's time to quit. Tonight I have to take Earl Wilson to Chasen's and the ball park. I'm not keen about it but he called me and I can't evade it. Being with a columnist for a couple of hours is a very trying ordeal. They expect you to be comic and entertaining. I'd rather be quiet and just eat dinner; however, I'm taking Ruby along to assist me.

Write soon and lots of love and kisses.

Your padre,
Hackenbush

Garson Kanin was a screenwriter and director married to actress Ruth Gordon. The Epstein twins were Julius and Philip Epstein, the screenwriting team. My half-sister Melinda was born on August 14, 1946, between this letter and the next one. I was at home for summer vacation at the time.

September 10, 1946

Dear Mir,

I was astonished at getting a letter from you so quickly and I can only assume that time hangs heavy on your hands. Alan was up to dinner the other night and I felt he had it coming for the $70. I took him to the ball park and I don't hear much from him now. I am taking him to lunch today—at the inevitable Copper Room. Since Ruby has departed for the East and the World Series, I have to eat lunch with someone.

This is a bad week for me. I have a "Command Performance" tonight with an early rehearsal; I'm working every afternoon with Kras, and Betsy Kelly phoned me to make a money pitch at a dinner for Patterson as a write-in candidate from the Sixteenth District. I told her I'd make the pitch if someone wrote the piece. She said "Oh, that'll be fine," and it wound up with Zelinka phoning me this morning, asking if I'd collaborate on the speech. My impulse is to chuck the whole thing for Friday and go to the ball game. I get sucked into more things that don't pay any money. It's strange how easy they all think it is for a comic to just stand up and be funny—the jokes will just follow along! Well, the hell with it!

Brecher dropped in last night to see Melinda and we had a very nice visit except that he brought Mrs. Brecher. The girls sat upstairs and talked for two hours and Kay claims that Mrs. Brecher is crazy. She said she didn't understand a word she was saying. I don't go by that,

92

however, for there's a good deal of me that Kay doesn't understand. The point of this whole thing is that Irv read your story and was flabbergasted. He was amazed at the talent you displayed in the story and marveled at the sadistic streak that you self-consciously disclosed. Anyway, he thinks you have a lot of talent and Irv is a pretty tough critic. I thought you'd like to know this.

My schedule now is a little busted up in the morning. Melinda awakens at 9:30 and, considering that she's usually wet and full of all sorts of debris (this is known as putting it nicely), she's a remarkably docile child. This morning Jeanette, who, by the way, is a wonderful woman, bathed her and I dried her. She is a remarkably good baby and rarely cries even when she's hungry. She's beginning to like her bath and kicks her feet. Last night I gave her her bottle and she makes the damnedest noise when she sucks the milk. It sounds exactly like a rusty farm gate and my hunch is that she's going to be a very determined young lady — as God knows all of them are. We still carry Kay upstairs but she now walks down under her own power. Some days when I'm not there, Jeanette and Brunetta carry her. It's quite a sight.

Zeppo, in case you're interested, got slaughtered at the ball park. He had Oakland for the whole series and they lost seven out of nine to Hollywood. I wouldn't be at all sure that the whole thing wasn't framed. Zeppo has now decided to quit this sort of gambling but I doubt that he can stick to it. Well, everyone seems to be a sucker for something. My weaknesses are women and the stock market.

I can't continue this any further for I have too much to do.

Lots of love and kisses and Kay says she'll write you soon.

Your padre

Betsy Kelly was the wife of Gene Kelly and a good friend of mine.

September 23, 1946

Dear Mir:
If the typing is different today it will because there is a new secretary in the office. I don't know her name but I suppose I will find that out one of these days.

I had a letter from Kurnitz from New York, in which he told me that the rumor that he was going around with Patsy Englund is true and I guess it's all right but it just seems strange. He sent the baby a beautiful blanket which I am trying to exchange for some golf clubs for myself.

93

I received your letter on equestrianism and this will teach you to stay on the right side of the horse. You didn't have to go all the way to Vermont to get thrown off a horse—you could have done that right in Beverly Hills. Your glasses, according to our former secretary, a Rachel Linden, were sent to you on Friday, the thirteenth, which is probably why you haven't received them. DID YOU GET THEM? Well, so what happened to the books and other paraphernalia—and did you get the grips with your clothes?

Wednesday I hope to finish up with Krasna. We have done two complete rewrite jobs and if it isn't any good now the hell with it. Nine weeks we were on it this time and about twenty in the other experiment. This is a good part of the year and it better be good or Krasna will know the reason why.

I don't know whether I told you but I am beginning a picture named *Copacabana* and I am sure it will turn out to be just as dreadful as the name implies. They sent me the first twenty pages last week but I don't want to tell them how bad it is until I sign the contracts. In this picture I make love to Carmen Miranda. I hope the weather is cool for this can be a pretty gamey assignment. If you are interested, Andy Russell is also in this opus, and Gloria Jean, Xavier Cugat, Bill Goodwin and some other hams.

The baby is blossoming. This morning I dried her, fed her and shoved cod liver oil down her throat. She seems to like it. Apparently she still doesn't know what it tastes like. She weighs seven and a half pounds.

Irene just phoned that Art won his match this morning in the Pacific Southwest. He won two singles yesterday and two doubles. He played a tough guy today—Jack Teuro from New Orleans. Art is playing well and I think his tournament experience is doing him a lot of good.

Yesterday I saw your friend Mickey Rooney play with Petra, the French champion who won at Wimbledon, against Frank Shields and Walter Pidgeon. Pidgeon looked liked eighty and hit the ball as though he was a hundred. Rooney, your old boyfriend, played surprisingly well and in addition, I came to the conclusion that I would rather see him on the tennis court than in the movies.

This is all for now and quite a good deal. I hope you are well and have abandoned trick riding.

Love and kisses,
Your padre

Kurnitz was Harry Kurnitz, the screenwriter, playwright and novelist.

94

October 3rd, 1946

Dear Mir:
I got your wire yesterday and a brief letter today. Your letter was very disappointing. It seems to me that after an intermission of three weeks you could think of something more interesting to write about than an MGM musical. I would rather you tell me something of your school life and your new associates and what you do with yourself. Writing about a musical, particularly one from Louis B. Mayer's menagerie, is about the same as writing about the weather. Kay said she wrote you a long letter but that she has not heard from you since then. This I know to be true because I too look in the mailbox.

Now, you inquire why Miss Linden is leaving. We are still good friends, but she's been promising to leave for the last three years though we always wheedled her into remaining. But this time she had that determined look in her eye so we had to agree to her going. I hope this clears this up for you.

About the picture I am about to embark on—it is called *Copacabana* and it is a musical in technicolor, if we can get the film, with Carmen Miranda, Andy Russell, Gloria Jean, Xavier Cugat and some other names that I don't recall—mine, for example. They have a fairly good story and I am sure it will be one of the worst pictures of the new season. Sam Coslow, the songwriter, is producing it and it will have his songs in it.

I finished the play with Norman and we both think it's good. As you know, I have departed from my original intention to appear in it and the chances are we will just put an actor in it. Appearing on the stage every night for a year doesn't strike me as being much of an existence. Kras is going to New York the first of December and even then is reluctant to go. After all these years he has discovered golf. He has joined Hillcrest and is now trying to get me to join. I don't think he's going to make it. That last experience I had with you and Arthur flogging through the hills of Brentwood is something that I haven't yet recovered from.

Arthur played in the tennis tournaments and was eliminated by Malloy 6–4, 6–2. He played quite well but he's a little rusty. Malloy has played in sixteen tournaments since last March and Arthur has played in one and it was too much of a handicap. Kramer won the tournament. Schroeder played brilliantly but he too suffers from tournament rustiness. In the semi-finals it was so crowded we could only get seats in the sun. It was 105 in the sun and I wore a pith helmet and sunglasses. It looked like I was right back in *Animal Crackers*.

I'm sorry you haven't received the books and records yet and my hunch is the same as yours—that they haven't been sent out yet. Glad to know you received the glasses. One would never suspect it from the letter you wrote.

I am campaigning in Fresno tomorrow night with Jimmy Roosevelt, Will Rogers and Senator Murray. The objective is to elect these candidates and if they are defeated they can blame it on my speech.

I could write you much more, but until I get a decent letter from you—this is it.

Love from all and thanks for the wire.

Your Padre

[October 15, 1946]

Dear Schmear;

The radio is playing "Blue Heaven," courtesy of Andrew Kastelanetz and the gas company. Kay is upstairs dressing and I am here writing, if you can call it that. Now that the air mail has been reduced to five cents I may write you more often. On the other hand, once the picture starts I may not write you at all.

I will try and endeavor to answer your questions. To begin with there is nothing new on the government capital gains case. I believe it will be thrown out and disallowed. There has not been a test case yet and until that time arrives no one knows what the ultimate decision will be. In the meantime I am not worrying about it, what comes, comes, as they say in Arabia, and the hell with it.

The present picture [is] called *Copacabana;* what the critics will call it is something to conjure with. At any rate, I am making it at United Artists, an extremely pleasant studio, unless one is unfortunate [enough] to bump into [Samuel] Goldwyn. There are parking places and a passable restaurant on the lot.

I am having a small dinner party Tuesday night. Kay is infatuated with Jimmy Roosevelt, so I thought it best to take the bull by the horns and throw them together. I therefore invited him, and who knows, maybe they will elope and eventually get married, and then if Jimmy should become president (stranger things could happen, he is a hell of a fellow) Kay could be the first lady of the land. Can you imagine the President's wife strolling around the White House on her hands? That hasn't been done since Dolly Madison. And can you imagine Leo Gorcey, if Kay should become the president's wife?

The script at the moment is brutal, and I have fired three of the writers and replaced them with others. I am not going to worry too much about the rest of the picture but it is terribly important that I emerge from it with honor and a few kudos from the public. Last night we journeyed all the way to the beach to visit the Kibbees. They provided us with a fine dinner and also inquired about you. They have a nice house there and the little mutt that they had last summer has grown into a big beautiful majestic German shepherd. He comes in the house when the door is opened for him, and at Kibbee's command he leaps up and shuts the door by throwing his weight against it. All in all, an impressive performance.

I had a small intermission just now, for I was listening to Fred Allen and he is still far and away the best performer on the air for wit and satire. Speaking of radio, did you hear the opening Crosby show last Wednesday? He had Bob Hope for his first guest and the show was great. The thing that makes it different is that the show is now a platter and is not a live performance and if this succeeds it may be the beginning of a new kind of radio with all the rest of the top shows demanding that they too be allowed to render theirs the same way. Henry Morgan now follows Bing at nine-thirty Pacific time Wednesday. If you are near a radio next week at that time you might twirl a dial and see how you like it.

I must close now as I am going out to dinner and I am still not dressed. Everything else is fine except the script I am doing. Melinda is trying to talk now and gurgles little sounds that only parents understand. Kay is fine and grousing about going out too much. Harpo is on his way to Baltimore to play two weeks and then he will be in New York, address unknown, for as yet he has no hotel accommodations. However, if you should get down you can find out where he is through the Max Gordon office.

All our love and write soon. Your ever lovin' Padre,

XXXXXXXXXXXXXXXXXX

Kisses.

Padre & Kay

Dear Mir;

I will do you the doubtful honor of writing you the first letter that
shoots off this new typewriter. I don't know whether I am really entitled to a typewriter, but I thought it over and I concluded that anyone
that can sell his writings is entitled to the best equipment that money
can buy, and since I have stuck many a magazine with my writings
over the years, I finally concluded, with very little arguing on my part,
that the best was none too good for me.

It is Sunday morning. It is quiet. Melinda is asleep—her customary
condition, by the way; Kay is asleep—she has a cold and I have instructions not to disturb her; I have just finished cleaning out the incinerator and burning some debris, and here I am at the machine.

Art and Ick were over last night to dinner and then we went and
saw *Caesar and Cleopatra*. I didn't understand all the military maneu-
vering, but the dialogue was fine, and I have decided that with the possible exception of me, Claude Rains is unquestionably the most
charming man on the screen.

We are supposed to begin our picture in two weeks, with a chance
that we may begin in three. We have about half the script; parts of it
are good and the rest is being altered to satisfy my demands. I saw Carmen Miranda in a Fox picture and my heart sank. In addition to looking like a dressed up bulldog, she sings each song the same as the
preceding one, and to top it off, she is supposed to feed me [lines] in
the picture, and I didn't understand a goddamned word she uttered.
Somebody will have to provide interpreters in each theatre to keep this
going.

Well, I won't bore you with my professional life. I must tell you that
I may be involved in another radio show before the year ends. Perhaps
even with Mickey Rooney. That's a nice pleasant thought to toy with.
I have given up on being a success on the air. The way I figure it out,
I just have too much talent for it; it requires a mediocrity that I can't
acquire. The fact of the matter is that I just take it when I can, as a
money making device, and do the best I can. I don't think I will ever
be a hit in radio. I have had many chances, but something seems to
go wrong every time. So now I grab what money I can and know that
in a few months the sponsor will listen one day, and there goes
Groucho Marx. I figured it up and despite the fact that I have never
been a success on the air, I have played over two hundred weeks in a
matter of five years, so I really have no complaint to make about it.

I accidentally heard Danny Kaye last night, that's the only way I listen to him; he was a guest on some show, and he still sounds like a cross between Cantor and Milton Berle—there's really a combination for you. Now if they could cross Ida with Berle's mother, they would have a new and sensational kind of monster for the Field Museum.

Tuesday night we are having one of the most ghoulish parties ever tendered in this town. We are having Henstell, Vurijnk and Leventhal, a bone specialist. I wanted to ask Schnaidt and Utter of Utter and McKinley but Kay vetoed Utter on the grounds that he might bring a sample with him. What a night to get sick, and God help any of their other patients.

Well, I must go to lunch now. Write when you can, and we all send our love. In case I forgot, they liked Arthur's outline and he has now been engaged at two fifty a week, less withholding tax of course, to write the screenplay. So you see that your brother is now a regular writer even though he is employed by Harry Cohn.

Love and kisses,
Your ever lovin' Padre

Harry Cohn was the head of Columbia Pictures through the 1940s. He had a reputation for being tough and was generally disliked in the industry.

October 25, 1946

Dear Mir:
This is not going to be a letter. It's merely a device to enclose some miscellaneous correspondence that concerns you more or less.

I wrote you so recently that there isn't much new to relate. I am busy bouncing writers almost daily and that consumes a great deal of my time. Ruby is doctoring up the song called "Go West, Young Man." You may recall that I chirped this from time to time at the Army camps. I am playing an agent in the picture, courtesy of Gummo Marx, and at one point I bring in an act to sell to the owner of the *Copacabana*. It turns out to be me in my old makeup. So you see, I am now playing dual roles just like Bette Davis and other expensive thespians.

The Friars Club has been organized to try to give the West Coast actors a taste of what they used to get in New York. A good many of the big names have displayed a willingness to join up. The clubhouse is a shanty—across from Ciro's. They are doing some rebuilding and yesterday I dropped by to see what progress was being made. A disheveled looking mobster in a turtled-neck sweater met me at the door and explained what a wonderful club this was going to be. He looked like Jessel and I wouldn't be surprised if they were related. One remark of his was unforgettable. He said, "Mr. Marx, you are going to love this place. We're going to be open twenty-four hours day and night, and at night, if you meet somebody and you don't want to take them home and dirty up your own house, why you can always bring them here." I just cite this to show what a crazy organization they are assembling. I am sure the Union League Club in Boston will have nothing to fear from this layout.

There I go—writing a whole letter. Lots of love and I hope you met some interesting boys in Pennsylvania. I have always heard that Pennsylvania is just full of interesting boys.*

Love,
Padre

* This doesn't mean you have to get married.

[November 4, 1946]

Monday Night.

Dear Mir;

A quiet evening at home. Kay is dusting off the books and has just gone upstairs to feed Melinda. The nurse went off this evening to converse with her Scotch friends in the neighborhood, and I have been reading the *Atlantic Monthly*. All very quiet and domestic. Brunetta is gone and in her place we have a new one named Dorothy. This is her first day and she seems quiet and contented, but you can never tell when one of them will turn into a Lizzie Borden and run amok.

Today was a typical one for me. After breakfast and reading the morning lies in the *Times,* I went and had my razor repaired at the Remington Rand place and then to a shoemaker to get the cushion in the big leather chair repaired. The shoemaker was too busy to sew it, so he lent me a needle and thread and I could be seen by any of my admirers sitting in a small shoe shop on La Brea sewing away for dear life. Then to the studio for a conference with the writers, and then I had to stop at the Farmer's Market on the way home to buy some things for dinner.

Arthur, in case you don't know, is now working at the Columbia Studio (courtesy of the Gummo Marx Agency) helping to fashion a new Blondie picture. He is getting two hundred a week, and if he makes good he will get two and a half. I hope he makes good for he needs the confidence of a steady job and the assurance that goes with it. He is a wonderful boy and I worry more about him that I do about myself. I suppose this is natural for all parents, especially parents who have children. This is a mild sort of joke that is hardly worth deciphering.

Charlie Lederer is working on the turkey that I am about to embark on, and whether he is any good or not, I can't tell as yet. Inside of a week I will give you the complete dope. In addition to him we have a Walter De Leon who talks like all the writers you read about whenever you read a funny piece about Hollywood conferences. The third writer is a Hungarian named Latzo something or other. He fancies himself a comedy writer and whenever I encounter him he says, "Here is a funny line." Can you think of an answer to that? Shades of Kaufman and Ryskind. The picture may be saved due to the fact that it has eleven songs in it, mostly sung by Carmen Miranda, who Lederer insists is a man dressed up in women's clothes. My advice is not to take any of your schoolmates to see this if it enters the confines of Vermont.

There is not much more of interest to write you. I did have a letter today from the fire department informing me that unless I remove the rubbish that I have been dragging across the street into a vacant lot, I have an excellent chance of being arrested.

Ruby is returning from the World Series tonight and I am glad he is coming back. I miss him a lot, for like two old dowagers, we need each other to talk to. I am getting him a job on my picture writing a song that I will do with the greasy Miranda, and I am sure that will make him happy. The producer, Coslow, has a wife, Esther Muir, that you used to play games with in a dressing room in Frisco, and if you hurry back, perhaps you can pick up where you left off.

I must close now and go to bed. Tomorrow is the last game of the series and I must be in shape for it. I am a Cardinal rooter, in case you don't know, and by the way don't you owe me a dollar?

If you don't hear from me soon, please remember that I am in the custody of the fire department.

Love and a lot of kisses from us all. Write soon.

Your Padre,
Padre
XXXXXXXX

Ryskind was Morrie Ryskind, playwright and screenwriter whose screenplays include Cocoanuts (1929), Animal Crackers (1930) *and* A Night at the Opera. *Every year my brother Arthur and I would bet our father a dollar on the Pennant and on the World Series. Our favorite team was the New York Yankees and they almost always won. My father hated the Yankees.*

101

[November 12, 1946]

Sunday afternoon around two to be exact.

Dear Mir.

Received your pencil-written letter from the infirmary and hope you are better by now. Last night unannounced and unheralded, Tin Can Joe breezed in. I was sitting with Sheekman discussing some business and I was annoyed by his uninvited visit. Well, after a half hour of various degrees of silence he finally left. He is a nice boy but he should learn that no one is welcome unless he is invited. Particularly by me, a character who doesn't care much for people that he has asked to the house.

Well, enough of this philosophy. I am working like a beaver whatever that means, on the script writing and memorizing and I have to level on it for the time isn't too long before Al Green, an ancient incompetent who is preparing to screw up the works (the director), shouts roll them, and four other mediocrities rush out to fawn at his feet and do his bidding no matter how lowly. He lives completely in the past and discusses nothing that has occurred since the first world war. If you get near *Harpers* for the current month, read a piece by Niven Busch about the directorial racket in Hollywood. Quite revealing. It won't affect any of the old directors for most of them can't read anyway. Maxine as you know is getting hooked up Friday, and it's too bad that you can't be there to see it. There is nothing women enjoy more than to see a groom that is roped and tied and ready for the halter, not a thing. That angers you, but you will admit sooner or later that there is something to what I say. In addition to that, I enjoy teasing you about women. Personally I am fond of them; they contribute certain things to society that man never can. My experience is that it's the women that dislike the women, rarely the men, particularly if they are pretty and well stacked. Speaking of well stacked, Earl Wilson sent me his latest book *Pikes Peek or Bust,* get it?, and the fascination that those two things have for Earl would, I believe, arouse the interest of a psychiatrist were he to go to one. The fact of the matter is he writes well, and it's a shame that he devotes most of his column to trivia. For example, a few weeks ago Pegler came out and attacked Roosevelt with one of the most vicious columns he has ever had, accusing the late pres of being drunk, etc. A few days later Wilson went after him and really wrote a wonderful column defending Franklin and attacking Pegler beautifully. I only write this to say it's a shame that he wastes his time when he has a lot of talent that could be used for a good purpose.

I might add, too, that in his new book he devotes a whole chapter to me, and if for no other reason it is worth getting. I was flattered, for I certainly have hardly any bust to speak of.

We had a small cyclone last week. It was called a high wind in the papers, but it took one of the big trees in the backyard and blew it, roots and all, over on Gabby Hayes' garage. My only regret is that the bearded Gabby was on the road, for otherwise it might have wiped out one of the most untalented actors in the movie industry.

I think this includes all the news of the past week. If I have omitted anything drop me a line and I will send you twenty-five cents in stamps to include the cost of mailing. So until next week at this same time this is Alvin Wilder signing off and telling you, "When you are sleeping on a Sealy you are sleeping on a cloud."

Love and kisses from me and the character on the bed—your stepmother. XXXXXXXXXX Kisses.

Padre XXXX

Gabby Hayes was an actor who appeared in over 200 westerns, most often as a comic sidekick to the heroes. He later starred in "The Gabby Hayes Show" on television during the 1950s.

[November, 1946]

Saturday night around six-thirty

Dear Mir:

Just arrived home from the day's shooting, sound like a hunter, and am glad to get off that cold dark stage. I must say that in comparison with the last picture this has been easy. There has been no physical work to speak of, however, later in the picture I will do a little dancing and rehearsing but that will be much better than swinging head down from a ladder and other comical stunts that writers dream up so glibly in an office. At any rate the rushes seem to be satisfactory to everyone concerned, and I do look astonishingly well. I look like a cross between my father, Mephistopheles and an opium peddler on the Mexican border. At any rate the backers, of whom there are many, all seem delighted with the fifteen pages I have shot up to now. Miranda is charming to work with, unspoiled and unaffected. I always had an idea she would be a roughtough dame, but she is far from that and photographically she has never been shot as well as this present camera man is doing it. All in all, this may be a pleasant surprise to a man who ventured into this just to get a little money.

The news about that girl is shocking, and I can imagine how her parents must feel about it. I hope you don't pick up rides on roads. There are just as many degenerates in New England as there are in California so be on your guard, and don't consort with anyone that you don't know, and well. Melinda is so smart. The nurse has taught her to put her hand out when you say how de do to her, and it looks like she will eventually end up as the smartest baby on Sunset Plaza Drive.

I have to go to the wedding and that cuts into my Sunday time. I have a hell of a lot of script to learn, and it's the hardest kind of dialogue, it doesn't make sense and has no logical sequence of words, so I keep plugging away, over and over again endlessly, but I must say it's a savage kind of satisfaction, when the day's work is o'er (poetry yet) and I can take a pencil and cross out a page or two and say well that's done, good or bad, it's done and it doesn't have to be memorized anymore. There is going to be a big crowd at the wedding, lots of people that I don't know and don't want to know, so after the ceremony I am exiting from there and having dinner at home, for I am shooting the first thing in the morning and I have to get back to my room, and then there's Fred Allen and a magazine or two and it's far more interesting than listening to a lot of strangers go on and on.

I am sending you ten dollars for a pair of snow boots, whatever the hell they are, and if this whole thing has done nothing for you it has taught you that ten dollars is a lot of money, and not something to be tossed aside like an old lover. Well enough of this philosophizing, the script is there looking at me coyly, and so here I go again. In case you care, my name in the picture is Lionel Devereaux, but I can still be addressed as Groucho Marx.

Love from all of us, and keep your feet warm.

Yours Padraically,

Groucho. ############### kisses.

The girl he refers to disappeared while hitch-hiking (the same weekend that I had hitch-hiked to Connecticut from Bennington — something I never told him about).

[November 18, 1946]

Dear Mir

Monday Morn the 18th

I usually write you on Sunday but the day went past and before I knew it I was at the Village Theatre watching Van Johnson and Keenan Wynn in *No Love No Leave*. The picture was generally panned but expecting nothing we had a good time. There was also something called *I Am Faithful in My Fashion,* a line taken from Cynara, and that line I can tell you was the only line that was remotely connected with talent.

Well, Maxine is now a married woman and can now begin to worry whether she is going to be pregnant this month or whether she wants to be a mother the following one. He seems like a nice fellow and like most nice fellows doesn't make too much money. I hope they make a go of it, for the divorces out here are coming so fast that it is impossible to know who to invite for dinner, although I must say that my crowd (the elderly literary group) are a way behind with the separations. I guess they are so preoccupied with their writings that they haven't time to run away from their wives. This morning's crop was Laraine Day and Ann Miller. I always felt that the Day thing wouldn't last, for he is a jerk and she is a tough baby with a tremendous amount of personal ambitions who figures everything out coolly and disspassionately (I am certain the last word is spelled incorrectly) that who knows. My conviction is that most marriages are decided in the bedroom, but like all generalizations that can be pretty wrong too.

I am sorry you have a hacking cough. I think you would be wise to quit smoking, if only for a while. I spoke to Henstell and he suggested you might try one of those heat lamps—they are made by Westinghouse and other concerns—Sylvania Electric, for example (I happen to be a stockholder of that company)—and they cost about two dollars. You screw it into your regular lamp (first removing the other bulb) and let it play on your chest (nice work if you can get it) for about fifteen minutes, and not closer than about eighteen inches. It may not do any good, but it is also good for drying hair and keeping your feet warm, all that and heaven too for that small sum. You also might inform me what the results are of your X rays.

Arthur (thank God) is still working on Blondie, that's the script, and now that he is on the way to being a father, he is going to need all the money he can get a hold of.

Speaking of writing, I had a piece in the Sunday syndicated *This Week*. It turned out only fair, I thought; it was funny when I wrote it, but it's been months since then, and now it just strikes me as a labored essay on a subject that doesn't seem topical anymore, even though the need for houses is more desperate than it was when I first wrote it.

I don't get much time for anything anymore. I have that goddamned script in front of me most of the day, and by this time every line in it seems so dreary and stale, as a matter of fact many of them are. This can't be much of a picture when one considers the cast, the director, the producer, the script, the physical equipment, etc. I have no right to complain, this is the best offer I had — hell, the only offer — and they are paying me considerable money, so I am working hard and hope by some mysterious chemistry in the shooting that it comes out as a great classic.

Well, I must go now and have a business lunch with Kibbee and Gummo. I hope you are all right and love from Kay who is lying on the bed in an extremely seductive pose, and from me who is beginning to resemble the Jews' answer to Canada Lee making up in white face.

Love,
Padre

Laraine Day was a film and television actress. Ann Miller was an actress and dancer who had appeared with the Marx Brothers in Room Service *(1938). Canada Lee was a black actor who had appeared in Hitchcock's* Lifeboat *in 1944.*

November 27, 1946

Dear Mir:
I enclose letter from Bye, which I am sure you expected — also a piece from the *Writer's* magazine.

I am not writing you a letter for Kay just wrote you. Bogart was at the house the other night and got completely drunk. This is a pretty normal thing for him. I don't think I'll ask him again. He's a bore when he's stewed and he's not a hell of a lot better when sober. I feel sorry for her; she tried to get him to go home, but he's a fighting stew. Even the mild and meek Kurnitz couldn't stand him any longer and finally told him off. The moral is don't go around with actors — with a few exceptions, they are jerks. I'll stick to writers. They are older and more settled.

Love and kisses,
Your Padre

106

[December 1, 1946]

Dear Miriam;

This is Sunday night around eight. Kay is on the bed pasting clippings and pieces of mine in a scrapbook for posterity. The fact of the matter is that some day, if I ever get the energy, I may put them all in book form, for I have been told that there is an audience of potential buyers for this classic that may put it in the same class with *Forever Amber* and *Gone with the Wind*.

I have just finished two days shooting on the picture and last night before staggering to my home I witnessed the first day's rushes, and was agreeably surprised with what I saw on the screen. I don't think that the the dialogue or story will ever get any awards, but oddly enough it might be an entertaining picture. What more could anyone possibly expect from an opus called *Copacabana*? I will say, however, that if one has an allergy to Carmen Miranda this is not going to be their dish, since she plays two parts in this one, instead of the orthodox one. She is very nice to work with and that's a help since I am with her in most of the scenes.

I am glad to have had a letter from you and the news that you are all right and that your cough has disappeared for the moment. See that you get enough rest and keep away from smoking any more than you have to. I don't know whether I have ever told you, but Krasna has quit smoking; he gave away all of his smoking equipment and has now become one of the most objectionable fellows in town. There is something about the missionary zeal that gets everyone and I can well understand that the desire to reform one of any vice (fancied or real) can be infinitely more enjoyment than practicing the act. I received all his pipes, a very expensive collection by the way, and they have all been cleaned and fumigated (I didn't tell this to Norman) and I am now beginning to smoke them. He also has taken up golf, and he will regale you at any time or place with his latest score and the trouble he had on the eighth hole through no fault of his own. He has been trying to persuade me to join Hillcrest, but I am not in the mood. I was a member once when the initiation fee was three hundred dollars. It is now six thousand and the way I play golf it isn't worth it. As a matter of fact, at the moment I have no great desire to play golf. I used to enjoy it a little, but I was usually in a rage before I got through, and it's so much less aggravation cleaning out the incinerator and doing odd janitorial jobs around the house. The slight need I have for club life will be filled by the new Friars club which from present plans will be completed some time after the first of the year. The club will be a pretty classy one judging from one of the conversations I was in a few weeks ago. Jessel is one of the prime spirits in the club, and naturally a good many of his friends and relatives will hold important posts in running it. One of them greeted me the other day and began explaining the many advantages this club would have over the Union League Club and the Harvard Club in Boston. I asked him how late the club would be open at night. He said, "Mr. Marx, we are going to be open all night and all day, we'll never close. Suppose you meet some friend in the evening and you don't want to take him to your home and dirty it all up, why you can just bring him to the club." Oh well, it will be better than the Copper Room, except that I understand that Harry Cohn is going to be a member.

I have no idea what to tell you about a job for the open season. You might try asking Ernst again, or Max Gordon, or Jerry Chodorov. My circle of friends in New York has dwindled to a straggly few. You might also ask Harold Ross and George Bye. I am sorry that you won't get a chance to see Melinda through these stages, but it can't be helped. She is very good and hardly cries at all. She makes spit bubbles now and may grow up to be another Harpo. Well, I have to arise at seven-fifteen so this is it. All my love to you and kisses, and that goes for Kay too. I will write you again next Sunday, unless I accidentally get a day off. Good night for now.

Your lovin' Padre,

Padre
XXXXXXX

Harold Ross was the editor of The New Yorker.

December 17, 1946

Dear Mir:
I wrote you the other day so I have nothing to tell you as you will discover when you read that letter.

I am enclosing a Christmas present which I imagine you prefer to some gewgaw I might buy for you.

Merry Christmas and love and kisses,

Your Padre

[December 24, 1946]

Sunday morning

Dear Mir;
This Sunday morning only differs from the previous one because it is
that much closer to Xmas. The tree is up. I had hoped with you gone
that I could buy a small tree this year, but I got hooked for just as big
a monster as when you were home. The whole thing has gotten so far
out of hand from an expense angle that I don't want to think about
it. Except for marriage, it's the most gigantic holdup of all, and there
doesn't seem to be any solution to it. Then Harpo and Zep had to go
and adopt six kids between them and all the other kids that I seem to
know better as it gets closer to Xmas, well the hell with it.

We are having what is known as a schlepper Xmas eve. All the semi
homeless, like Margaret Dumont and Selma Diamond, and a slew of
others. As soon as they all go home, I am going to sneak off and go
to the Jococo Room and dance my fool head off.

We saw *Margie* last night. It's not great but it's pleasant; it's a movie of the 1920s, and it doesn't have [Betty] Grable or Alan Hale playing
a bartender in a Bowery saloon. It's a cute picture, although a little too
sugary for a steady diet. Anyway, it's the first movie I have seen in
more than three weeks, and I only went because it was Saturday night
and as you know we don't shoot on Sundays.

Kay is appearing in the picture so that she can get enough money
to get her mother a new set of teeth, or approximately that, anyway
a number of teeth. I think she will be good in it, she is going to do a
little singing and a little dancing. I note what you say about giving you
additional money on your three months layoff. I purposely made your
monthly allowance a liberal one, I remember how affected you seemed
by my generosity, and I don't think you should even suggest any more
money. I am not going to bore you with a lecture on the value of money. I am sure you are aware of its value at this time, and I suggest you
learn how to budget your allowance for the times when you need it
most.

The wedding I told you about that I attended was either Maxine's
or Kay Marx's. At any rate, they are both married. I suppose pretty
soon there will be more children to give Xmas presents to.

In case this letter strikes you as grim, let me give you a faint idea
of how many people I pay tribute to. There is Kay's and your allowance, alimony to your mother, commission to the Marx office, a
secretary, Lester Roth, a lawyer, a tax man, Salwyn Shufro for in-

vestment services, a cook, the federal tax, the state tax, a tax on the dwelling I live in and the nurse for the baby. All these items I have mentioned do not include living and medical and clothing and charities and a thousand other things, and they pile up so that I don't like to think of them.

This isn't a very cheerful Xmas letter, and I am sorry that it all sounds so sordid and commercial, but unless I explain things to you, it is impossible for you to see my side of the logic. I am glad to know you are going to be somewheres where it looks as though you might have a good time.

If you write me and let me know when it is a good time to catch you I will phone you during the Xmas week. All my love and from the rest of them too, and write soon and a Merry Xmas, even though you must think I am a Scrooge.

Your loving Padre, ****************************Kisses

Padre

Selma Diamond was a friend and comedy writer who had written for "Blue Ribbon Town." Kay Marx was Gummo's stepdaughter.

January 15, 1947

Dear Mir:

I get very little mail from you these days and you get very little from me, so it all comes out about even. Your mail has been going to Bennington, which is why you haven't been getting your allowance or anything else. I neglected to tell my secretary that you were in New York City.

I expect to be through with the picture in about ten days and am looking forward to it. Not the picture, just the ten days. Every morning at seven I arise and go to the studio where a bald-headed makeup man with halitosis slaps a cold wet sponge on my map and applies what he calls Max Factor pancake. He also keeps insisting that I should feel the little new hairs that are coming out on top of his head. He has discovered a new cure for baldness and is convinced that it will only be a few months before he has more hair than Gene Tierney. The next thing on the program is the filming on the song "Go West." I have already recorded and now the tough part begins. You see, the lips have to match the record. Kay is pretty jealous. She says my lips should only touch hers.

Kay was over to Virginia's the other night. Kay came home and threw up around five in the morning and Virginia got a lemon seed lodged in her throat and is now taking sulphur. Kay has decided to eat at home in the future. This is more expensive but safer.

What are you doing? Do you have a job? If so, what is it? Are you actually working for Krasna? If so, are you getting paid? I hope you are not wasting your time in New York without working.

Melinda is getting cuter every day. I guess all babies do. I think she recognized me for the first time yesterday, for the minute the nurse brought her in she socked me in the eye.

There's lots more I could write you but I'm so busy that I can't waste any more time with you.

All my love, and let us hear from you, even if it's only a request for money which, I can assure you, will be turned down.

Your Padre

P.S. I am enclosing your dividend check from the Standard Oil.

P.P.S. Just received your letter, written in longhand, so disregard everything in this letter.

P.P.P.S. Have you hocked your typewriter?

February 4, 1947

Dear Mir:
I've been in the country for the past few days looking at nature. It was very nice there and we played golf. Kay played with us. She had never played before so that will give you an idea of what we went through. It reminded me of those old days when you used to accompany us and carve up the fairways. She was in a rage most of the time over her inability to hit the ball. It's a strange thing about golf. People don't pick up a violin or a piano, if that were possible, and grow angry because they can't play it as well as Heifetz or Horowitz, but once they grab a golf club they instantly assume that they should play as well as Snead and Nelson. Kay, also, as soon as she hits the ball off the tee, leaves the tee and the other participants stand there undecided whether they should hit the ball and kill Kay or wait until she has disappeared into the rough. Arthur also played. His game is somewhat like Kay's and considerable misery. At nights we went to the village and saw Pat O'Brien, Roy Rogers and Trigger. There's a remarkable similarity between the three of them.

There were two young writers there. I kept thinking of you and

111

wondering if I could marry you off to one of them. One was Jim Henderson and the other Bill Pepper. I kept calling him Bell Pepper, which got no laugh. At any rate he's engaged so that's closed. Tremendously attractive fellow with a black mustache and raven black hair. He comes from a very wealthy family in West Virginia but the tale I heard was that his folks were euchred out of their dough. I missed you up at the farm. You would have enjoyed it there. They had some feeble saddle horses and the customary cows and chickens. At night we discussed everything from Karl Marx to Senator Taft. Peggy, the girl that Bell Pepper is more or less engaged to, has thick ankles and this might have been just the spot for you. I don't know why I write you all this. It certainly can't be of any interest to you but it certainly does help to fill up the pages.

Salpeter, nee Gordon, told me that you were living in squalor. For a while I thought he meant a small town in New Jersey, but it seems he was referring to your room. Then your letter came and I was concerned about it because you wrote that it was a very tough, dangerous neighborhood. Max said he was trying to get you something else. It seems to me that there must be a room for rent someplace else in Manhattan or even Brooklyn that wouldn't have so many disadvantages as you mention.

Regarding your mother, it seems to be a pretty helpless problem. She can't be cured of anything unless she is willing to cooperate. Unfortunately, she doesn't seem to be in this kind of mood.

Irene is beginning to expand and before you know it I'll be a grandfather. I don't mind it much for I've felt that way for years. Melinda is so cute. We were gone for six days and apparently we made a much better impression on her than I imagined. I didn't think she'd remember us. She can push herself up, but instantly falls down. This is all pretty dull unless you're a parent.

I love you very much and hope to see you one of these days. We're going to preview in a couple of weeks and my future plans will depend a good deal on the reaction to *Copacabana* and to the treatment of Krasna's show in New York, for if the critics slaughter him I doubt if he'll be in much of a mood to do ours very soon.

Love from all,
Your Padre

Feb 22 Washington's Birthday [1947]

Dear Mir;

I wired you last night and expected an answer, but up to now I haven't heard from you. . . . Anyway, I am planning to come to New York, and I would like to know whether you are going to be there or back at Bennington, and if you are back at school, would you be able to come in Friday, Saturday and Sunday for the three weeks I contemplate being there?

I wrote you an angry letter last week chiding you for not writing more often, and since then had a short letter from you telling us very little. I also sent you some lingerie for Valentine's Day (Valentine's Day was merely an excuse) but we are still uncertain as to whether you received that or not.

I note what you say about Kurnitz throwing a party for Patsy [Englund] at the Stork Club, and to me it looks like Patsy is hooked or is it Kurnitz? What does she tell you, or are you sworn to secrecy? I would like to get some info (that's the way they talk on *Variety*) for Mabel Englund, or is she too keeping things from me? I suppose you wonder why I am so inquisitive about Kurnitz's love life. Well, the fact of the matter is that some years ago he gave me some framed letters of W. S. Gilbert and at the moment they are resting in the cellar gathering dust and assorted microbes, and I thought if Harry gets married again and settled down in a house of his own, I could give them those letters for a wedding present. My cellar is terribly crowded now with an assortment of old sporting paraphernalia left over from my old and more active years, sun lamps, old radio scripts, cheap domestic wines growing cheaper and more domestic all the time, a pair of galoshes that I am saving until I move East again and many other items and I would like to clear the cellar of as much junk as possible.

We previewed *Copacabana* the other night at Glendale and for a first preview it was astonishingly good. The chief trouble was that Carmen sang too often and too long, and this we are remedying for the second preview which will be Tuesday night in Pasadena. It was a good thing we previewed in a large theatre, for there are so many producers on this picture that we required almost ten rows just for them and their wives and children. Anyway, it was a fairly satisfying trial spin and I think with judicious cutting and trimming it can be a fairly good picture. If it is, it will be an astounding achievement. For you must remember that they had no story and no names and no money (this last fact I wasn't aware of until we had been shooting two

113

weeks) and we were surrounded by incompetents. The only reason I took the job is because it was the only offered to me, except for making a Marx Brothers picture, something I have no more desire for nor interest in. And Russell is quite good in the picture and if it wasn't for his protruding teeth he could go quite a ways in the movies. As it is, I don't think he will go much farther than the dentist. I have been offered an opportunity to do another picture with Carmen, but I don't think I will take it. To begin with, she is no particular draw anymore, the bloom has worn off, she is no novelty as she was seven years ago, her singing is so stylized, and in a definite groove, and as a straight woman for me, it is frequently difficult to understand her, and this is an additional handicap for a comedian. It is hard enough to get a laugh when the audience hears what the straight man or woman says; if they don't hear the feed line, obviously it is considerably more difficult.

It is too bad; I like Carmen, she is a nice woman and very easy to work with, but I have to look out for myself. At the moment she is hardly an object of pity for she is getting fourteen thousand dollars a week singing in a cafe in Florida.

Last week I bought Melinda a playpen and she seems very happy in it. Kay has rearranged your room and it looks quite nice. If there is anything you want in it (other than Gregory Peck) let us know and we will fix it up so that it resembles Marie Antoinette's boudoir.

Anyway, all my love to you and also Kay's and Melinda's and try and write more often. Your loving Padre Groucho Marx of the Marx Brothers.

Padre XXXX

This is Sunday morning, your wire just received and also the news that the lingerie hasn't been received. We will investigate that tomorrow. Now about coming: I am not sure when I can come until the previews are over (or did I mention that in a earlier part of the letter)? If you could come down Friday, Saturday and Sunday for the three weeks I would be in New York I would prefer to come around the first of April; if this isn't possible I will come earlier while you are still employed in New York.

You might also call up Max Gordon and investigate the possibility of getting a bedroom at the Dorset with twin beds if possible, one bed if no other is possible; at any rate, let me know. I will see what railroad accommodations are, and if that can't be arranged I would be forced to fly. (The hell we will, love Kay.) The short interlude is by Kay, which you can disregard. I will take the train if it can be arranged, but if necessary I will fly. This is all pretty mixed up but I think you can untangle it, if not I will send an interpreter on ahead of this letter.

Again, love and kisses, Padre and Kay.

Mir;
Don't worry about us flying, because I will not, and will not let him. We will come on the train, or else. Can't wait to see your new haircut, everyone tells me you look wonderful. See you soon.

Love and Kisses,
Kay

February 28, 1947

Dear Mir:
Finally got a letter from you and I hope you have completely recovered from your flu attack. I will be glad to pay your doctor bill, particularly if it aids you in recovering.

It is extremely gratifying to me to learn that you are now keeping company with four different men. I can understand your going around with Stanley, Al and John. John you say you met in an elevator. Was the elevator going up at the time, or down? This is very important, for going down in an elevator one always has that sinking feeling and for all I know you may have this confused with love. If you were going up, it is clearly a case of love at first sight and it also proves that he is a rising young man. I am a little baffled as to why you see David. A fat young anthropologist, probably covered with germs, doesn't sound like a very attractive suitor. Perhaps what your doctor diagnosed as intestinal flu was too close contact with David. As for the Japanese, I frankly don't know how I would feel having an enemy as a son-in-law. Of course I realize that most sons-in-law are enemies anyway, but this could be an extremely sensitive relationship. We may be having dinner together some night and I might accidentally bring up the subject of Pearl Harbor and in the confusion all of the sukiyaki would fall on the carpet. At that, it would be a relief to meet someone older than me. At the moment practically everyone I know is thirty or forty years my junior and at times it makes me feel quite ancient.

We are planning on leaving here on the tenth and arriving in New York by train, weather and engineer permitting, on the thirteenth. As yet, however, we have no sleeping accommodations. I have suggested flying to Kay, but she resolutely declines to go up in the air. In fact she goes up in the air when I mention it. We may have to walk. However I will wire you before arriving.

You say you are going to quit your job on the seventeenth. I should arrive in New York on the thirteenth and I would like you to quit then so that we can spend some time together. If you then have to return to school before I return here, you will just have to make the trip weekly, with me, of course, defraying the expenses. Don't worry about that part of it. I miss you very much and I am very anxious to see you.

We previewed the picture for the second and last time last Tuesday in Pasadena with a house full of typical Pasadenians. You know, that young hoodlum crowd that screams hysterically when Andy Russell, or anyone like him, makes his appearance. They seemed very well satisfied with the picture, that is the producers, and the audience loved it. *Copacabana* is no great noteworthy artistic achievement, but it will make a lot of money and [is] a vindication of my determination to veer slightly away from the old character. I have some other movie plans brewing and will tell you about them when I see you.

I hope you will be able to live with us at the Shufros. I don't remember whether I wrote you that he had volunteered to let us use his apartment, as most of the time I will be in New York he will be in Florida with his family.

At any rate, give all your suitors my best and let me know what shows you haven't seen so I can get you seats for them. If some of those you have seen you want to see again, that too can be arranged.

Love and kisses and I hope you are all better by now. I am glad you liked the lingerie. You can give me a style show when I arrive, in a nice way of course.

Your Padre

March 7, 1947

Dear Mir:
It was nice to hear you on the phone, and yesterday I received your letter. I hope you are taking care of yourself and that you don't give the flu germs an opportunity to play a return date.

When I told you I had planned on being in New York on the thirteenth, everything was all right, but Kay has been in bed for five days with the doctor appearing each day. She has had a combination of the flu and strep throat. She is subject to these attacks and has them frequently. I fear that one of them one day might be very serious. I don't

116

know whether it's just her lack of resistance or the climate, but after she emerges from this I am going to insist on her taking every conceivable kind of inoculation possible.

So — at the moment I won't be in New York on the thirteenth and I will lose some of the time I was going to spend with you. Obviously I can't leave Kay while she is ill. I will try to get a reservation for a few days later, but everything is pretty much in the air right now. As soon as I know something specific I will wire you. Thus the best laid plans of mice and men, etc. etc.

I am having lunch today with your brother and sister-in-law. She is beginning to take on that top-like shape that all six-month mothers eventually acquire. She is a very nice girl and I am extremely fond of her. I didn't care much for her when I first met her. She is a very determined young lady and I have a notion she makes most of the decisions. Of course Kay does too. I have come to the conclusion that most women do. Most men are just putty molded the way their wives wish. I think the great wars are the ones fought between the sexes, not between nations. I honestly believe that men and women dislike each other and only go around together for sexual reasons. If it weren't for that I think men would avoid women as though it were a plague. I personally know of about four women I would like to be with. I know fifty men that I could have around me. Well, it's late in my life to start talking this way.

Take care of yourself. We'll get there as soon as we can. I told the Rube Goldbergs to call you so don't be surprised if your phone rings.
Love and kisses,
Your Padre

Sunday morning the twentieth of April [1947]

As yet I haven't been out of the house. We arrived here Thursday night around two in the morning. The plane trip was pleasant, and I have been spending most of my time sleeping and reading. Today I am going to the Sunday doubleheader at Gilmore Field. I have spoken on the phone to a few people but I have very little desire to see anyone for a while.

I received your wire about the car and I hope it runs all right. Before driving it let me know the engine number and all the other information so that I can get you covered with the insurance company. You see, even now driving begins to take on additional burdens. I hope you drive more carefully than you did when you were out here. The only advice I can give you is to slow down, whenever you are in doubt give the other driver the right of way. I remember I once read somewhere, "I am never going anyplace that is more important than not getting killed." With this pleasant piece of philosophy I will drop the subject, knowing full well that you will do as you goddamned please.

Melinda is very cute, and she knew us immediately when we got in the house. We woke her up at two in the morning and she was smiling and just as agreeable as (write your own simile). Yesterday I took her in the little carriage up the mountain road. She wore a little poke bonnet and seemed so interested in the surrounding scenery, as though she were a little old lady.

I had no idea how tired and nervous I was until I got here. The two broadcasts and the quarreling and the constant running to the theatre and dressing for restaurants and the crowds on Broadway, well, the whole thing is not for me. Even though I wanted it, my health wouldn't permit me to do a show, with the fierce rehearsals and nervousness of the tryouts, and the physical strain of battling the audiences night after night (assuming that we ran that long). I could make some money that way, but I'll wait and see what other means there are to make a buck (as Gordon would put it).

Arthur and Ick are fine. She is expecting in about two weeks, and Kay is giving her a shower. This is a device to gather a lot of presents by the investment of some sandwiches and ice cream.

Arthur isn't working and I imagine he worries about it, but he doesn't display his emotions casually, so it's hard to tell whether he is disturbed or not.

Shufro is here and he is going to the Valley today to spend the day with the Garritys, as they are known out there. He will be home in a few weeks and you can then find out all about your mother from him. From what Arthur said the other night, she seems to be behaving pretty well.

I won't write any more as I am tired and nervous and I just want to sit and stare. All my love to you and write soon. I am sending you two hundred dollars instead of one seventy-five. This will enable you to get license plates and driving card, etc., perhaps even one gallon of gas.

Good-bye for the moment.

Love,
Padre

The Garritys were my mother and her second husband.

118

April 30, 1947

Dear Mir:
When the bill came from Saks, I was shocked to find that you had spent over $100 more than I had asked you to. At first I was going to skip sending you your monthly allowance for being a sucker, as all parents are, but I decided to send it. However, I am writing Saks and notifying them that in the future nothing is to be charged to me unless it has my personal okay since I can't trust you. I thought I was being good to you, but apparently it wasn't good enough.

Am glad you like the car and presume that by this time you have it insured. I am working hard with Krasna and we have thrown out practically the whole second act and have started almost from scratch again. This is the fourth time we have done this play and it's now been ten years since we started it. I had better hit the bull's-eye this time, for I'm sure we will never take another crack at it. Krasna's persistence is astounding. He was just offered $10,000 a week to write and direct a picture for Warner Bros. and turned it down to keep hacking away at the same old play. I guess it must be me. When he writes a play alone he writes it in three months, and with collaboration takes ten years.

Well, I have an awful lot to do. Glad your writing is improving. Send on the second piece when you get it. The Krasnas thought your first one about the train was very good.

Love and kisses.

[May 17, 1947]

Dear Miriam
Happy birthday and this is your last year in the teens. Well, everything ends and that's the finish of that. I have passed so many milestones that I don't pay any attention to them anymore. I saw Arthur and Ick's baby last night at the Kahns' and like all babies at the age of nine days he is cute and husky.

Since I get no mail from you at all I will make this short. I realize that you are busy but I am too. I work all day with Norman and guest shots, etc., but I can always find time for you. I suppose it is silly for a parent to complain about a child of theirs not writing. If the desire is there the letters will come through. Well, the hell with it, I don't want to make this a preachment. We seem to have a pretty rugged relationship as it is.

The play is coming along pretty good now; we have made drastic changes and it better be right this time. We estimated the other day, in one of our daydreaming moods, that we began this ten years ago. And here we are, still hacking away at it as though it were an idea we had dreamed up yesterday.

Arthur is still out of work and it is one of my big worries. He is twenty-six now with a family and no income at all. I try to pull strings to get him placed, but jobs are pretty scarce now for young writers. He works all day and doesn't seem worried about it but he doesn't talk much about his affairs.

Melinda is a little doll and smart as a good college president. She dances and seems to be aware of an awful lot that most kids her age are not hep to. This could be just the pride of an aging and doting parent, but I don't think so. Our ball club is right back in its customary position, last place, and there is a good chance that it will remain there for the balance of the season. The niggardly bastards who own the club won't spend any money for ball players, so every night we go out there and spend a miserably cold evening rooting for this raggedy collection of misfits.

Chico is leaving on the *Queen Elizabeth* Monday for six weeks in England. Chico, with his customary regard for his own welfare, is taking with him enough food to feed all the displaced people in Germany, but thank god he isn't doing that.

Harpo has a script now that was written by Ben Hecht; it is pretty good but still needs a lot of fixing. Now if they can get a studio to put money in it, he will be all set for the beginning of a new career. Oh, I forgot: Chico too is in it.

I think this covers all the Brothers and their activities. I am taking care of your plane reservation and will let [you know] later all about the details. Love and kisses to you and happy birthday and drive slowly.

Your loving Padre Groucho Marx

Arthur and Irene's son Steve was born on May 8, 1947. The play he mentions here and a few times previously was A Time for Elizabeth.

May 23, 1947

Dear Mir:

I received your letter of apology and don't believe a goddamned word of it.

I feel pretty good this morning. Hollywood won its last three games after losing ten out of the previous eleven, and your brother just sold a comic article to *Cosmopolitan* for $300. This will give him a lot of confidence and you know how important that is to a young writer— the assurance that something he pounds out has a market value. That is why poetry is such a nebulous art. Nobody buys poetry so you never know whether it's good or bad, except, possibly, the reaction from someone you are living with at the moment. This, I concede, can be considerably more important than a princely sum from *Life* magazine, but I am certain that no poet can ever be sure that what he has written is any good. This all sounds pretty materialistic but, little girl, that's the kind of a world you are living in. It's a jungle and it is up to you to claw your way through. Those kindly shy fellows who barely subsist usually have shiny blue serge suits and hop the bus. Maybe they're better off at that.

I certainly have drifted far away from writing a letter. I had dinner with Billy Wilder last night and he told me he had read Arthur's screenplay and was surprised how good it was. I guess Wilder has always visualized Arthur as a fellow with big feet, rushing the net with a tennis racket. I guess, at that, it is hard to reconcile that sort of picture with literary talent. Anyhow, I am greatly encouraged by his recent activities.

Kay sent you a birthday present and we still don't know whether you received it. It certainly was nice of Jeanette to remember you. I don't know what she sent you, but apparently you were satisfied with it.

Tin Can Joe dropped in yesterday with a plea to use the typewriter for a few hours. We sent him upstairs and locked the door so he couldn't sneak out to raid the icebox. He wanted to use my room, but I am not keen about strangers prowling through my desk. It's horrible enough when I have to look at some of the things I have there.

Well, the time grows short, the letter grows long and I am off to Krasna's. All my love and kisses. This, too, from Kay and Melinda. Write soon.

Padre

[June, 1947]

Dear Mir;

After many weeks a letter arrived from you, and not a very pleasant one either. I feel very sad about your mother and am going to have a long talk with Arthur about it. I am sure that if it continues Jack will

121

leave her, and then she would be a lost soul. You see, everyone has his own worries. Arthur, for example, has a baby now and is working at the moment for Mannie Manheim, and these two things keep him occupied. Oh, I imagine he worries about his mother, but he isn't the forceful type and would rather drift along than take any direct action.

Now on to another problem. I don't believe there is any great friendliness between you and Kay. I notice you two used to correspond but even that has ceased. I asked Kay about this. Miriam, she said, "Is nice to me when she wants something, otherwise she treats me with kind of studied contempt." I believe there is some justice to her complaints, and I couldn't argue with her too much, although I did. . . . As usual I am in the middle of all this feminine internecine warfare and I am sure it is all based on jealousy, but nevertheless, no matter what it is based on, it exists. . . .

You know all this sounds silly. Unfortunately, it isn't. The period in New York was a trying one for all of us, and I think a similar one can be avoided if we all work a little at being reasonable.

I would like you to write Kay a letter, a friendly one. You know except for her jealously she isn't hard to get along with, and a nice letter from you would soften her up instantly. I don't want another divorce, and a bitter feeling between you two could easily lead to one, through a series of steps that I can see in my mind's eye.

This whole letter may come as a huge surprise to you. You may even think that this is all part of an imaginary struggle that doesn't exist. But you are a pretty smart kid, as evidenced by the pieces you have written for the magazine, and I am sure you are as much aware of this as Kay is. So if you love me, as I know you do, try and make your stay here a pleasant one for all of us. I am anxious to see you and I want you to have a good time.

I am still working with Kras and after ten years of writing and rewriting, we are only now beginning the third act. He is wonderful to work with, so smart and so interesting, there is no situation he can't extricate himself from, and perhaps that is our trouble. He is so nimble mentally that he leaps around like a mountain goat, to coin a goat. Anyway, we have been working now for seven weeks again, and if it isn't right, we will have to abandon the project this time and say to hell with it.

You mention the Yankees and you forget to mention the Giants, a team that is closer to my heart. Speaking of the Giants, I don't think that Jane Stoneham is connected with it anymore. I don't remember who told me this but I didn't make it up. Art is working now for Mannie Manheim and this week he did the sketch alone, and he told me that they liked it a lot, so maybe he has caught on to how it's done. I thought your car looked pretty classy in the mag. And for all you know, it might be a cut down Rolls Royce. Well this is a pretty long letter for a playwright, but I haven't written you in so long that I had a lot to tell you. Love and kisses from all. I conveyed your regards to the Scot on the upper floor, and to all the other inmates who inhabit this little place, and try and write more often.

Love and kisses,
Padre

Mannie Manheim was a Hollywood writer. Jane Stoneham was the daughter of Horace Stoneham, who owned the New York Giants baseball team.

[June 17, 1947]

Dear Pooch;
I am furious at my stupidity. I wrote you a long brilliant letter yesterday full of charm and wit, and on my way to the mailbox I dropped it or mailed it and forgot that I had, although I have no recollection of it. You may still get the letter for it may have been picked up by someone and mailed after they saw it was a letter. At any rate this is just a note to tell you that I wrote you yesterday. I haven't got the time today that I had yesterday so this will be brief.

Your letter came and it was a good letter and made a lot of sense. Far more than mine made that I wrote you. You just have to realize that Kay is a good girl with a good character, but she is so afraid of losing me that she gets a little crazy at the thought. . . . I showed your letter to Kay—I didn't see any reason why I shouldn't. Since she read it she hasn't commented much about it, but I think she is looking at the whole problem a little more clearly. *Time* reviewed *Copacabana* in the current issue and if you are interested in seeing your father's photo you might buy a copy, although I imagine it won't be easy to purchase one when the news gets around that my picture is in it.

I wrote you a long letter yesterday, two pages, that's par for me, but now I'll have to quit and rush to Kras's for the finale. We should finish up this week and I will be so happy—we have been at it eight weeks this time. It had better be brilliant. Hollywood is in fifth place, and all I can say is goddamn the Yankees and their third-rate ball club.

Love and kisses and see you soon. Your Padre as of yore,
Padre XXXX

[June 20, 1947]

Monday morning.

Dear Pooch;
Your letter came and it made a lot of sense. As you say, all of Kay's
fears stem from insecurity, and that is the reason for her foolish fears.
I am perfectly satisfied with her, and I keep telling her that I have no
intention of running away with a new dame the minute one gives me
the eye. I think things will work out once she is convinced that her life
is safe. The Friars opened up Saturday with a packed club and I believe
it will be a success. I M Ceed (as the columnists put it) the show with
Jessel and I was very good. I am always nervous about those things,
for I am not in the business of nightclubbing and I get uneasy when
I know I am sucked into one of those spots where I have to face the
audience without material. Fortunately, I have such an abundance of
charm that I simply overwhelmed the audience and I was voted the
boy most likely to succeed in the forthcoming years.

I received your Father's Day wire for which thanks. I got a sweater
from Melinda which I shall return to Pesterre in the morning. Arthur
gave me two sleeping coats and I am beginning to believe that there
is more to this Father's Day racket than meets the eye. I also got your
latest effusion on girls getting beautified and found it genuinely amusing. There is no question that you will be a writer, and the kinds of
things you are doing are not the easiest type of writing, but one that
there is a demand for. Who knows, you might even wind up writing
jokes for some third rate comic with Selma Diamond. She calls up occasionally and asks for you and when you are returning to Calif.
That's California in case you don't get it.

Arthur showed me his piece last night that he had sold to *Cosmo*
and it was very good. I had no idea he could do it that well. It is now
getting to the stage where both my children write better than their father, and all I need now is for Melinda to start writing pieces. Well
anyway, I can look forward to all my talented children supporting me
and sending me scads of pin money every week. In some circles this
is known as the Oh yeah, or You-should-live-so-long department.

I expect to finish with Kras this week, and this will conclude another eight weeks on the chain gang. If you have a copy of the current
Time mag. you will see a review of the *Copacabana* picture and also
a snapshot of the fair Carmen and me. The trade reviews on me were
uniformly good and it means that some other gent will be after me
with honeyed phrases to do a picture for him. I have a couple of deals

in the fire but there is no sense of telling you about them until they are further advanced and I have an advance in my pocket.

Ben Hecht, who is doing the picture with Harpo and Chico, is dangerously ill in a New York hospital. He has been getting transfusions and all those things and it's quite serious. He is a wonderful guy and I would certainly hate to see anything happen to him.

I don't know whether I told you that Tin Can Joe has been over here a few times recently asking about you and using the typewriter and pleading with me not to do anything about my teeth for he will be a dentist in a few years, and that he will do the job better and cheaper than anyone I could possibly get.

You don't write me anything about your car. How does it run, have you had much trouble with it? Let me know all the details, for an old car is much more interesting topic than an old woman, for example, and frequently looks better. I have to close now, don't worry about anything, live for today, Hollywood won a doubleheader yesterday, all's right with the world, it's later than you think, the only thing to fear is fear, you get out of life exactly what you put into it. Love and kisses, and I love you a lot.

Your Padre.

################################

The picture that Ben Hecht was writing for Harpo and Chico was Love Happy *(1950). Groucho appeared in it as well in an effort to boost box office appeal.*

Fourth of July [1947]

Dear Schmir;
At the moment Melinda and her mother are asleep and all that can be heard is the mumbled singing of Jeanette as she goes around the house brushing imaginary dirt off the furniture.

This is a busy day for me. This afternoon there is a double header at the ball orchid, and tonight I am going to a surprise birthday party for Gloria Sheekman, who was born on the same day as George M. Cohan and I presume many other people.

Finally got a brief letter from you written with a carbon so dim that I had to drink a whole bottle of cod liver oil (Vitamin A) before I could distinguish the letters. Are you now using the ribbon from your hair for the machine? Or have I finally gone blind? I am glad to see that you have discovered Thomas Wolfe. I could have told you about him

125

when you were three years old, but I knew it was no use, so I just kept my mouth shut and bided my time.

I sucked myself into something that I now regret. When the Friars was formed I was fool enough to consent to act as one of the board of directors. The result is that I now find myself one night a week, a night that could be given over to baseball, the movies or just plain sitting home and sitting, attending a board meeting with a group of fairly dull men discussing the finances and operation of a club. This club is a tremendous project and requires all the skill of an expert hotel operator to direct and to watch that it doesn't go into bankruptcy. And for no reason at all I find myself worrying about its fate. If it continues I will be forced to resign for the membership of a big club isn't too attractive, I mean any big club, and I don't want to be bothered with it. We had a stag dinner for Jack Benny last night. The speakers were Pat O'Brien, George Murphy, Jack Benny, George Burns, Cantor, Goldwyn, Parkyakarkus and me. Most of the speeches were lewd, a little too much for my taste, but the members roared, and I was embarrassed at the finish when I realized how clean my speech was. In a few weeks they are giving a dinner to [Walter] Winchell and I suppose I will be hooked into appearing again, although I will try and duck it. I guess I am just not a club man.

Tuesday night I am doing "Command Performance" with Glen Ford and some assorted actors. This thing still drags along. I don't think they find it as easy to get actors to appear as they did when the war and hoopla was at its height, but every week, rain or shine, war or no war, they drag on with these transcriptions that are sent to hundreds of thousands of boys that apparently are still planted around different sections of the world.

I was supposed to do a picture with [Maurice] Chevalier; the deal was about set when he abruptly took a run out powder and screwed back to France. He said he has a picture coming out with direction by René Clair, and before he signs a contract he would like to see how this picture is received in America. I think he is stalling to see what other offers he has before he is reduced to appearing with me. Well, I am not going to worry about it. If nothing else comes up, I can always get another job on "Command Performance."

I see very little of my grandchild Steve, principally because I am so busy with Melinda. I guess a grandparent shouldn't have an infant of their own, but that's the way it worked out.

Are you flying or training? I couldn't find out much from that dim

126

letter you wrote me. Get a new ribbon and tell me the news. Love and kisses and I am anxious to look upon your face again.

Your Loving Padre Dr. Hackenbush, sometimes known as S. Quenton Quale,

Padre

S. Quenton Quale was the name of the character Groucho played in Go West.

[September 4, 1947]

Wednesday afternoon

Dear Mir;

I was going to write you a long angry letter pointing out to you how thoughtlessly and stupidly you acted on your departure, but since you wrote and admitted all this, there is no need to continue the lecture.

I hope you write your mother once a week and that you also wrote Ethel Johnson.

It is murderously hot today and for the past few previous days, and since my room is one of the few cool spots in town, you can attribute this letter to that fact.

I am glad that the Sullivan episode is over or at least I hope it is, for I like Sylvia and Ed and it would hurt me to have anything happen to change that relationship. Plus this, it would then be very difficult for me to get my name in his column. I think you gave him quite some encouragement, and I hope you realize that it is always easier to lure a married man than a single one. So don't take too much credit for that conquest.

I bought a ping-pong table today and now the yard has two swings, a sandbox, a barbecue, a rock pile that Kay hauled over from Catalina (courtesy of five policemen) and enough other furniture to make it impossible to move more than two feet in any direction without stumbling over some hard, unyielding object.

Had a wire from the French government's movie or cinema representative inviting the Marxes to participate in the French festival at Cannes. All expenses paid, and nothing to do but show our bodies. I would have gone, but Harpo refused, said it was too damned much trouble and that it would interfere with his golf.

Other than this there isn't much to relate. I resigned from the Friars and my guess is that it will fold up quickly. Of course my resignation may be just the spur it needs to roll up a record membership.

Kaufman was here to dinner last night along with the Chodorovs and about eighteen others. We had a Chinese dinner served outside and it was all very pleasant. Sorry you couldn't have been here; however, they all asked about you and you can take that for what it is worth.

I am enclosing a piece from the A[tlantic] Monthly. It struck me that the relationship between the father and the son closely resembled ours. However, even if you don't think so, I think you will be amused by it.

Arthur's piece is in the current Cosmo and if you like it, you might write him a letter telling him that. He may get a job in the shorts department at Paramount, through Sheekman. I will let you know in my next letter.

Love and kisses and write soon.

Your Padre

P.S. I was at Chasen's last week and sneaked out some garlic bread and layer cake to your itinerant dentist. Best from Kay and Melinda.

Ethel Johnson was my step-grandmother, married to my mother's father, Oscar Johnson. The "Sullivan episode" refers to columnist Ed Sullivan making a pass at me in New York, which I had rejected.

[September, 1947]

Saturday night

Dear Mir;

In song and story this is always mentioned the loneliest night of the week. Tonight that isn't true for we are going to the Sheekmans' for dinner, and I know six other couples that are headed in the same direction, but anyway it's a way to begin a letter.

I am sorry that you didn't think I reminded you of old man Sitwell, but that instead you regarded me as a kindly old dope. Frankly I don't know which category I prefer. Anyway I thought you would like to read the next installment, which will fall out of the envelope when you slit it. I have had a nice week with Schnaidt. Apparently the two weeks' vacation he had had done things for him in the way of renewed strength, for he really went after me, with his drill and his little brass hammer, but I must admit that he did a fine job in excavating two old fillings and replacing them with two burnished gold inlays that are the envy of every colored houseman west of the Mississippi. The only reason I can spell Mississippi with such confidence and assurance is because I have never forgotten the lyrics of the song that Frances White of Rock and White made famous many years before you were to see the light of day around Mt. Morris Park in upper New York.

I have one more little job for Schnaidt, and then he thought I would be free for about five years or more. What a prospect to look forward to.

Sheekman got Arthur a job at Paramount for five hundred dollars writing a short around a set of scenery that they had left over from a picture they shot years ago. It's a gypsy set and it has to have a love story, four songs and a hell of a good part for some Romanian actor that they have under contract and have no work for. The story has to be about a drunkard, for that's the only part that this ham can play, but unfortunately the Breen office of censors (despite *Lost Weekend*) insists that the short cannot be made if the character is shown as an habitual souse. So that is really an assignment for a budding young writer.

As yet we haven't signed any contracts with Douglas to portray the part of Davis in *Elizabeth*, but he has told us that he is going to do it and I see no reason at the moment to doubt his word. He seems to be a very nice fellow and I think we will get along swimmingly. However, if the play flops, I assure you that I will campaign to defeat Helen Gahagan for Congress if it takes every cent I've got.

Arthur Schwartz just arrived and after asking for you, he asked me if I would play the lead in his new musical he is doing with Dietz. It is going to be a musical adaptation of *U.S.A.*, the John Gunther book, and he claims he has Bea Lillie for the female section. I turned him down, for to do a musical revue is not the thing I am after. It is flattering to know that there is still a demand for the old comedian, but as long as inflation doesn't ruin me, I intend to duck all musicals and particularly revues. I am still negotiating with Cowan to do a picture and I should know something definite in a week or so. I have heard nothing new about the quiz show I auditioned for the man with the toupee, but they seem to think they are going to sell it. I have been fooled too often to take much stock in that kind of optimism. When I sign a contract and am getting paid and the money comes rolling in I'll be inclined to believe it.

Melinda as you know can walk now and has a sort of a cross walk between Karloff stiff legging his way through a graveyard and a stewed sailor with two days' shore leave. She is mad about me, but then who isn't? Her social life is much livelier than mine. One day she goes to

Judy Garland's, then Frank Loesser's, and many others that I can't think of at the moment.

It is now seven-thirty and we are supposed to be at the Sheekmans' at seven, so I will knock off. With this little missive I am also sending two pieces, one by a writer named Diamond (it's not a new subject, but I think very amusing), the other is about Jane Russell's climb up the pole of publicity.

Love to you from all of us, and write when you get time. Your superannuated Padre #################### These are allegedly kisses,

Padre

Douglas was Melvyn Douglas, an actor. Helen Gahagan was his wife, a congresswoman for California. Cowan was Lester Cowan, who produced Love Happy. *The quiz show he auditioned for was, of course, "You Bet Your Life."*

[September 25, 1947]

Wednesday afternoon and hot as hell

Dear Mir,

We received your letter from you yesterday and we are relieved to know that you haven't been blown to pieces yet by that demon you are driving. It seems to me that you should never venture forth without a fireman in the rear seat (if there is such a thing as a rear seat) and a Red Cross kit. I thought once you had a new engine head that you were rid of your troubles and that you could roam the countryside lightheartedly and with a song in your heart. Why don't you turn it in and get a washing machine in its place. You wouldn't then be able to see the scenery, but at least your clothes would be clean, and you wouldn't blow up. I am going to see Avak the healer sometime this week and ask him if he has a representative in New England that could lay hands on it. Have you tried talking softly to it? Instead of your customary longshoreman profanity, perhaps a few gentle words would do the trick. How about reading aloud to it from Shelley or do you think that would make it even more erratic? There is no question that you have a problem machine on your hands, and that it cannot be cured by any of the orthodox methods.

September in California is almost as erratic as your bus. It is a blazer today, and we sat in the grandstand at the tennis club and watched the tournament grind its way to its inevitable conclusion, Kramer ver-

130

sus Parker or Schroeder. They are doing a hell of a business this year and though I have ducats for Saturday, I have been unable to stash any for the finals. I don't imagine you are going to lie awake at night worrying about my problem, and I don't think I will either, but I like you to know that though there is misery and unrest in Europe, we too have things to worry about. . . .

The Lester Cowan deal was finally signed and some time this winter Harpo and Chico will appear in that Ben Hecht story, with me doing a brief appearance as the commentator. Don't pay any attention to any items you read in the theatrical sheets, for they are all the imaginings of my press agent. I am so confused by the pieces I read about myself that I have decided to fire him, for it is getting so that I don't know what my next move is.

This is the last week of the ball season and next week begins the winter season. This embraces some small intellectual parties at small unpretentious homes and semi-weekly trips to the Oriental Theatre where the seats are not only cheap but uncomfortable. Henry Morgan said last night on the air, "They have double features in the theatres, so that you can see one picture that you have already seen and one picture that you won't enjoy."

I don't know whether I wrote you that I bought a ping-pong table a few weeks back, a beauty too. There is only one drawback: there is no one to play me. Kay began, but shortly after that took sick with an infection, so here I am with all this magnificent equipment and no worlds to conquer. Chico is still overseas and what with the food shortages in England I wouldn't be surprised if they ate him. At any rate we don't hear anything from him, and unless the Tax Department relents I wouldn't be surprised if we never heard from him again.

Why don't you try and write a piece for a magazine (a commercial piece about you and your car)? I think it could be sold—the piece, I mean, not the car. It could be very amusing. Think about it.

I am happy to know that you are now an editor of a magazine, or at least an assistant one, and who knows? You may turn out to be the next Robert McCormick of the *Chicago Tribune*. I would rather you wouldn't, for then you would have to live in the Middle West, and it is terribly hot there in the summer and vice versa in the other season. Must close, no more paper, love and kisses, write soon,

Padre

Oct Second [1947]

Dear Mir;

Received your letter on my birthday and it was much better than a telegram, and as you said, considerably cheaper. Telegrams should be used for business and not sentimental purposes, and it was a very nice missive.

This is a busy week for me, there are so many things going on. To begin with there is the World Series with Brooklyn finally winning a game today, making the score two for the Yanks and one for the Bums, and whoever tagged them as the Bums certainly knew what the word meant. In addition to my sentimental interest in the National League I bet fifty dollars on the Brooks against ninety. The broadcasting of that game takes at least two and a half hours, today it was over three, and then it's time for lunch.

I am signing definitely for the radio quiz show for twenty-six weeks, after which the sponsor has the privilege of tossing me out if he isn't amused or satisfied. It will be on Monday night and I believe the opening show will be the twenty-seventh. This is my last fling on the air; if I don't click this time, I will be convinced that it is not the medium for me, and confine my waning talents to other fields.

Sunday Kay and I are flying to Frisco to play five hospitals in three days (I'll never forget you doing the sketch on the aircraft carrier) and then when I come back I am doing an air show for the boys overseas; it's a Xmas show and luckily for me will not be heard on this continent.

Then we have to get ready for the radio show, and in between I have to make an appearance at an orphan asylum, so I'll keep busy in the near future.

I read in the school paper that you defaulted in the tennis tournament. Were you ill or just indifferent? Gonzales's play in the South West was brilliant, I think he has a good chance of becoming the number one player in a year or two. He is six-foot two and except for a scar he received when he was a boy delinquent, quite handsome. It was gratifying to hear that tony crowd that goes to those matches cheering for this kid from the other side of the tracks. Kramer played brilliantly and I hope you get a chance to see or him and Riggs when they play in New York this winter. Budge told me at the matches that he thought Bobby would get too many returns back and discourage Kramer, but Jack is awfully good and game too, and I think he will make quite a match of it.

Ruby is unable to go on the tour to Frisco for he is working at Metro on the Kalmar and Ruby opus, so I was compelled to take Walter Jurman, Virginia's friend, with us. He plays well but it is all in a semi-continental style, and when I sing Hackenbush, it may come out like the "Blue Danube Waltz." Tonight is my birthday so tonight I am taking Art and Ick and Kay to see *Call Me Mister*. The kids haven't seen it and although I am sure it is not up to the New York company, I believe they will have some fun at it; if not, they can always sue me.

Melinda babbles now and this is the prelude to a steady stream of conversation that the female is addicted to. Everyone raves about her and apparently she has inherited most of my charm.

The fish I caught in Yellowstone arrived today. The bill was forty-three dollars. If I had had an idea that it was going to be so expensive, I would have eaten the goddamned thing when I hooked it. Well, instead of me hooking the fish, I was hooked by the thief that stuffed it. Anyway, it's a thing of beauty and I predict will look far better on the wall than many of the photos that I have in the library.

Well, write soon and all my love to you, and hope to get a chance to see you this winter. Love from Kay and the baby, and best from Harry Lauder. Yours,

Padre XXXXXXXXXXXXXXXXXXX
XXXXXXXXXXXXXXXXXX

Harry Lauder was a Scottish actor and singer (this probably refers to Melinda's Scottish nurse, Jeanette).

[October 12, 1947]

Dear Mir;
I have been planning to write you much earlier in the week, however, when one is a radio star (the sponsor hasn't picked it up for next year yet) one hasn't much time for correspondence.

Kras is going to New York the seventeenth to consult with Rodgers and Hammerstein on his new musical with Berlin, and I will try and find out where he will be, and perhaps you may get a chance to see him.

Chico is on the verge of going to Australia this month for a four-week jaunt, and if he goes he may take Harry Ruby along to work with him. At the moment Ruby is working at MGM on the scenario for the picture of the life of Kalmar and Ruby.

We had a party last night. Among those who entertained were Green and Comden (who told me they met you in New York with the

Kellys, I believe) and they thought you were a nice girl. Obviously they don't know you as I do. Johnny Mercer and Loesser sang, and Jules Munshin, who is very clever and who was asked at Kay's insistence, did his stuff, and the inevitable routines by Kay and me, and Ruby was on, and we all wound up singing quartet songs. It started out as a dinner for all the Brothers, but it grew until we had thirty-two people at the table.

I am going to have a welcoming party for you when you return, so take heed and prepare for it. You can sing "Show Me the Way to Go Home," or if you prefer, "Onward, Christian Soldiers."

Tonight we are going to the Norman Panamas' to dinner, and tomorrow if it is a nice day I am going to the Gilmore Stadium and watch our team lose another game with the greatest of ease. If it is cold, and it is recently, I am going to stay home and read and listen to some music.

Kay at the moment is sleeping in the back room, for her mother burned her hands on a roast while removing it from the oven, and since both hands are bandaged to the hilt, she is unable to do any housework and she is staying with us. The twins too are here, for they live with Kay's mother and there is no one there to take care of them, so Jeanette helps them with their schoolwork and other things. Jeanette is quite a woman. She is a little on the garrulous side, a trait, by the way, not unusual with the feminine sex (I know that will burn you), but she has so many redeeming features that she is certainly worth putting up with.

I am sorry that you are having so much trouble with your car, and next year or season if I am still on the air and making money, I am going to take steps to get you a good car. I have one and Kay has one, and I want you to have a conveyance that you can ride in with confidence and even a bit of joy. We will discuss it when you come home. Kay suggests that since you spend half the night talking about life and other things that you should room with her when you come back, and just leave your things in the back room.

How do you like school now that you are back? Do you miss New York and that lovely climate it threw at you this season? From what I read and saw in the news reels it really was a dilly. I have to get dressed now, it is late, so take care of yourself and write soon. Love to you from all of us.

Yours,
Padre

134

Green and Comden refers to the stage and screenwriting duo of Adolph Green and Betty Comden. The Norman Panamas were screenwriter, producer and director Norman Panama and his wife. The twins were Kay's nieces.

[October 15, 1947]

Dear Mir;

Was pleasantly surprised to find a letter from you when we got back from Frisco, and sorry to read that you are having so much trouble with your monster. Now it's the battery that is dead or dying. Are you sure that your generator is all right? You see, the generator stores up the juice, that is, it generates the juice that flows into the battery. This explanation isn't the technical one that you would get from Kettering of General Motors, but it may be the key to what is wrong with your car. Anyway, I would have it investigated. I think too that you should be certain that the place that looks at your motor is a reliable one, and that they are not out to bleed you.

We are both exhausted from the trip up north. We flew both ways and it only took an hour and a half. When I think of how long it used to take me to drive that distance. Ah, the plane is indeed a wonderful thing, and worth the slight risk involved. We played five hospitals in three days. We used to play only one hospital a day, and that was enough. Anyway, they were all so grateful for those ancient jokes we threw at them that we had our reward. Kay was out last night making a recording of a Sam Coslow song (whatever that means), and if it turns out well, we will send you some of them. You see, Kay gets a half a cent a record, and if you can sell twenty of them for her, she will get ten cents royalty, or almost enough to buy the mustard for a hamburger at Delores.

Thanks for the maple candy. I am eating it warily and with great deliberation: no one is going to make a diabetic out of me.

Thanks to Chico I lost fifty dollars on the World Series. He told me that it was virtually impossible for the Dodgers to lose, so my fifty went down the drain. I must say, though, that I had fifty dollars' worth of fun. In all my years of listening to those games, I have never been as excited as I was last week. I spent the whole time glued to the radio, and was pretty sad when the last game was over and the Bums defeated. I don't know whether you know it, but Brooklyn has never won a World Series since the beginning of organized baseball.

I am sending you a dollar for the series outcome, and I think that makes us even on the year. I spent all day yesterday working on the

135

radio stuff; you won't think so after you hear it, but even a poor show requires a lot of time. Where the commercials should go, how long they should be, should they be integrated, etc., etc. We are trying to get them to put the show on wax, like the Crosby show, for then if there is something indecent or mediocre, it can be clipped before the customers ever hear it. They are holding out for what they term a live show, but we hope to talk them out of it. We begin October twenty-seventh, on ABC chain, eight o'clock your time; the second show for the West Coast will be nine, that of course will be a record, for there is not a man alive that could wrangle through two quiz shows in one evening.

Melinda is a big hit all over; she babbles and gurgles and I must admit is extremely bright for her age. She is the hit of every party, and she goes to many more parties than we do. Arthur told me yesterday that Steve sits up in a high chair now and is beginning to look around. I hope someday that you too will have a baby. I do think, though, it would be nice to wait until you get married. . . .

The third page of this letter is missing.

[October 18, 1947]

Dear Mir;

Well, this is quite a place today. Kay has been in bed ever since we returned from Frisco with the same kind of cold that she had when we were in New York. Melinda, for the first time since she was born, had an inflamed tonsil and a fever at one time of a hundred and five (it has now receded to a hundred), and finally last night I got a regular old fashioned cold, the kind that a man of my age should get.

Well, I guess we will all recover, and soon be as good as new again. I damned well better be, for next week I have three rehearsals for my quiz show, a Jolson rehearsal and show for Wednesday and Thursday, and a few confabs on the Ben Hecht story, that is the story that he wrote for Harpo, and finally Chico got in it, and then I suddenly found myself in it for a brief bit. When you sign the contract they always say it won't be any work at all — this is so that you will work cheap — and then after the papers have been drawn and your signature is on it, you suddenly realize that there is a lot of work attached to it.

To begin with, I want it to be good for Harpo and Chico, so I not only worry about my own part but also about theirs. It won't be shot,

136

fortunately, until next March, which will give me a lot of time to get the quiz show going smoothly.

Frankly, I don't see why the quiz show should create any furor, it's just another one, there are a hundred on the air, and they all give away money. They are all quite similar in content and shape, and I can't see anyone rushing to the radio on Monday nights, eight o'clock American Broadcasting Company, to listen to something that they can hear almost any time they flick a switch. Of course, I didn't tell this to the sponsor when we were negotiating with him for the contract. We told him that this was a brand new road in radio, one that had never been travelled, and the only reason he was able to purchase it for that price was because we saved money by taking in each other's washing. The sponsor is a Hungarian named Gelman, and he has a tremendous plant in Chicago, which I am afraid I eventually will have to go through, making all the appropriate ahs and ohs about the size and beauty of the place. I remember doing this for Pabst just before I was replaced by Danny Kaye. However, all this whining and complaining can be ignored for I know it's sophomoric, but I love radio. If the show clicks it's better than any kind of show business. Particularly for a man of my years. It means no getting up early in the morning and making up and memorizing and all the physical discomforts that the rest of the business presents. So I am going to work hard at it and try and do it as well as I can, and not insult anybody that is connected with the show in any way.

I am sending you a check for fifty dollars to help you pay some of the unexpected expenses that you had on repairing the monster. I hope this is of some help; if it isn't you can always get yourself a banana split with the cash, or hang it on the wall as evidence of your father's generosity. Chico was over last night to dinner. He brought two Scotch records of Will Fyfe for Jeanette, a necktie for me and a print for the wall. Right after dinner he fell asleep and the next thing I knew we were saying good night at the threshold.

Well honey, take care of yourself, and write soon. I miss you and hope to make New York some time this fall, but as yet this is just a hope. Love and kisses from all, your Padre.

Padre

I am going on the Jolson show I believe it's a week from next Thursday, I will let you know definitely just when it is. I have heard no offers as yet from the Crosby show for the coming season, but they will run out of guests before the season is over, and will come running to me.

This Tuesday I am doing the Xmas show for "Command Performance." This is a big show that is piped overseas to the unfortunates that are still marooned in foreign lands. Fortunately it isn't heard in this country, so I can still walk with my head held high.

Well, I think that covers everything. Kay has a little cold; other than that we are about as well as one can be and remain alive. If you can figure out that last sentence, I will send you a half-pound box of chocolates and two seats to any radio show, except the good ones.

All my love to you, and best from Kay and the baby. Write soon. Padre. ##########

The show for Pabst he refers to was "Blue Ribbon Town" ("The Pabst Show").

October 29th, 1947

Dear Mir:

Finally got a letter from you after two weeks. There's no excuse for this at all. I know I can't type nearly as quickly as you can and I can write a letter in ten minutes. But then, I'm a parent and you're the child and I suppose that does make a difference.

I sent you a blouse from Chinatown in Frisco. I don't know if you ever received it. If you didn't, it's lost because I failed to remember the name of the store I purchased it in.

If my present plans materialize, there's a strong likelihood that I may be in New York for February and March, two very pleasant months, by the way. I can see it all now: Kay in bed with a hot water bag, Vic salve, nose drops, goose fat, penicillin, copavin, sulphur drugs and midnight visits from the doctor. Her coughing will be heard clearly over the whining of the winter winds as the doors and windows all rattle at ancient old Dorset. I should know in about a week or two if we do this. When I say "we" I am referring to Krasna and myself. This means that I will have to do my radio show from New York, but since we rely mainly on the contestants this won't be too much of a problem, although I imagine I will be fairly busy.

I am doing a bit on the Art Linkletter "People Are Funny" show Friday, six P.M. here, probably nine P.M. in the east—NBC. If you don't hear it you won't miss much. It is mostly a plug for my new radio show, "You Bet Your Life," copyrighted by Elgin-American of Elgin, Ill. One of these days, if the sponsor doesn't sour on me, I'll wangle a compact for you.

I am glad to read you are making such good progress with your new

138

story and that you labored so diligently in New York to the exclusion of everything else. This, of course, I take with a large bag of salt, but it's interesting anyway.

The baby is wonderful. She fell flat in the mud this morning and started crying—apparently she doesn't like mud. This means she won't read the columnists when she grows up.

Kay is moderately healthy for a change. Her old lady got married last week and I had a rehearsal the day of the wedding so fortunately I had a good substantial alibi for not attending.

Arthur is working on a story with some chap whom he claims is very talented—he seems very optimistic about himself.

I must close and run now, or I must run and close now, whichever you prefer.

Loads of love, even though you are a louse. Let's hear from you from time to time. Your letter is one of the few letters I get that isn't a bill, although even that one frequently is.

Love,
Padre

[November 8, 1947]

Dear Mir;

Leaving for Palm Springs in a few minutes and know I won't write while there, so therefore this brief message from my sponsor. "When buying compacts, remember a woman is judged by the compact she carries, and it is absolutely essential that she have one for daytime, playtime and nighttime." What they mean by nighttime is a little beyond me. Are you supposed to carry one in the hay, can it be filled and used as a hot water bottle? Who figured this all out, and how impressed are the potential customers with this sort of nonsense? Well, the goddamn things better sell or I will be back in the bedroom playing on the guitar, such things as "When the lights go on again all over the world."

Did you hear the second show and how did you think it was? We already waxed the third, and you can hear it next Monday night if you are in the neighborhood of a radio and also in the mood.

Quite a hegira going to the Springs, where I haven't been since the town was an armed camp during the war. I need the rest badly—I have been working very hard for the past few months and the strain has

139

been great. If it does me any good I may do it frequently this winter. The way my schedule works out I will have four days' rest each week.

I am proud that you have been selected to teach English and grammar, and also that you have been accolated by the dean or somebody for the fine writing you are doing. Who knows, I may be harboring an incipient Edith Wharton or a spare Bronte in my midst.

I still don't know definitely what my plans are about the East junket. But the next few weeks will bring a decision that will be more or less definite.

I received the Low cartoon, and I must say I didn't think the picture did me justice. I am glad you received the waist and I hope you fill it out accordingly.

Melinda is a knockout. I never thought at my age I could knock off anything as brilliant and beautiful as she is. She is quite spoiled. Yesterday she threw quite a tantrum while out shopping because I wouldn't let her handle the wheel of the car. I tried to explain to her in small words that the police disapprove of babies fifteen months old driving Cadillacs, but she was furious and I had quite a time quieting her down.

I can't write more for we are late and I must be off before the sun sets in Palm Springs. Lots of love to you and write, even if it's only a letter. Your Padre, and Kay and Melinda.

November 14, 1947

Dear Mir:
The pictures arrived and they are very good. I don't think your choices are the best, however you will have to decide this for yourself. I don't know why you want a dozen made up, unless you have more boyfriends than I know about. It seems to me that this will be enough of the 8 x 10. Arthur wants one and I want one. However, if you think it vital that you get a dozen I don't want to stop you. . . .

We got our first Hooper rating yesterday. It was 6.03. This is phenomenal. We expected around 3 and for a Monday night on ABC and a new show, we wouldn't have felt too badly with a 2. It's very encouraging, and if there's anything to these ratings it will make the sponsor very happy. So you will have some idea of what I'm talking about—Morgan, who has been on two years, got a 5, and Jack Paar, whose show costs $16,000 weekly, got a 5½. I'm ashamed to tell you

140

how much more expensive the Paar show is than ours, but with the difference in price one could buy a small GI home weekly. Have you heard any of the other shows except the one you wrote about?

How is your car running, and how are you? Is there anything you desperately need for Christmas — other than Gregory Peck or a mink coat?

Lots of love to you. You might try writing more often even if it's only a four-page letter.

Love,
Padre

November 21, 1947

Dear Mir:

It was a strange dream. You came into the room and I asked you where you'd been. You told me you were over at Hillcrest. I said, "What doing?" and you said, "I just read *John Loves Mary* for the second time and liked it even better than when I first read it." So I decided to call you up. You sounded like you were talking from under the bed.

Kay and I will look around for a coat for you. It's rather a strange way to buy one, but it may turn out all right.

Glad you liked the last radio show. It seems like it's catching on.

This is just a note. I'm late as hell. The script comes on Friday, and Saturday, Sunday and Monday are given over to repairing some of the jokes. Don't let it get around, but it's not all ad lib.

I read someplace last week that the Bennington College girls are considered more sophisticated. I hope this doesn't mean what I think it does.

I am enclosing a poem from the *New York Times,* which I am sure you saw.

Take care of yourself. Lots of love, and always wear your earmuffs when you are out driving.

Padre

December 10, 1947

Dear Mir:

This is just a note to ask you whether you received the red coat, or are the red-coats still coming?

141

I am sending you a "Fibber McGee" script which I found in my dressing room last night. I thought perhaps you, or someone in the school who is interested in radio writing, could from this get a good idea of how a top professional show is constructed.

I hope you heard last Monday's show (December eighth), for I think it was one of our best.

I will write you the latter part of this week, when my time is freer. Love and kisses and write soon.

Melinda sends her love, and Kay does too.

Padre

[December 12, 1947]

Dear Schmear;

You are the only one I write to personally. All my other correspondence is dictated. I don't know what this proves; maybe you can figure it out.

I had a notion when I started on this show that it would take up very little of my time, but I find that it keeps me just as busy as any other show I have been on. As Jimmy Fiddler would say, "Don't get me wrong," I am not complaining, I am having the time of my life doing this show. I like the radio and what is just as important is that all my friends seem to think that I have found my metier at last in this business. They all like the show and that gives me a glow, for I would be unhappy doing a show that they were all contemptuous of.

Anyway, we are moving into the Jack Paar spot after the first of the year, and that will have me preceding Bing Crosby. We will have tough opposition in the East with "Mr. District Attorney" against us, but in radio if you get a good time, you cannot avoid having something good opposing you. I hope you hear the show we have tonight, for I think it's the best one we have had to date. Well, enough about me.

I wonder if you didn't make a mistake in abandoning the column you did for the school paper (even if you only did it every other week). I think it was good practice for you and accustomed you to writing under pressure, a valuable asset for a writer. I realize you are busy, but offhand I think you should try and squeeze it in.

Kay bought a coat for you. It's a red one with a collar that turns up and I hope it is warm enough for you. I know it's a dangerous way to buy you clothes, but Kay has good taste, and my hunch is that you will like it. You may have to wear five or six sweaters under it, but no one will see that except your best friends, and by this time you may not have any.

Are you working this year when you go to New York and if so have you given any thought to where it is going to be? Grace Kahn just returned from New York and she told me that she saw you and that you are getting prettier all the time; is this true or is Grace's eyesight failing? Please let me know about this, for I know a very good oculist out here, and I might want Grace to pay him a visit.

Other than this there isn't much to tell you. Harpo is still playing golf, Chico is still being chased by the man from the income tax department and Melinda knocks hell out of my room whenever she enters it. Kay is taking a flu shot today, and took one last week too. I also took one not because I contemplate acquiring the flu, but I am mad about having quacks stick needles in my carcass.

Arthur has finished a screen treatment of a story in the James Cain tradition. I think it is good, and I hope to god he sells it for what it would do to his bankroll but also to goose his reputation along. After that he can turn Communist and get fired for being subversive.

Lots of love to you and write soon, and let us know what you think of the coat. Melinda sends you a big kiss and knows your picture now and she will surely know you when she sees you.

Your loving Padre, that quizmaster
and fun loving sex fiend, Groucho
XXXXXXXX

Jimmy Fiddler was a Broadway columnist.

[December 29, 1947]

Dear Mir:
It was nice to hear your voice over the phone, even though it was the usual cry of insolvency. I saw your mother at the Kahns' Xmas day and she told me that she sends you money frequently. I realize that things are a lot more expensive than they were two years ago, but I remember when you asked me about going to Bennington you said if I would give you twenty dollars a month that you could get along fine; instead of that I gave you eighty, and this has been occasionally supplemented by dividend checks and other contributions, and you are now at the stage where you don't have five dollars to get your radio out of hock.

Why don't you have Price and Waterhouse come in once a month and audit your checking account? I hope you get a job soon in New

York for I don't want you hanging around there without one. There was no mention of this in your letter or phone talk, and I am wondering if you have something lined up to surprise me with? Shufro wrote me that he spoke to you and that you seemed in fine fettle, whatever that means. If the reports of the snowstorm are accurate, you may never get this letter for your mailbox must be buried under an avalanche of snow. Someone said they finally got that goddamned white Xmas that they have been yearning for all these years.

It was eighty-five here for the past few days and I spent most of the time in my shorts in the backyard, clipping the tender shoots of the rose bushes. It hasn't been so hot in years and it was doubly enjoyed by the contemplation of the blizzard in the East.

As I told you over the phone, we will probably be in Chicago around the second week in February, and perhaps we will get together there for a reunion at Henrici's or even one of the more fashionable restaurants.

Dick Comen dropped in Xmas Eve for some turkey and trimmings. He seems happy and busy; he still works at Chasen's and I imagine that money comes in very handy that he makes there.

I am sorry that you didn't like the coat, but I must admit that it is a difficult way to buy one. I am awaiting it and I hope I don't have any trouble with Haggerty's, where it was purchased, for it has been a long time, and I wouldn't blame them if they were difficult about it.

I will send you the hundred dollars but I want to be sure that the money is spent solely for the coat. You see, I like you and love you and worry about you, but unfortunately I don't trust you. If I sent you the money, I wouldn't be surprised if you spent sixty for the coat and the balance down the bottomless well that apparently sucks away most of your money.

So you look around with those expert clothing stylists and when you encounter something that seems to fit your carcass, communicate with your Padre and we will make a deal.

Arthur told me quite casually the other night that you broke your arm. I thought he was reciting part of a new story he had concocted, but last night I heard the same story again, this time from Sunny Sauber, who incidentally looked better than I ever thought she could, and had a nice looking fellow with her to boot (if she enjoyed booting her escort around). I was at the Biltmore Theatre to see Chevalier in his one-man show and I must say he is still a hell of an artist, in the true sense of the word. Only a great talent could come out with no makeup, scenery or orchestra and hold the audience (at four dollars a throw) the way he did.

Well, this is a lot of letter to write by hand. As a rule, I slip this chore to Sara Roberts, but lying there with your broken arm (I have a hunch it is only sprained, at least I hope so), you can read this letter over and over again. This week if you are interested we are on Wednesday night, right before the Bingle, and a Happy New Year, and write soon. Yours, Padre, and Kay and Melinda.

I don't mind your not having sent anything to Kay and me, but you might have kept out three dollars to buy something for Melinda. I was a little embarrassed in front of Kay.

XXX Padre

January 3, 1948

Dear Mir:
The coat came and I took it back to Haggerty's and so far I've heard no complaints. They hadn't examined it for fruit stains by the time I left the store so the case of the coat will probably be settled amicably.

This won't be much of a letter (very few of mine are). This is just to send you $100 for the coat and, as I wrote you before, I don't want $83 spent for the coat, nor $72, nor any other sum. Not that I doubt your honesty (which actually I do), but I'd like a receipt showing where and how much the purchase was.

The new year arrived bringing with it income tax reports and quite a headache for Kay. She took one too many New Year's Eve and was very funny. She is slowly recovering from it and has sworn off alcohol. Like most of her resolutions, I don't take much stock in this one.

I hope you hear next Wednesday night's show, for I think it's the best one we've had. I know you don't care much for it, but out here it is a veritable sensation. As you know, I was embarrassed about doing a quiz show, for it is considered the lowest form of radio life, but all of my friends, the ones who make big salaries and listen to "Information, Please" and the other erudite programs, are nuts about this. I just don't understand it, but apparently the quality of ad-libbing on the air is so low that if anyone comes along with even a moderately fresh note he's considered practically a genius. Don't be surprised, but I think your old man has finally arrived in radio. You could knock me over with a microphone.

I hope your arm isn't troubling you; that you get a nice warm coat and a nice warm job; that you have some nice warm boyfriends; and that you have a very happy and warm new year.

I expect to see you in Chicago in February.

All my love,
Padre

Dear Miriam:

Under separate cover I am sending you the December issue of the *Atlantic Monthly*. Your dad thought you might be interested in the articles by the authors checked on the cover.

How long do you plan to stay in New York? I have a very nice brother in New York. Shall I have him get in touch with you? Do you have a telephone number through which you can be reached? If you're interested let me know.

Sara

January 9, 1948

Dear Mir:

I am sending you $50.00. This should provide you with enough money to see twelve shows. As you know, Arthur and Irene will be in New York and you probably will want to be with them. Arthur has very big feet and if he can only get two seats for a show you can always sit on Arthur's foot.

I hear very little about the overcoat that you were going to buy with the hundred smackers I sent you. I have instructed Irene to give me a full report. They were over to dinner last night and we went to see *The Senator Was Indiscreet*. They liked it, but I didn't. I thought for a combination of MacArthur, Nunnally Johnson and Kaufman it was an amateurish job. It was almost as though a group of college boys had gotten together and decided they would show Hollywood how to make a picture. I hope for their sake it does business, but I doubt it.

Thanks for the Van Gogh. It's very cute.

Love from all,
Padre

Groucho and Ruth Marx, mid-1920s.

*Miriam Marx with
her uncle, Harpo
Marx, circa 1930.*

*Miriam Marx, circa
1931.*

Groucho, Arthur, Miriam and
Ruth, circa 1931.

Miriam at five, 1932.

On the set of Duck Soup: *Ruth, Harpo, Groucho, Miriam and Arthur, 1933.*

Miriam, Arthur, Ruth and Groucho, 1935.

Groucho, Ruth, Arthur and Miriam on the tennis court, 1936.

Groucho and Ruth at a masquerade party, circa 1937. Groucho is Rex the Wonder Horse.

The family playing pool at home, 1937.

A family portrait, 1937.

The house on North Hillcrest Road, Beverly Hills, where the family lived from 1937 to 1948.

Miriam in front of the Hillcrest Road house, 1937.

Ruth, Miriam,
Groucho and Arthur
at home, 1938.

Miriam and
Groucho in Palm
Springs, circa
1940.

Clark Gable with
Miriam, circa 1944.

Miriam after
graduating from
Beverly Hills High
School, 1945.

Groucho at Grant's Tomb, New York City, mid-1950s. The inscription reads, "Dear Mir, This is to show you who's buried near Grant's Tomb. Love XXXX, Padre."

Miriam and Gordon Allen's wedding photo, 1955.

A typical sign-off from a letter to Miriam, with an atypical self-portrait.

Miriam Marx Allen with some of the photos in her collection.

[January 12, 1948]

Dear Mir;

I am sending you twenty dollars to see a few shows, and beginning the first of next month, I am sending you a hundred and twenty dollars instead of eighty. I am not too bright, and it just occurred to me that your living must have gone up, the same as everyone else's. I didn't mind your living in comparative squalor, but complete poverty was too much even for me.

The fact of the matter is that your note to Jeanette in which you wrote "how happy you were to get the cigarettes and how much they meant to you" touched me and made me realize that you were certainly living a beggarly existence, therefore the increase in your allowance.

Please don't acknowledge this raise, for Kay would then want more money, and God knows she is doing very well. Any thanks you may want to convey you can do by smoke signals, or you can tell Arthur and he can whisper it in my ear when he returns from the frigid East.

I had a wire from Art and Ick notifying me of their safe arrival, and I hope you are all having a good time together.

Our Hooper went up to ten and three points, which is phenomenal. Our show, I won't say is the talk of the industry, but it is getting an enormous amount of favorable comment, and it looks like I may have finally found the golden formula.

Anyhow, we are all very happy about it, and can only hope it continues. The Chicago trip, which you mentioned in your last letter and I mentioned in my previous letter, doesn't look so good at the moment, and except for seeing you I am happy about that. I have very little desire to see Chicago at any time, but Chicago in the winter, ugh is all I can say. This trip isn't definitely off, but there are problems involved that have to be solved, and unless they can be ironed out, we just won't be able to go.

I saw *The Senator Was Indiscreet* and they were certainly indiscreet to put that out. It was amateur night on the screen, and from what Nunnally Johnson told me, it will be a disaster financially.

I must close now for I have to go to work on the script. Love to you all and write soon, and have a good time together.

Your loving Padre

Ick: I will go over and see Steve today, and see if Grace is taking proper care of him.

Padre

147

[January 16, 1948]

Dear Mir,

You must be going mad, two letters in one week and long ones; time must indeed hang heavy on your hands. Speaking of time, this is Thursday afternoon around four o'clock, and I have just come back from a long walk up the hill.

We got our new Hooper today and it is the talk of the radio industry. It was ten and three percent, after thirteen weeks on the air, and on the smaller of the three big networks. I know this sounds childish to you, and would indeed to me too, except that the sponsors and ad agencies swear by these percentages, and whether I remain on the air or not depends on these figures.

The show seems to have hit, there is a great deal of talk about it and about me, and it's never happened before in all the years I have been hammering at the gates of radio. Well, the hell with me. Now about you.

I saw the *Junior Bazaar* and your picture and I thought you looked right cute. By the time this letter arrives you will have Art and Ick around and will know all the news that is fit to print. Did you read my story or piece in the anniversary *Variety*? Probably not, but if you are around one read it, it's one of my lesser works, but still brilliant. . . .

Kay is upstairs cleaning out the closet. She feels that she has cleaned me out and that now there are new worlds to conquer. She took a flu shot some weeks ago and though around us people have been dropping off like bananas that are too ripe, she is still well, and as happy as any woman could be, lucky enough to have me for a husband.

I asked her about writing you, and she said she wrote you a long personal letter, which required a long personal answer, and until you deigned to do that there would be no further correspondence between you.

I also saw Dick Comen, and he wanted to know whether you received the Levis he sent you for Xmas, and what were the chances of getting an answer to the series of letters he's sent you over the months.

I am sorry you have so little hot water at your present residence. If this condition continues I could perhaps pour some in a hot water bag and ship it to you. Let me know how you feel about this. Or would you prefer a bag of cold water that you could heat yourself? You are certainly living under primitive conditions, but someday you will laugh at all this, either that or shoot yourself. Seriously, think of all

148

the interesting stories you can tell your children when you are old and gray, or do you expect to be old and gray without children? Let me know how you feel about this.

Well, I think I have told you (in my halting manner) all the news so I will address the envelope and close, hoping the weather has eased up a bit and that you have a good time with those two Western characters, and write soon. Yours with love, Padre, Kay and Melinda, who can now say "ball."

Padre

January 28, 1948

Dear Mir:

A quick note just to send you your allowance. I was going to write you personally, but the weeks roll around so quickly. Maybe Sunday I'll get a chance.

Had a letter from you. Glad to note you're moderately happy. Hope you're enjoying the New York winter. I love it from a distance. Remember when we were up in Maine and you said "I'll schenk you Maine"? Well, that goes for that New York winter.

In addition to my other tribulations, Dr. Salinger, Max Gordon and Abel Green (from *Variety*) are all in town. The cook (Brunetta, that is) walked out owing everybody on Sunset Plaza Drive. I think she even borrowed money from the mailman. She's a nice woman with a streak of larceny as wide as the rear end of Archie Mayo.

Today is a big day in my life for we should be getting another Hooper. If it goes down I will cut your allowance again, and also my throat. If it goes up I'll take Kay to an expensive restaurant—not that she cares much about them. She's really drive-in happy. Any time we pass a wiener roast or a hamburger stand she wants to stop. It doesn't make any difference if she ate a half hour before. I guess it's that old life at the El Jardin.

Well, I'm late so ta ta. Kiss your brother and Ick for me and write soon.

Love,
Padre

"Schenk" is Yiddish for "give."

February 10, 1948

Dear Mir:

Received your letter yesterday about your experiences at *Yeomen of the Guard* and laughed inordinately (as soon as I finish this letter I'll look this word up). I'm glad you liked the show. When I say "the show" I'm referring to "You Bet Your Life." The standard is not quite as high as Gilbert and Sullivan but the money is steadier.

Art and Ick are back and told me all about your visit to the Big Town (Lardner, 1938). You know, Irene always had a dream about living in Connecticut on a farm hard by New York. I questioned her about this on her return. She said, "Are you mad? No son of a bitch will ever get me out of this state again." Arthur says the backyard tropics of Southern California will be all that he wants in the future.

Nothing definite or even approximately so, but Guedel, my partner, is trying to wangle a two-week fling in New York in April. I will see him tonight and question him further.

I hope your financial situation has eased considerably under the new deal.

Kras and I are going away tomorrow for five days to do further work on our play. There's no kidding this time. We've already picked a theatre in Frisco in August so you'll probably be present at the birthplace of America's biggest flop.

By the way, I read a review by Hoffman this morning, Irving that is, of a new play by Jean Sartre dealing with the Negro problem and Hoffman just raved. By a Frenchman, yet!

I don't know whether I told you that I saw Betsy Kelly in *Deep Are the Roots* and she was lousy. She acted as though she were doing a Robbins ballet. I've seen Gene a few times and we speak about you. Kurnitz, too, always asks how you are and where.

The baby is wonderful and kisses me all day. I guess it's just a way I have with women. I never thought I could take on a new one at my age, but she's quite a gal.

I'm glad I'm leaving for five days, for Kay is fixing the house again. She runs around all day in her pajamas with a hammer in her hands. Her hammering usually starts about midnight. She should have married an owl.

This morning, incredible as it may seem, two cats were having an affair in our backyard. The black cat, the female, belongs to Gabby Hayes, and the white one is a male from across the street. I told Kay this morning that it was very interesting and actually was the only sex life that was occurring around our premises. Say, maybe I've been running a cathouse all these years.

Well, enough for today. Happy Valentine and all my love to you and I hope you've recovered from your recent intestinal disorder. Anyhow, it's getting close to the time when we'll see you again.

Love,
Padre

P.S. Kay has gradually removed everything from your room and hung it in other places and I predict that by the time you return you'll either share the room with Kay or sleep with the maid—something I've been doing for months.

Guedel was John Guedel, the promoter and originator of "You Bet Your Life."

February 25, 1948

Dear Mir:
I meant to write you personally on my own little typewriter, but just too many things pile up and I couldn't get around to it. However, I did instruct your brother Arthur to write you a stop-gap letter. I presume you have received this by now.

Fay Barrett just left the house. Her name at the moment is Connelly. She came to see the baby and she said to be sure to give you her best. She is married to a drunk from whom she is getting a divorce. It was her first time out and she said he was hopeless. She even had him put in a sanitorium so she is back working again. I thought to myself, when Fay told me all this, that perhaps her husband had seen her one morning just as she was and decided that drink was the only escape. Anyway, that is the Saga of Fay Barrett.

I've been working like a stevedore. Three days a week on the radio show and three days a week with Kras. Over and over and over we keep writing this turkey of ours. Tomorrow I start again. We have again rewritten the first two acts and are now off in a cloud of uncertainty on the third. We hope to finish up this week—I don't think I can take it much longer. The two jobs together are just too much. My feeling about the play now is that it will be a relief to have it open even if it closes the following night. At least I won't have the nightmare of writing facing me anymore. Kras is a relentless collaborator and there's no goldbricking when he's around. We certainly deserve a success. I suggested that we call the play *Life with Krasna*. Eleven years is a long time!

151

I'm sorry you have been ill. Apparently you are subject to colds or flu. I took one flu shot last December and so did Kay, and all our friends at various times have been laid low by colds, flu and Virus X — all but Kay and myself. We've gone through the winter like Michigan went through the Trojans.

When do you go back to school? There's still a likelihood that I might get to New York in April. I will know more definitely this week. Don't count on it though. The best laid plans of mice and radio comedians, etc.

I delivered your kisses to Melinda and in return she bit me. Do you still hear the radio show? You don't mention it so I presume you have scratched it off your listening schedule.

Well, write soon and all our love to you. We are all goddamned sick of the constant sunshine. Each morning we look up at the sky for a stray cloud but I guess the jig is up and I wouldn't be surprised if, before August, the whole goddamned state blows up, including the farmers. It serves them right — who told them to be farmers?

Love and Kisses,
Padre

P.S. The *Silo* arrived with your story. I thought it was beautifully written and good enough for *The New Yorker*. Does the fact that it was printed in the school magazine preclude the possibility of it being sold to a commercial magazine? I am curious to know how a mag like *The New Yorker* would react to it. On second thought, they would probably object to its length because it is quite long for them. However, I think you can feel very good about it. Some of the characters are slightly familiar and you must soon stop writing about them and strike out for newer and fresher material.

These are my opinions, for what they are worth. I think you have a good chance of becoming a first rate writer and I am very proud of you.

Love,
Padre

March 1, 1948

Dear Mir:
Just a line, for I wrote you a long letter a few days ago.

There happened to be a couple of pages in the *Saturday Review of Literature* about Thomas Wolfe. I know how interested you are in this tall, fat man. This summer I am going to give him a whirl.

Went to a big party at the Perrins' the other night and the conservative Eileen Ruby, who is usually sober, took three fast swigs and wound up dancing on the table. What liquor will do to people! Tears down all the inhibitions.

Love and kisses and write soon.

Padre

P.S. Sara Roberts' brother, whom I don't know and apparently you don't know either, would like to take you out. Why the hell don't you answer the phone? Says he can't reach you and I will give him your number — or are you already married? Anyway, love.

[March 6, 1948]

Saturday morning around ten

Dear Mir;
Had a letter from you a few days ago, and sorry to know that you almost sheared your hand off taking a bath. People bathe too damn much anyway. I believe they do it so that they can brag to their friends that they took a bath this morning, etc., etc.

I sent you some handkerchiefs for Valentine's Day, but I never heard from you as to whether you received them or not.

Unlike you, I hereby acknowledge the receipt of the picture of yourself; it is very pretty, a real glamour girl, so help me, and it is now roosting on top of the piano, where it is generally admired (*Iolanthe*).

The baby is a cute dish and smart. Yesterday she discovered that there was candy on the coffee table in the living room and when I wasn't watching she sneaked out, grabbed two pieces, stuffed them in her mouth and at the sound of my footsteps, she scrammed down the hall toward the kitchen and protection, but I nailed her with a flying tackle at the pantry door and held her upside down until she disgorged the loot.

I mislaid your last letter and don't know when you are returning to

153

school. If you in your next letter will tell me when you are around I will phone you, just for the sheer delight of hearing your dulcet voice. I am enclosing a clipping from the *Nation* with which sentiment or argument I am in full accord.

Speaking of politics, Ryskind was here the other night. I had been hooked into making a radio appearance for the Bev Hills tubercular drive, and Mary was on the committee, so we were lightening up the script a little. Anyway, I complained about Fairless boosting the price of steel five dollars a ton, and I said even Taft (no shining liberal) was indignant about that. You should have seen Morrie's face (none too good at best) when I cracked at Taft.

I am also sending you a clipping from *Variety,* and a copy of the *Screen* magazine, which I think you will find interesting; if not, let me know and I will refrain from sending it anymore.

By the way, Mary Ryskind read your story the other night and liked it enormously; so did Art and Ick.

Kras and I have finished our play for the eleventh time, and I would send it to you, but I have only one copy and I need it for my own amazement.

We hope to snare the Marches with it. Fred read it before and didn't care too much for it; we hope he will like it under its new writing. We have built up the woman's part considerably. I have a hunch that was one of the objections to the previous version.

Well, enough for now. Write soon and I love you and would like to see you one of these days.

Yours,
Padre

The Marches were actor Frederic March and his wife, actress Florence Eldridge, who frequently appeared together on the stage.

[March 22, 1948]

Saturday afternoon.

Dear Mir;
The Giants and Cleveland are playing at Wrigley Field, and I was dying to go down, but I have had a cold all week and wasn't up to the trip, thereby disappointing Ruby and myself.

We have had wonderful weather for months, in fact too dry, but as soon as the big league clubs arrived in town, it began raining, delighting the farmers and dairymen no end, but embittering every fan in Southern California. Well, that's life, or something approximating that.

Tonight we are journeying out to the Valley, Arthur at the wheel, to the Don Kahns', where we are having dinner. We accepted this right before we had an invitation to the Gene Kellys' for a big birthday party also for tonight.

Melinda is in the room while I am typing this, and I have to stop this every few minutes to watch what new mischief she is in. At the moment she is sitting on the guitar, so there will be a slight pause here for a moment while I tap her with an old golf club that luckily I have at my side.

Sheekman was impressed with your piece and threatened to write you. I'll wager it will be a long professorial dissertation. If a fellow ever was cut out to be a pedagogue, it is Sheek. He loves to advise on any matter of that sort. His opinions are sound, but even if they weren't he would give them just the same. Well, if he ever resigns from Paramount (where incidentally he is their top writer), he can get a university position for at least thirty-eight fifty a week.

We had a letter from you last week, on that cheap yellow paper, but your letters are always welcome, even though it is on that cheap yellow paper. Where do you dig it up? Do you have a boyfriend in the Philippines that smuggles it to you by way of Manila? Or do you steal it from the wrapping paper at Gristede's grocery store?

I hope you realize that I am just trying to be funny, and that I adore the stationery you write on. I do wish the pages were a trifle larger, however, for then I could use them to wrap my laundry in.

Well, enough of this unfunny and forced routine. I was happy to read that Marquand's son, a proper Bostonian no doubt (I am willing to hear more about this), enjoyed the radio show. Apparently most people do, for we are getting a lot of wonderful reports on it. It is more than likely that your old man (after all these years) has struck a formula that may keep him engaged on the radio for years. I don't know what this proves except that I was way ahead of my time, and that America is just getting around to appreciating what a clever and interesting man I am. However, if the sponsor doesn't pick up the tab for the thirty-nine weeks in the autumn (poetical for fall), forget all about what I have said and please destroy this letter.

Kay and I are brushing up on the routines for the war with Russia, and we would like to know whether you would be interested in playing in the Lockheed sketch on an aircraft carrier in San Francisco Bay.

Well, I think I have told you all the news. Write soon, and lots of love to you from both of us, and the little Melinda too, who just ripped one of the strings off the guitar—God, she's cute. Write soon. I hope this reaches you before you blow for Vermont.

###############kisses,
Padre

Marquand was novelist John P. Marquand. His daughter Christina and I were good friends at Bennington.

March 22, 1948

Dear Mir:
This isn't a letter, for I wrote you a letter a couple of days ago.

I'm sending you a couple of diminutive checks from two giant industrial corporations who, it seems to me, could do better than this by you. Also, a small piece from the *Saturday Review* and a very funny speech (I thought) written by Ken Englund who, at the moment, is in New York. I'd tell you to give him a ring but I don't know where he's stopping. Patsy left for England this week. Strange she should have the same name.

Anyway, love and write soon.

Yours,
Padre

April 9, 1948

Dear Mir:
Just a line to enclose this fascinating photograph of your father and two girls. I really have a mustache. The smear on the upper lip by no means represents the actual foliage, but was placed there by a jealous scoundrel.

Next week is our last show. This will be heard on April twenty-first. I expect to be back in the fall, if not for Elgin-American for some other sponsor.

Earl Wilson called me the other night from New York. One of those unfunny interviews over the phone which I am afraid will eventually wind up as a column. Apparently there aren't enough loose-heads in New York—he has to reach all the way out to California on the chance that I might, over a period of ten minutes, say something funny. Brother, was he fooled.

There's no news of any importance to write. The world situation is certainly not worthy of discussion. My family life is quiet, uneventful and routine. Let me hear from you when you get the time.

Love from all,
Padre

The photo enclosed showed Groucho with Mary Alice Keene ("UCLA's most beautiful co-ed") and Peggy Lee, who, with Groucho, had judged the contest.

[April 16, 1948]

Thursday evening around six

Dear Mir;
Well, the last radio show is over (it will be heard next Wednesday) and I feel like a boy out of school. I am terribly tired and have that letdown feeling that I hope comes from relaxing the muscles. I have been sleeping badly lately, and I am curious to see if I will do any better now that the strain is off.

Cantor's dinner was given last night at the Biltmore Bowl. There were over twelve hundred people present, and I must say that I acquitted myself creditably, considering that I am not a professional banquet speaker, and the competition was George Jessel and a few more of the same kind.

I am proud to say that I indulged in none of the maudlin sentimentalism of the others and relied on being humorous. In the talk there were no mentions of Ida and the five girls.

By accident Ida snared me for a moment, before the dinner, and upbraided me for being responsible for Janet leaving the Cantor manse. Eddie was present too, and I said, "You must expect your children to be on their own when they grow up," and they countered with, "We would like her to be home," and I bluntly told them that she wasn't happy there, that she was an individual and that she had a right to her own life, and all the other cliches that always are said during that kind of a discussion.

Your letter regarding the political situation was a small sensation around here. I had it at the Hillcrest Club and Kras read it and was so impressed that he asked me to read it to the crowd at the table. Among those at the table were George Burns, and Lou Holtz, and a son of Harry Hopkins (Roosevelt's Harry Hopkins), and Milton Sperling, and Buzzell, and others. After I finished reading the letter, Milton Sperling (who is married to one of Warner's daughters) said that that night he was giving a dinner to Senator Pepper and some assorted Democrats, and would I lend him the letter and he would return it the following day. This he proceeded to do, and he sent a note with it which I am enclosing. You can feel very flattered by this. Politically, my position is one of standing off. I don't want to vote for Truman, or for most of the Republican candidates. I am going to wait and see what the Philadelphia convention brings forth. I personally believe that the Demos are depending on Eisenhower to run, and I really think he will run, but that he is playing the game cagily, and feels that he can't afford to commit himself at this time. I also read in the *Nation* that many of the big city bosses in Chicago and other large vote centers have definitely decided that they can't win with Truman and are going to lay it on the line for Ike.

Your writing has certainly improved enormously in the past year and I think (if you can think of something to say) that you have a good chance of earning a living writing, if that is your ambition.

Your friend Dick hasn't been around here in recent months. It seems that he barged in one morning while Kay was in a state of semi nudeness and Kay bawled him out. I think he is offended. He shouldn't be; he is a man now, and if he wants to visit us, he should phone first and warn us of his impending arrival. If you write him, you might explain that to him.

He is a nice boy and I don't want to hurt his feelings. He has been doing (along with his other activities) baby-sitting for Art and Ick, and they tell me he does a very good job. I would be suspicious of one who was that proficient at baby-sitting. Perhaps he has a family that you know nothing about?

Well, here I am at the end of two pages and I must get dressed. We are going to the Beechcombers with the Krasners. Wish you were along. Love and kisses from all—Padre. Write soon.

Kisses,
Padre

Milton Sperling was a producer and screenwriter.

April 27, 1948

Dear Mir:
I didn't mean to surprise you so abruptly, but up to the time this letter was written my plans were still nebulous. I am leaving Thursday and will be in New York Sunday, and you'd better be there when I arrive. I am going to the Hampshire House, which overlooks Central and on a clear day you can see the Polo Grounds, where I expect to be Sunday afternoon. Maybe you can stay over until Monday and go back Monday night or Tuesday morning, or something. Anyhow, it will be nice to look at your dour kisser again. It's very convenient having a daughter on each coast. As I leave Melinda with heavy heart here, I run into Miriam at the other end.
 The sixth of May I am doing the Jolson show. I may do "The Charlie McCarthy Show" the thirtieth—if I don't I won't stay quite that long as you will be coming home soon.
 I get no mail at all from you but I suppose you're busy. Anyhow, that is your customary excuse.
 Won't write anymore, for I'll see you soon.
Love and Kisses,
Your Padre

[May 28, 1948]

Dear Mir;
Home again and glad to get here. The air trip was smooth and dull. The modern plane flies so high that it is impossible to see anything but an occasional cloud and they can get pretty monotonous after a while. I can see by the beginning of this letter that there are going to be plenty of mistakes and I attribute the whole thing to Communism.
 I often wonder what they used to blame everything on before there was such a word. Well, I'm up and about again. This is the first time I have been up and around since I have been home. I caught a cold, either from weariness or nerves or whatever one catches a cold from, and I have been reclining on the mattress, reading and thinking (not much thinking), mostly reading. I think most people read so that they won't be thinking; anyway, that's why I do. It's far more pleasant to read someone else's thoughts than to think of your own. I have been reading the war memoirs of Winston Churchill, and whether you admire him or not (and my hunch is that you don't), he is a fine writer and tells so vividly of those war years that you really live them all over

159

again, if that's what you call having a good time. Other than Irene and Steve and Arthur, I haven't seen anyone since I arrived and have settled for a few brief telephone calls to my friends. Not even a ball game, although the Hollywood Stars seem to be able to lose with just as much regularity whether I am present or not.

Chico is still in Australia and will be for a few weeks yet. He is a big hit and will probably return there after the picture is completed. The picture is going to start the latter part of June and will be made at the same studio that hacked up *A Night in Casablanca*. I hope for the boys' sake that the picture is good, but I am happy that I will only have two weeks' work in it. I am in no frame of mind or physical condition to go through one of those eight-week schedules. Plus this, I have the play with Kras to contend with and I have all the work I need for the summer months.

Kay, too, is tired and has a cold, and the baby is just emerging from one. She comes to visit me from afar and it kills me, I want to grab her and kiss her, but I know I shouldn't go near her while she has the cold, and she can't understand why I stay away from her, it's all too confusing. Someday I'll explain it to her, but I'm afraid by that time she won't be interested in whether I kiss her or not.

Kay is going to finish off this letter. It was certainly nice seeing you, and I hope your trip back to Bennington was pleasant. Love and kisses and don't drink too much, it's a terribly easy habit to get into. Love, and write soon,

Padre

The next voice you hear will be Marie Marvis—

Dearest Mir;
I planned to write you a long note, but don't feel up to it today, having a bad cold, so forgive me and I'll write soon.

Love and kisses,
Kay

Marie Marvis was a second cousin of Kay's.

[June, 1948]

Dear Mir;
I received a notification from Bennington that tuition was due for the next year. I told you last year that I had paid two years and that your mother should carry you the rest.

When we separated I gave her over two hundred thousand dollars and insurance policies. In addition, despite the fact that she is married to another man, I have paid substantial sums every year, not just token payments but big chunks of money. I think this is almost unheard of in the histories of alimony. I am now supporting your mother and a strange man. I overlook the point that she should have pride enough to refuse this money, but I can't overlook the point that since you are her daughter as well as mine, and the kind of a financial settlement she made, she should contribute toward your education. I am therefore returning the papers from Bennington for you to send to your mother.

About the airline travel. There was another wreck yesterday someplace in the Far East, a Pan-American liner, and as far as I am concerned I would just as well you took the train, even though it meant seeing you a few days later. I know there are many people travelling who don't get killed in planes, but I only have two daughters, unlike Cantor, who has five, and Joan Davis, and I would like to keep both of them.

I just got through writing you two letters, one that you didn't get (I lost it somewheres), and one that I presume you didn't get.

I finished with Kras yesterday and am weary. I didn't realize how tired I was, but I guess I was sustaining myself by working, and now with the knowledge that it is over, I just collapsed.

Kras and Harpo and wives are going fishing at June Lake for a few days and then we will plan our course of action. I leave everything in Norman's hands for he is so much smarter than I am. Jesus, what a mind. I love you and am awaiting your arrival eagerly.

Padre####

Joan Davis was a radio, film and television comedien who had her own television show, "I Married Joan," during the early fifties.

June 28, 1948

Dear Mir:
Just a line. I am back working with Krasna and have neither the time nor vitality for a long-winded letter.

I thought you might be interested in the enclosed piece from the *Nation* sizing up your candidate. Just remember this appraisal does not come from the *Los Angeles Times,* the *New York Times,* nor McCormick's *Tribune,* but I thought you might be interested as I was in reading it.

161

We have found flaws in our second act and since the cast doesn't begin rehearsing until next week we thought we had better try to plug up the leaks. It will even be a relief if the show opens and closes. Eleven years is too long to work on a play. It's astonishing how many people dislike this play, but Krasna and I are putting our own money in it as a gesture of nose-thumbing and defiance.

Arthur, as you know or don't know, sold a piece to *Redbook*. This delights me no end for he was getting pretty discouraged. It takes an awful lot of courage to sit day after day in a room and hope that something you write is going to sell.

Arthur has promised to meet you and greet you at the depot. I will greet you from my bedroom—or maybe the living room. I am glad you are taking the train if that makes you any easier in your mind. I would still rather fly.

I note what you say about the Yankees and will point out to you mathematically that it will be impossible for them to win the Pennant.

I have to knock off. Love and kisses,

Padre

September 3, 1948

Dear Miriam:

When you phoned and asked me for fifty dollars, I sent it to you. I was going to deduct it from your allowance, then I decided not to because of the heat. I just got into my office and found a bill here for you from Chasen's for $67.55. I think you have a goddamned nerve to do this. I am good and angry about it. I have no intention of letting you get away with this and I am deducting this from your next month's check.

In addition, I want you to stop phoning long distance. You have a typewriter and if you are too damned lazy to write just forget about it. My phone bill this month, thanks to your long distance calls, was $59.00.

Padre

Chasen's is a restaurant that we ate at frequently when I was growing up. Kay and I had fought that summer and hadn't spoken almost the whole time. At the end of summer we made up, got drunk together and had an expensive dinner at Chasen's—which we charged to Padre while he was away.

[September 10, 1948]

Dear Mir;
Wednesday evening—this is the first night I haven't been to the Biltmore Theatre, for we have done all we can with the play and this is the way it will open at the Fulton Theatre the twenty-seventh.

I received your letter today and I am sorry that I got so angry at you, but it did burn me up when I saw that bill from Chasen's.

However, I forgive you and I will send you your full check for the next month. I am terribly tired. I have a radio show tomorrow night and Saturday I have to shoot on the boys' picture so that they can preview. I have to memorize this dialogue, and then Monday I cut another radio show, and Tuesday night Kras and I fly to New York and land at the St. Regis Hotel sometime Wednesday. It's a relief not to see the play tonight. I saw it forty-three times and I am damn sick of it. I am dead tired so I won't write anymore, but will tell you all the news that is when I see you next week.

Other than that we are all well, and hope this finds you in the same condition. I will be in New York a week and then have to fly back to complete the Cowan picture and cut the fourth radio show. All my love to you from me and all the rest.

Yours,
Padre######Kisses

[October 9, 1948]

Thursxday afternnoon

This is a brilliant beginning. I have written two words and have already made two mistakes. The hell with it. This is the first time I've been at the machine in months and I am a little on the rusty side.

Just a week ago today I was sitting in a plane winging through the air and it was certainly nice to get out of New York and those reviews. I am just beginning to recover from the effects of the pannings. I had no idea how deeply it had left its scars. Fortunately, I am so busy I have very little time to brood about them or the play. I think the critics are unfair bigoted bastards and I don't want any more of them. Let younger fellows take those whippings. Fortunately, I have other ways of making a living, and I don't want to be subjected to their not so tender mercies again. Tonight I have a radio record to cut, and when I am through with it no one compares me with Shaw or Sheridan, or

163

Pinero or even Molnar, but they all say how clever I was and what a witty man I am, and that's enough salve for my ego at my age.

Haven't heard hide nor hair from you since I departed and I hope you are still alive and editing that magazine in your customary manner. Monday I begin a week of shooting for Cowan which he has coming and then I will have a rest, for I will have nothing on my mind but moving into a new house, with all that that entails, memorizing eighty-five pages of dialogue for the picture I am doing for Cummings, and my radio show. I am not complaining. I am glad I have the jobs and the money that goes with them, but I will be busy.

It is as hot as August here today and if I had a beach house and the time I would go down to the sea and help Governor Warren pick grunion.

There is not much to tell you that you don't know. [Robert] Mitchum is still off the weed, the Yankees are conspicuous by their absence from the World Series — I hope you are ready to concede that the best team won, although the picture of poor DiMaggio limping around the outfield with that charley horse will always be one of my sadder memories. The regular number of divorces, pregnancies and marriages are taking place out here, Susan Marx is recovering and is contemplating returning home this weekend (you might drop her a line) and Melinda grows cuter and smarter every day.

She is acquiring the characteristics of most of the other children that are not born in poverty; she doesn't want to eat, and insists on animal crackers every time she enters my room. She will always associate me with animal crackers, and I don't mean the picture or the play.

Take care of yourself, don't drink too much and write occasionally even if it's only for money.

Love and Kisses,
Padre

Dearest Mir;
This isn't going to be a letter, but just a note to tell you that the new house has taken all my time, and when I get a breather, I'll sit down and write the goddamndest letter. Maybe six pages long. Until then, take care of yourself, BE GOOD.

Love and Kisses,
Kay

This was written after the play A Time for Elizabeth, *co-authored by Groucho and Norman Krasna, had opened in New York and been panned by the critics. Otto Kruger, a fine actor, had played the lead, which was originally written for my father. When Groucho played the part himself later in summer stock, it was fairly well received because, although it wasn't a great play, he suited the role. My father always wanted to be a writer—far more than he wanted to be a comedian—so it was a great disappointment to him when his play flopped on Broadway. The picture for (Irving) Cummings was* Double Dynamite *(1951). Susan Marx was Harpo's wife.*

October 29th, 1948

Dear Clunk:

I shouldn't write at all because I rarely hear from you and when I do it's about the Yankees. It seems to me that a girl who is editor of a college magazine should be able to write a letter to her father once every two weeks about something more interesting than a seedy ballplayer. Why don't you write me something about your life at Bennington? You must have some contacts that could conceivably interest me. Suppose I wrote you about nothing but the Hollywood ball club? You would be justified in throwing the whole thing in the ash can without reading it.

Speaking of cans, I have had all the toilets removed from the new-old house that I recently got stuck with, but with these new toilets you will practically be sitting on top of the world—courtesy of A. A. Hokum, plumbers. Plus this, one of the seven dozen workmen infesting the premises discovered a nest of termites in the timbers, which means ripping up quite a piece of cement and other pieces of foundation. I discovered, also, that the roof leaked, all the windows jammed, the heating plant had to be modernized, electrical wiring was inadequate for the amount of outlets I required. But I shouldn't complain, for they threw in the billiard table and sixteen balls. The house will stand me about $700,000 by the time I move in. Kay has that wild look that comes to a woman's eyes . . . when she visualizes how she is going to transform the house with drapes, carpets, shades, antique furniture. Luckily, I am so busy and weary that I haven't much time to brood about this new madcap enterprise of mine, but I predict I will be licking my wounds for years to come.

Grace Kahn postal carded that she was in New York and would like for you to get in touch with her on your next trip in. She will be at the Hampshire House until about the fifteenth of November.

This script I am about to embark upon is beginning to be botched up by an itinerant gag-writer by the name of Crane, a friend of Sinatra. Apparently he is one of the 700 screenwriters out of work and since Frankie Boy always takes care of his friends he cajoled Irving Cum-

mings, the producer, to hire this lad. This will be the first unpleasant-
ness of my new chore when I tell Cummings what I think of Crane's
interpolations.

I could write you a great deal more, but I'll save some of it for Chapter Two. I am sending you some Chesterfields and my love and write
soon.

P.S. The four freezing months, as I remember, in New England are
December, January, February and March and those four months I
think you would be wise in garaging your car if you expect to have one
in the spring. If necessary, I will pay the $12.00 monthly garage rent.

Love,
Padre

December 8, 1948

Dear Mir:

I am sorry you had such a disappointing Thanksgiving, but things
won't always be that way so cheer up.

I am terribly busy and terribly tired. The last two days I spent walking on a treadmill with Frank Sinatra. I dreaded doing it but it wasn't
nearly as bad as I had anticipated. Very few things are. I walked approximately forty miles. And who do you think staged what little stag-
ing could be done? Your old friend Stanley Donen. A nice guy and I
think some day he will be a very good director. We have quite a lot
of fun on the set. Sinatra is an exceptionally nice chap to work with.
Laughs easily and is surprisingly smart. Don't be amazed if he too
winds up a director some day. He knows a lot about the camera and
the technique of movie making.

Three days have elapsed since I started this letter. This afternoon
I spent reclining in a tub of hot water with all my clothes on. I emerged
none the worse for wear but it isn't very pleasant. All those connected
with the picture seem to be very happy with it. But you know I am a
skeptical character and extremely suspicious of pretty enthusiasms.

I'm sorry you got so annoyed at *Copacabana*. It seems to me that
you had seen this some years ago. Was this a return trip, or was this
your maiden voyage?

This is a bad week for me. We are moving Friday and we are coming down the stretch on the picture. I am a little weary but there's nothing wrong with my condition that a few weeks of solitude won't
repair.

The next time I talk to you on the phone I want you to hear Melinda speak. Her words are really beginning to take shape. I took her over to Harpo's Sunday and Alec (Harpo's five-year-old) fell for her hook, line and sinker. They had quite a card game and when I suggested that we leave she kept right on playing. She gave me the brush quickly. I practically had to drag her out of the house.

I'll be through with the picture in twelve days. When I am, I will write you a more comprehensive and detailed letter. This is just to let you know that we miss you and that when you were small you were just as cute, although I must say that you have outgrown it, but I love you just the same.

> Love and kisses,
> Padre

January 2, 1949

Dear Mir;

This is the first letter that I have attempted in weeks so there will be more than the customary quota of errors. It's the day after New Year's. Melinda is on the couch reading Mother Goose, at least looking at the pictures, I am taking Ruby over to Hillcrest for lunch, Kay is asleep and I am glad the holidays are over.

I thought the article in *Silo* was quite good, but don't you think you could quit writing those somber, almost morbid, pieces and write something a little jollier for a change? After all, everything in life isn't sad, clinical and depressing. If only for a change of style, try something else.

While dining at the Derby last week I encountered Mary Hammond (I believe that's her name) with her husband. She looked about the same, although I didn't know her until she told me who she was, and her husband seemed like a nice chap. She said "you owed her a letter" but I imagine you are accustomed to that accusation by this time.

Dick Comen was here for lunch yesterday and then saw the football game on the television set. I watched it for a few minutes and then staggered off to my room for a nap. He said "you owe him a letter."

I was over to the Kahns' (among other places) New Year's Eve, and they all seemed to be having a good time. Art seems to like his job at the studio. I asked him if he heard from you, and he said no, "you owe him a letter."

Later we went to Krasna's. In evening clothes, no less, and he had

167

his customary and good food. Their party broke up around two. I spoke to Ruth and she wanted to know when you were going to answer her letter? Then we went to Frank Loesser's house and among those there was John Steinbeck, drunk as usual—brilliant writer but a nuisance, for I have never been around him that he wasn't stewed, and he is the pugnacious souse. One has to be careful what they say in his presence. I admire his writing but personally you can have him, and as far as I know you may have had.

Then home and up at noon, a rare thing for me; I am doing the Jolson show on the thirteenth, and the Crosby show with Judy Garland shortly after. I don't know whether you know, but I won the newspaper critics award for the best quiz show in radio. This is an empty honor similar to the Oscar in the movies, but it does impress the sponsor and the general public and that's about all I want to impress.

I wish you would write more often and tell me in one of your letters what your plans are. We all send love and hope to see you one of these days.

Yours,
Padre

January 18, 1949

Dear Mir:
Enclosing a piece by Ken Englund. Thought you might find it amusing.

Kay wrote you a long letter and I wrote you a short one so there's nothing new to tell you except to reassure you that Art Linkletter will not be on the show again.

Love and kisses,
Padre

February 25, 1949

Dear Mir:
You will receive a gold pencil sometime in the near future, which was presented to me by Irving Cummings for shooting *It's Only Money* so swiftly. I had no use for the pencil and thought perhaps you could use it. My guess is that it won't bring much in hock.

Glad you heard the "Lady Be Good" broadcast. I was so busy I forgot to inform you. It turned out pretty well considering what we originally started with. They have asked me to do *The Mikado* on April fourth for the same sponsor and if it can be cleared I probably will accept.

I have been terribly busy the past few weeks. I had extra shooting to do on the boys' picture and extra narration to write and mouth, plus the guest shots I have done—I am really beaten. I will never again permit myself to get involved in so many activities simultaneously. It's just too much for me and my nature doesn't permit me to relax very much. The trouble with show business is that you are either very hot and many people bid for your services, or you are practically washed up and nobody wants you. I must concede that my position is the better one, but I am going to try to dole myself out more carefully.

I took Melinda to the Griffith Park Zoo the other day. I had been promising her this for a month. I knew if I didn't fulfill this promise pretty soon she would lose all faith in me, and besides I would be too old for the animals. I had never been to this menagerie, but as a veteran of the Bronx and Central Park zoos this is certainly a moth-eaten layout. They have one old elephant, three mangy bears, two ditto camels and the customary farm animals and deers and wild fowl. But no lions, tigers, hippos or rhinos. We had a lot of peanuts to throw to the animals but her aim wasn't very good so she ate most of them herself. Then I took her to the Derby where she had matzoh ball soup to celebrate Israel becoming a country. She is quite a kid and follows me around the house like a trained dog. I'm sorry you've seen so little of her since she was born, but I hope you will be able to spend some time this summer in your own room, with two beds no less.

From your letter your place must be quite a shambles and you must be quite a cook. God help the man that you prepare food for. He had better own a bicarbonate mine.

My plans are pretty hazy. I don't know just when we will go off the air. I have been toying with the idea of going to Palestine this summer and playing a week for the Airlift boys in Germany. This is an extremely nebulous expedition at the moment as it involves Jessel so I will just have to wait and see what happens.

How are you doing with your shorthand? I read very little about it in your recent letters. Have you given it up for cooking? Did you ever go to see Abel Green about a job for this autumn? And what are you doing about your future life? Since I am your gay provider, more or less, you might reveal your plans.

169

All my love to you and the best from the five women in the house—
Melinda, Kay, Virginia and two [maids].

Padre

It's Only Money was the original name for Double Dynamite. *Virginia was Kay's cousin, Virginia Semon, who lived with them and helped take care of Melinda.*

April 6, 1949

Dear Miriam:

I thought I had sent you a record. Anyway, it was sent off to you to-day. I also found a cute snapshot of you somewhere between the age of two and eleven. I'm not very good at appraising women's ages until they get to seventeen.

Your dissertation about my spoiling the baby I thought was a bit on the jerky side. The old saw about a little learning being a dangerous thing also applies to a smattering of Freud, so I would appreciate not having any more of that particular kind of nonsense.

About your graduation. I will try to unfold it to you by slow and easy stages. My first news of it was when Shufro came back from having dinner at your mother's and quoted your mother as saying that she did not want to go to your graduation—not because she doesn't love you, but because of the expense—and if I were going she would prefer to stay home. Since then you told Kay on the phone (according to Kay) that you weren't particularly eager to have your mother come on whether I showed up or not, but in order not to offend her we were to let her know through Arthur that I contemplate going. As I wrote you, my health is nothing to cheer about at the moment. There's nothing specifically wrong with me except that I am not as young as I was thirty years ago (this is a particularly shrewd bit of news) and the thought of travelling east in the middle of July is one that I don't feel up to at the moment. I know you place great importance on the graduation but (this comes of having a father who is a combination egomaniac and introvert) I have to dole out my vitality sparingly. I hope you understand that this has nothing to do with my love for you, for if I didn't love you I certainly wouldn't send you a record that cost me ninety-three cents wholesale. As I wrote you, I even rejected the invitation of the Peabody committee to present me with their award for the same reason. During the war it was called occupational fatigue, and it still is. Plus this, I hope to see you this summer. If I weren't I would probably go east in July.

170

When you answer me, please let me know that you understand what I have just written. I don't want your mother to be hurt. Art will tell her that I am going, even though I am not. Your mother will be happy. You, I hope won't be too much hurt, and I will be resting— something I need badly.

You can hear me on the Jolson show April seventh just by turning on your radio. It really isn't worth it, but if you have nothing better to do, he and I croaked through a song together like two elderly bullfrogs.

I was thinking of getting you a television set for your graduation. You can then stay home and watch the Yankees lose the Pennant, or anything else that strikes your fancy. If you have other notions about how I should spend the money let me know. Only I do not want to give you any cash for you to continue to subsidize your girlfriends.

Love and kisses, and hope you are well,

Padre

May 17, 1949

Dear Mir:

Your last two letters were dillies. Your first one told me you were kicked out of college and your second one that you ran over a cat. Some day I may tell you how I felt about both of these incidents, but we will skip it for the nonce.

This is Tuesday noon, it's raining just beautifully and in forty-eight hours you will be twenty-two—so I am sending you a check for $100 which will give you sufficient margin to run over another cat and a half, figuring $40 to a cat.

My phone bill last month was $88. I would like you to eliminate the surreptitious phone calls to Kay because the Miriam to Kay phone bills alone were $35. If you have anything to tell her you have a typewriter and ten healthy fingers. As Billy (Beeftrust) Watson would put it, "nuf ced."

I wish you would let me know approximately when you are coming home. I will then adjust my own plans accordingly.

I don't know why you ever left the other apartment you had. I thought it was just beautiful. It overlooked two garbage cans, a public utility pole and the week's wash of two immigrant families.

I am glad you had such a good time with the Aces and enjoyed your

171

revel in your rooting. You must know that they are not going to stay up there forever.

I am doing the Jolson show on tape this Thursday, which will be heard the following Thursday (the twenty-sixth) on the air. I don't recommend it particularly, but I never pass up an opportunity to make an honest dollar.

Lots of love—happy birthday—and will be glad to see you,

Padre

My expulsion from Bennington was due to a series of alcohol related problems, but I certainly didn't tell my father that. Billy (Beeftrust) Watson had a vaudeville act that featured several very heavy women. The Aces were Goodman (Goody) Ace and his wife Jane. Goody was a radio writer who had a show called "Easy Aces" during the 1930s and 1940s. He was a close friend of my father's.

June 6, 1949

Dear Mir:

About fifty percent of every letter you write tells in great detail why you have not written. I am fairly good with the typewriter—not nearly as speedy as you are—and I can knock out a moderately interesting letter in seven or eight minutes. Therefore I take very little stock in your protestations as to how busy you are and all that sort of thing.

I am glad you are at labor—no skip that, it sounds like you are having a baby which, as far as I know, could be. What I meant to say was that I am glad you are working and I am sure the additional money you make will come in mighty handy. I still think you are foolish not to take up shorthand in a serious way, but I can only suggest it. I don't know what your new apartment looks like but it cannot help but be an improvement over that dungeon you were living in when last I saw you.

Kay is making feverish plans for a vacation. Last summer when it was raining she toyed with the idea of going to Catalina. Recently we have had a heat wave and she now is thinking seriously of going to Palm Springs. I imagine as soon as Big Bear freezes over she will want to go there for the swimming. Kay is nuttier than ever and has the goddamndest excuses for everything. I said, "Why don't you wait until next week if you want to go away and I'll take you to Victorville or someplace." She said, "No. I want to go without you." I said, "Am I that much of a bore?" She said, "No, but if we go together people will know I am Mrs. Groucho Marx." That one I still don't understand.

As you know, you will become an aunt again inside of a week or so. I have a hunch it's going to be another boy. This is based on nothing except that male offspring seems to be characteristic of the Marxes, except in my case where I had two girls and one boy. But since you live in New York it doesn't count.

I met Maxine and she asked for you and wants to know why you don't write her. I could tell her but I had no intention of going into that. I also met Dick Comen who threw the same question at me and who also got the same answer—nothing.

I am scraping and repainting the white furniture in the backyard. One of these days I am going to drag out the golf clubs and find out if I play as badly now as I did when I played regularly. Krasna keeps pleading with me to journey around the course with him. I will eventually but I am not in the mood for it yet. I have a lot of odd jobs to do around the house—playing with the baby, planning the meals and cleaning the incinerator. This doesn't leave much surplus vitality for anything as useless as golf. But I joined the goddamned club and eventually I will have to begin torturing myself with my own mediocrity.

I taught Melinda to do a grind and few other tricks and she is getting to be quite an entertainer. She may be the Shirley Temple of 1965.

Well, I think this covers the domestic situation pretty thoroughly. Love and kisses and take care of yourself,

Padre

I had decided to move to New York after I left Bennington and look for work there rather than return home.

June 22, 1949

Dear Mir:
Received your letter and will answer you in a couple of days.

In the meantime, why don't you leave your car there, fly on here and spend the six weeks it will take to have your car repaired, and then go back. And don't worry about the $100 insurance, I will pay that.

Love and kisses. Will write you in a few days.

Padre

My car had been hit by a train in Massachusetts where I was visiting a college friend. I was drunk, and got stuck on the tracks. My friend and I were able to jump out of the car before it was hit, but the car was badly damaged. I hadn't

173

told my father anything about it until Walter Winchell mentioned it on the radio, at which point I had to give Groucho my own edited version of the events. He never did find out the truth about what happened.

[July 3, 1949]

Dear Mir:

I am sorry that you are going to be delayed so long, but there is nothing I can do about it that I haven't done.

I wrote to Joe Stone to get a move on and wrote to Shufro to see that Stone is prodded in the right places. I know how impatient one can get in that kind of situation. I told Stone to try and get a cash settlement from the company, but since tomorrow is the fourth, I won't know what he has to say until the fifth, when the United States mails will be back in action. Although I am not a Yankee rooter, I am just as thrilled as the rest of America at the magnificent comeback of Joe DiMag. The story of a great champion rising off the floor, no matter what the sport may be, is always an exciting one, for it is living proof of the durability and courage of man.

You should have heard the cheers the night they announced at Gilmore Field that he was back in action and that he had knocked off a double and a homer in his opening game. Now that that is out of the way, I still hope that they lose the Pennant to some city that hasn't had one in years, and where the bankroll isn't so long and green.

I had occasion to speak to Frank Herbert; he is one of the editors of the *Readers Digest*, and an old friend of mine from years ago. Despite the fact that he is on the *Readers Digest* he is a very nice man, and I told him that you would write or go to see him about a job, and he said be sure and do so, sooo don't neglect this. . . . I suggest that you write him a very clever letter that will impress him.

From the local weather reports the weather in the East must really be a preview of Hades (hell to you) and we are lucky having our regular climate. Hot during the day, but wonderfully cool at night.

Every time I consider going East, I think of those nights in New York, and then common sense takes the place of madness and I say quiet you foolish fellow and be thankful for where you are.

I have been playing golf a few times lately and I play as badly as ever; there is very little difference in my game now than when I played regularly. I will take you on when you get back, if you ever do.

Steve spent the day here yesterday with Melinda and they play together beautifully. He is a nice boy and rather quiet, on the style of his father.

Irene seems to be taking the disaster with her customary calmness, and it's quite a relief. The Kahns certainly are stoics when something grave happens. I remember how Grace and the kids took Gus's death. I know how they suffered, but with them it's always beneath the surface. I took Art and Ick to Hillcrest for dinner last night. It was the first time Ick had been out since she left the hospital, and she enjoyed being away from the bed for a while.

Harpo and Chico are a big hit at the Palladium in London, which makes me very happy. What makes me even happier is the fact that I am not with them. As long as I have this radio racket, I have no desire to appear publicly. I think the ham in me has simmered down to just a strip of bacon and it's just as well.

This is all that I have time for now. Write soon and remember, any time you want to live in California, it can be arranged. My guess is though that except for a visit, you would never be satisfied here again.

All my love to you and kisses, your handsome Pappy,

Padre Groucho

Joe Stone was my insurance agent. Arthur and Irene had lost their baby.

July 25, 1949

Dear Mir:

I won't write you a letter because I am just as busy as you are and, incidentally, just as lazy.

I am sending you the Shapiro check, your monthly allowance and $100 to keep you from starvation on your trek westward. This will eliminate any likelihood of your bleached bones being found on the great American desert. Try not to have anything happen to you on your trip west. Don't cross any railroad tracks without first consulting the timetables and remember always jump in time.

Will write you as soon as I get a decent letter from you.

Love and kisses,

Padre

[September 27, 1949]

Dear Mir;
This is the first time I have touched the machine in months, so I will
have to learn all over again. Luckily I have nothing to say. I won't talk
about Yankees after what the Red Sox did to them. I must admit, for
the first time in my life I was rooting for them. Not so much for them
as for Casey Stengel and what he has gone through. I am still hoping
that they win the Pennant but it looks bad with DiMaggio in bed and
the rest of the team crippled. Well, if they don't win, send on the money, I can use it. The Dodgers too look in a sad way and it looks now
like the Red Sox against the Cards. As for the Pacific Coast League—
you will notice if you look at the standings that Haney brought them
home under the wire, despite all the croakings by the local wiseguys
that they were lucky and would never stand up in the stretch.
    The name of the man that you seek is Frank Herbert. But perhaps
you have a job by this time.
    There is not much news to write. Nothing ever happens out here:
a few murders, a few divorces, a few cocktail parties and into the next
season. You might also call Earl Wilson about a job, he may be able
to help you, and call Irving Hoffman. You must try all contacts, you
can never tell where you will be lucky. Get up your nerve and talk for
yourself, that's the only way you are going to get ahead.
    Melinda has asked about you a number of times, and seems to
remember you. Back again to the other theme. Call Shufro about a
job, he has a lot of contacts and might be able to throw something
your way. My mind isn't functioning today, so there is no use in con-
tinuing this any further. Will send your check soon. Love and kisses
and take good care of yourself. Your loving Padre ##############
these, believe it or not, are kisses

September 30, 1949

Dear Mir:
Enclosed find check.
    Melinda started kindergarten today. The bus drove up and there
was a girl on the bus she knew and an empty seat next to her; but there
were two boys down at the front end of the bus in cowboy suits and
she made a quick dive for them—launching a career as the youngest
nymphomaniac in America.

176

I have done three shows so far and you can hear the initial one next Wednesday at nine P.M. EST.

Nothing more to say.

Love and kisses,
Padre

October 18, 1949

Dear Mir:

The World Series is over; Stengel is back in Glendale; I am out six dollars (according to you); and it was very interesting to read that you are on a strict Mohammedan diet—no meat and plenty of rice.

I was happy to hear that you are again in the ranks of the employed and I am sure you will lift *Mademoiselle* to a proud position. I am telling all my friends that you are the editor of the magazine and not the janitor that you said you were. Editor sounds so much better—and, who knows, if I keep on saying this you may eventually inherit that job.

Melinda is now a schoolgirl and every morning at a quarter of nine a bus picks her up and delivers her back at noon. She sings "My contrary 'tis of thee." This I assume she gets from "Mary, Mary, quite contrary" and is a little confused between "country" and "contrary." It's not hard to be confused at the age of three. I am still confused at the age of 103. Last week in the bus she sat next to Frank Loesser's daughter, who is six and one of the most spoiled brats that rich parents have yet produced. As soon as Melinda sat down next to her, Susie slugged her. So now Melinda sits with the driver and peace once more reigns in the bus.

I would thank Goody Ace for being so nice to you in New York, but over the past two years I have written him three times with nary an answer. He either despises me or he despises writing. I wish you would tell him this—it might force a letter out of him. He is one of my favorite people and I do miss not seeing him.

We are having a little sponsor trouble. Gellman is turning out to be a typical Hungarian. He is now asking, in return for our release, a substantial sum of money. This is similar to the hijacking that went on in the New Jersey post roads during prohibition. The honest thing would be to either let us go or retain us, but he wants to exact tribute from us so our relationship may end up in an obscene squabble.

Nothing else of note to relate. Hope you feel better.

Love and kisses,
Padre

November 10, 1949

Dear Mir:

This is quite a world we are living in. You earn some $30 a week and you contemplate spending $45 a week for an analyst.

I wrote to your mother today and explained your situation and asked her to pay half of this. I don't propose to put a time limit on your visits to the doctor but perhaps after a while they can be reduced in number. I don't know whether this form of treatment will do you any good but I am willing to go along with you for a reasonable length of time until we can judge what results are being achieved.

There's no question that there is a definite psychological barrier between all parents and children regardless of how close we were to them in their childhood. I find this is true with Arthur, just as it is with you and, I am sure, will eventually be with Melinda. I have spoken to other parents and their views in most cases are precisely the same as mine.

From your letter you will have had your initial treatment by the time this reaches you. Don't worry about it, I am sure we will be able to work out the financial end of this to a satisfactory conclusion.

It's raining good and hard today and it is a welcome visitor. We haven't had any for seven months and the surrounding forests have been on fire for the past month. . . .

Kay has her customary cold. Melinda also has one and I have been flirting with the edges of it for the past few days. But I am made of sturdy peasant stock and don't surrender too easily.

Election returns in the various states pleased me no end.

I will write you again when I hear from your mother.

> Love and Kisses,
> Padre

December 7, 1949

Dear Mir:

I am going to try something revolutionary in the form of swindling. I am going to send you $250 a month. Therefore I will supplement the check I sent you on the first with the additional money, which includes your $90 allotment for Dr. Gross. After you are through with Gross I will send you $160 a month instead of $120.

Now for the swindle. I am going to try to put this on my income tax as a deductible item and what you have to do, if you want the additional $40 a month, is to write me two pages of gibberish each week.

Suggestions for improving the program, gags about carpenters, plumbers, housewives, etc. The point is that when the revenue men come around with their bloodhounds I will be able to show them pages of suggestions, dialogue, etc., that you sent me weekly. This will ease my burden a little bit which, as you may or may not know, is fairly heavy. There's no certainty that the tax department will allow this. My only hope is (you are, more or less, a professional writer on a New York magazine) they may allow it. The worst that can happen is that if they throw it out I may have to commit suicide.

I hope Gross is doing you some good and I hope that you have written your mother a letter telling her that you love her and that you miss her. This you may find difficult but swallow your pride. If she died today I know you would feel sorry and wish you could undo some of the harsh things you said. Remember, she's probably going through change of life, is stiff some of the time, and is none too bright to begin with. So get off that pathological horse of yours. She will be awfully happy if you write her a kind letter. You don't have to mush over her but she hasn't got too much so do this for me instead of her.

Enough of this sermonizing (sermonizing — isn't that what you have done to your car?). I am sending you a coat. Hope it's warm enough and splendid enough to suite your regal tastes.

Love and kisses,
Padre

December 23, 1949

Dear Mir:

Glad you like the coat. I sent you some money for Christmas but you forgot to mention it, or perhaps you haven't received it. One can never tell with you.

The joke thing you can do this way. Instead of getting old joke books, you listen to the show and write down hunks of it and send it to me. I will put it on file and if there's any question about this we can always show them that the stuff had been used.

Melinda has a cold. Kay I presume you know a good deal about since the other night she said to me, "Wait until you see the phone bill for December."

The Christmas thing really has me down. This is just the time of the year when I start getting presents from grown-ups. Other than my family and employees I have always thought it absurd to give presents to my friends. Unfortunately, some of them don't feel this way, which necessitates my rushing out and buying gifts in return and the whole thing is a goddamned nuisance. I wish it was Washington's Birthday because that's one day I don't have to give anybody anything, even Washington.

I have to make this brief. This is the day I record the show and I have so many things to do.

Your letter sounds fairly cheerful for you.

I hope you have a good Christmas and New Year's.

> Love and kisses from all,
> Padre

January 17, 1950

Dear Mir:

Received your copy of my script and read it all avidly. I had no idea I was that amusing.

Shufro wrote me about your tax problem. You are now in the high brackets and you have the same problems that Bobo Rockefeller, DiMaggio and Arthur Godfrey have. In case you don't know, Godfrey's salary for the year is $900,000, so you see, he makes more in one week than a United States senator gets for the whole year, and after listening to them both I am inclined to think that Godfrey is worth it.

Your letter sounded quite happy and it's a shame that you don't get more chance to see Melinda. She is now doing tap dancing of her own accord. She has been watching it very closely on television and I imagine she finally concluded if they could do it she would give it a whirl. She does some kind of an Ethiopian shuffle that slightly resembles the levee scene in *Bye-Bye Blackbird*. Who knows, she may be the next Bill Robinson. She has many outfits and I said to her this morning, "You have so many disguises I don't know what to call you." She said, "When I wear pants I am Hopalong and when I wear a dress just call me Melinda."

Getting back to the tax problem, you figure out how much you can skin the government out of on your statement and I will pay your tax. Five hundred was paid to you in 1949 at writer's fees.

Kay is slightly better but it's been quite a month. For a while she was so full of bromides, sleeping pills and assorted sedatives that she didn't have the faintest idea what she was doing or saying, but the doc-

180

tor she is now going to has apparently helped her to discard a good deal of these props.

I had two letters from Goody and I answered one of them. If you see him give him my love. I didn't want to say this in the letter but the United States mails are very severe about his kind of missives going through the post office.

Love and kisses and write when you feel like it.

Padre

Arthur Godfrey was a radio and television personality who hosted "Arthur Godfrey's Talent Scouts" from 1948 to 1958, among other shows.

January 20, 1950

Dear Mir:
Kay told me that you phoned her last night and that it was necessary for you to go to a dentist and you were reluctant to tell me.

I wish, in the future, when you have a problem you would discuss it with me directly rather than with Kay, for she is erratic enough as it is. I don't think it is wise to burden her with more than she can absorb.

You can always reach me at the Hillcrest Country Club . . . if your news is too personal for public consumption.

Love and kisses,
Padre

January 30, 1950

Dear Mir:
In the future, when sending the jokes back it isn't necessary for you to include the quizzes. In some cases it might be well if you don't include the answers of the contestants but just my questions. Don't do this with every joke but with some so it doesn't look too prepared.

I will think about the television thing. The one I have upstairs it turns out I need, but I will try to work something out. You may wind up with a one-inch set. If so I will get you one of those glasses that a watchmaker squints through.

Yesterday was a rainy Sunday and I spent it working with Bing and Charles Coburn. I have two more days of shooting but I am afraid I'm

181

going to have a good deal of rehearsing. I am doing a number with Bing with a small dance.

Other than this my life is an open book. I wrote Goody Ace and expect to hear from him some time next year.

About coming to New York: at the moment I am not up to it. Perhaps in March or April.

Why don't you tell me something about your analysis and the progress or lack of it that you are making. Pull down that Iron Curtain.

Frankly, I don't know too much about the Alger Hiss case. According to Eleanor Roosevelt in her column the other day, she thought he was getting a dirty deal, and if she thinks so I am inclined to agree with her. I don't know why they don't put Chambers in the can too. Now they're after Acheson for defending Hiss. The witch hunt gets hotter and hotter.

Must run. Love and kisses,

Padre

February 17, 1950

Dear Mir:

It was nice to speak to you and I am sorry to hear you are so homesick. Although I have been toying with the idea of going to New York I have shied away from it for a number of reasons. Since I spoke to you, however, I have definitely made a commitment. It means a great deal of additional work and, frankly, physically I don't feel up to it, but I will do it anyway.

I am planning to leave around the middle of April and I will have to do two extra shows before I go and I must say that I dread going east. Unfortunately I have no buffer between me and the public and I get the goddamndest collection of requests, phone calls, nuisances and jerks. In addition, there are people I want to see—Kaufman, Goody Ace, Jerry Chodorov and, most of all, you.

I don't know whether you have seen *South Pacific*. If you write me a list of the shows you haven't seen, or care to see, I will buy three seats for these shows instead of two.

I am going to try to be there [in] about two weeks. I chose the middle of April because, by an odd coincidence, the ball teams are in full swing by that time.

This can't be a letter because I have too much piled up at the moment. I contemplate writing you next Tuesday and maybe by that time I will have heard from you.

Stiff upper lip, watch your love life, and all my love.

Padre

February 24, 1950

Dear Mir:

Don't worry about the dentist. When you are through with Weinberger let me know and I'll send him $175. There's an old Jewish saying which goes, "So machula, so machula." If you don't meet any Jews and should encounter any Russians (White ones, of course) you might throw this one at them. This is courtesy of Sara Roberts, the demon secretary. "Payem resh, ne payem resh, lutcha pitta."

Unless I drop dead, I am definitely coming to New York the middle of April. I will go by train, for Kay is afraid to fly and I am afraid to leave her alone on the train. She might marry the engineer, elope with the brakeman or jump out of the window. However, coming back I will take pot luck on Kay and let her return alone. She says she is only going for a week. I plan on spending two weeks there and she said she doesn't think she can remain that long away from the analyst. I don't know whether it's ever occurred to you, but I am probably the only eccentric comedian in the United States with an analyst on both coasts. This is a distinction I never thought I would achieve.

I don't think I told you that Arthur was working. He's doing a Blondie at Columbia. I once did a Blondie at Columbia but I wasn't working. By this time I think they've made about fifty Blondie pictures. She must be pretty gray by this time.

Love and kisses and don't worry. The H-bomb is just around the corner.

Padre

March 1, 1950

Dear Mir:

I am flying to Phoenix Friday with Krasna, the boy writer. Pretty soon we will have to stop describing Norman as the boy writer. I think he's forty now and almost as bald as Dudley Field Malone, who was formerly Collector of the Port of New York and who, if I am not mistaken, shuffled off some months ago.

I haven't had a vacation since *Time for Elizabeth* and that was a mighty fine vacation — sequestered in a small inside hotel room, reading those reviews and wishing I had taken up some pleasant vocation like cleaning out sewers.

I will be gone five days. Originally we were going to Palm Springs but it takes four hours to drive there and one can fly to Phoenix in an hour and forty minutes. Plus this, the New York Giants are spring training at Phoenix and mornings will be spent watching them, while the afternoons will be given over to looking for a small white ball in the rough.

I was happy to read you have become such an efficient hostess, housewife and cook, for some day, who knows, you may make some young fellow a fine helpmate. (Hey, what gives?)

I have taken note of the shows you want to see and there's a couple on there you might have to see without me. I will only have about twelve nights and I may skip *Kiss Me Kate* and the Lunt play.

I am late as usual. I saw the Jerry Chodorovs last night and Reba wondered why you never get together with her. I told her you were reluctant to force yourself on your father's friends. She said they liked you for what you are and would like to hear from you. They will be here for a month. And that's that.

Love and kisses and will write you when I return from Phoenix.

Padre

March 17, 1950

Dear Mir:

I don't hear from you any more so apparently you have another father in the east.

My plans are still to come to the Waldorf in the middle of April. Will let you know definitely just when I arrive so that you can roll out the red carpet at either the airport or the railroad depot. Kay doesn't want to fly but will if I definitely decide to go that way. Every time I contemplate taking the train I start thinking of those three nights in the berth and the change at Chicago and I lose my enthusiasm for railroading. Anyway, we are getting two bedrooms at the Waldorf, courtesy of CBS, so for two weeks you can sleep with Kay and compare analysts. I told someone that I was rather proud of the fact that

I was the only man I knew who had an analyst on both coasts. That is real wealth.

Phil Silvers is flying to New York tonight to see his friend Sinatra open at the Copa. If you want me to I will have him ring you. I frequently have people going to New York and I don't know how you feel about these ad lib phone calls.

There isn't much news to relate. We still have halibut on Fridays with stewed tomatoes. I go to bed early trying to figure out how to skin the stock market. (Shufro is here at the moment giving me his 1950 brand of double talk. He said he saw you in New York and that you seemed in good spirits.)

Arthur is still on the Blondie picture. Frace is in Mexico. Chico is in Vancouver. Kay is at the analyst and I am on my way to Hillcrest where we will discuss one of three subjects: sex, Milton Berle or Wall Street. The whole thing is beginning to smell like 1929, at which time, fortunately for you, you were babbling in your crib.

Love and kisses,
Padre

P.S. The current issue of *Look* magazine (March twenty-eighth) has the life of Groucho Marx, which I presume you are fairly familiar with.

April 5, 1950

Dear Mir:

There's a song in the Bing Crosby picture called "Life Is So Peculiar." Well, I never thought two weeks ago that Norman and I would both be getting divorces. I was going to delay telling you about mine until I saw you, but Kay being a woman couldn't wait to apprise you. I feel very sad about it but there isn't much choice. Kay wants it. Her analyst told me that the only way she could possibly become an adult was to be on her own. What she says she wants is a little apartment where she can do her own cooking and not entertain friends, nor go to any of their houses. I don't believe we had too much social life but apparently this is a psychological strain on her that I don't quite understand. She is going to have Virginia and the baby with her, which is the way I want it. I couldn't stand her being alone. It would worry me too much. She has given me many scary nights in recent months. . . . I suppose if I were a young man I could survive these brainstorms, but I am fifty-nine and one doesn't bounce back so quickly at that age.

I am in a nervous business—radio. I live by my wits and if I lose those I will have no job or income. I know she loves me, but we have no other choice. My life seems to be made up of a series of schlimazels. When I think of dissolving the family and living separately I get pretty blue. But then I think of Kurt Weill who died yesterday at the age of fifty and I try to adopt a more philosophical attitude. The nights are tough with this thing facing me.

I am really not in very good shape to undertake the New York ordeal but I am going. CBS is paying my expenses and they are really laying the interviews on me. I think they've lined up ten for me for the first ten days. At each of these I am supposed to be witty, charming, debonair and hilarious. I doubt if I make any one of the four.

I arrive Friday night, the fourteenth. If you want to come to the airport do so, otherwise I will meet you at the Waldorf, or I will see you Saturday, whichever you prefer.

Don't worry. Everything will turn out all right. Remember, every day is velvet that doesn't see the hydrogen bomb.

Love and Kisses,
Groucho

May 16, 1950

Dear Mir:
I can't seem to find time for correspondence. Either that or I am too damned lazy.

You damned near broke me in New York, but in spite of that I am sending you fifty bucks for perfume, or chicken salad or Mother Sells Sea Sick Remedy, in case you cruise around the world.

Kay seems to be in fine shape. She cooks almost every night, and good (that goes for your cooking too). She is still going to the doctor and whether it's doing her any good I don't know. At any rate, I don't think it's doing her any harm. I don't know how long the novelty of doing her own washing, cooking and cleaning will continue but at the moment she is contented. I miss the noise in the house of those tiny feet pattering up and down stairs, but I certainly don't miss the quarrels, discord and friction that constantly existed. We are very friendly and lovey-dovey but it just didn't work out. I hope you have written her or will write her. Things do change. Her last month in the house, the phone bill was $121. She showed me the phone bill for the first two weeks she's been living in the apartment and it was $2.30. It makes a difference, I guess, whose money you are spending. Well, I'll be careful but I don't expect to get married again for another three months.

I am taking your small sister to lunch and am enclosing a couple of things that she struck off. These will never put Van Gogh out of business but he's dead anyway.

The Goody Ace thing is too bad. I would have liked to have him for a son-in-law. Had a letter from him as I stepped off the plane but I just haven't gotten around to answering it.

Love and kisses. Happy Birthday, and don't get any older; you will only regret it.

Padre

May 25, 1950

Dear Mir:
Just a line to send you a couple of amusing lines from the *Atlantic Monthly*.

I got a brief letter from Betty Forsling but haven't gotten around to miscellaneous correspondence.

I was in Las Vegas for a few days, contracted a deep cough and decided to come home and go to bed. I am just now recovering, fortunately, for tonight I have to do a show.

Mrs. Arthur Murray, alone and sequestered at the Beverly-Wilshire Hotel, phoned me to have dinner with her. As soon as I discovered that it was she on the phone I put on a coughing fit that hasn't been equalled since the early days of tuberculosis. Had it been Jane instead of her old lady, I would have been there before the receiver was hung up.

I am taking your little sister to lunch and to the park. I miss seeing her as often as I used to. On the other hand, it's mighty restful going to bed at night and being assured that Kay isn't going to start tossing the lamps through the corridor. She seems quite happy and apparently that is one of my chief concerns. If she gets along all right I will manage very well. And God, but it's restful.

I hope you are enjoying the Yankees' thin lead, which I predict will melt before the season is over.

All my love, and regards to your girlfriend and your boyfriend.

Padre

June 1, 1950

Dear Mir:
I received the piece from *Mademoiselle* and it was very good. Also your mother's letter, which I read and I don't know what her finances or resources are any more but the hell with it. You go ahead to your analyst and I will pay the additional money.

I must say you have been very lax in sending me the material from the show which I was supposed to receive every week and which I haven't received now in over a month. I am not going to lecture you about this, but reciprocity is a two-way street and I hope I don't have to talk to you about this again.

I have been much upset recently, emotionally, and I have a show tonight so this accounts for the brevity and perhaps for a little of the terseness.

Dick was over to dinner the other night and packed away a very substantial meal. He's a nice boy and I am confident he will be a success at whatever he tackles.

Love and kisses,
Padre

June 27, 1950

Dear Mir:
Thanks for the Father's Day wire, the piece by Arthur Miller and the memories. Also the bill from Dr. Weingarten.

Had a postal from Comen, your dentist friend, warning that he was descending on you (in a nice way of course). The whole thing was a little mystifying. . . .

You are going to have to give me a definite date when you are going to be here and how long you intend staying so I can adjust my plans accordingly. I contemplate going away for a week or two with Melinda and naturally I don't want to be gone while you are here.

I am going to be on television this fall and because of that I am going to have to start recording and filming much earlier than I formerly would were I just on radio, so my vacation will be a very brief one, much briefer than I hoped for. I am good and tired. Between the trip to New York, the interviews, the divorce and the negotiations with NBC, I've had a very arduous and nerve-wracking year and I could use a few weeks to unwind. This is extremely difficult because there are so many new problems in connection with television that have to be talked out and over.

Lest you get the impression that I am dying, I want you to know that Krasna and I are taking two beautiful babes to an opening at the Biltmore tonight so please disregard everything else that I've said. Krasna and I are going very steady and I told him that if we ever got married and weren't happy at least when we split we could each keep our own money.

I really shouldn't write you at all. You send me the garbage from the show without even a six-line note and it's pretty revealing.

Please don't ignore the information I am asking for about your arrival — if and when.

Love and kisses,
Padre

"I am going to be on television this fall" refers to the debut of "You Bet Your Life" on television.

August 8, 1950

Dear Mir:
Received your letter and contents barely noted.

I just returned from seven strenuous days at Alisal Ranch. I rode, swam ate and dressed and undressed Melinda eleven times a day. This included strapping on a life preserver that had six straps on it. It was a lot of fun, wonderful experience and all I need now is two or three weeks in a quiet sanitorium.

I don't quite understand your sudden resolve to move back to the coast. Not that I don't want you out here, but you seemed so conditioned to a metropolitan existence and the excitement of working on a magazine. But I suppose there are other motives that you haven't disclosed, at any rate to me. I would like to know, however, just how serious your intentions are with Dr. Comen. I have been going to the same dentist for fifteen years and it's a radical change for me to switch to a comparative tyro after so many years of satisfactory treatment. As you know, this involves putting a new cap on one of my front teeth and unless I am certain that eventually he will be my son-in-law and that he will be supporting you, I will stick with Schnaidt. So if he sets his cap for you he can set a cap for me. This is not much of a joke but it's a very hot day and with the taxes increasing all the time I can't afford to be too funny.

I am delighted to see the Yankees getting the hell knocked out of them although I am saddened at DiMaggio's decline. It is always sad when a great figure slips into the shadows, but thirty-six is a ripe old age for a ball player and he has had a wonderful career. My guess is he will make a fine manager some day.

Kay is pretty angry at you for taking her coat and not returning it and I think it would be a nice gesture if on receipt of this letter you would wrap it up immediately and send it back to her.

I would also like our front door key unless you have sold it or given it to Stuart. I must say, shyness or no, I have rarely had a guest in my house as chary with his thanks as your friend Stuart. My guess is he is a fairly thrifty fellow and if he ever gets into dough could conceivably wind up as the richest man in the world.

Love and kisses, and let me hear of your plans.

Padre

My motive for returning to California was that my drinking was becoming worse and I hoped (erroneously) that a change of scene would help. I moved to the Los Angeles area, where I worked as the tape editor for "You Bet Your Life," which is why only a postcard from New York follows for the next three years.

May 7, 1951 [postcard]

Dear Mir:
New York is lovely and I am enjoying it. Brief moments of glory and being a big shot—ego lifters. . . . I love you quite a while.

Padre

February 5, 1953

Dear Mir:
I haven't written you because I wanted to give you a chance to adjust yourself to your new life and surroundings.

Arthur was much impressed with the place and seems very optimistic about you and the institution. He told me he didn't see much of you in Topeka, but that's the way they wanted it—so I had very little news about you. He's doing a piece on the place for *Collier's*. He's also doing a piece on Pancho Gonzales, the tennis player. I hope he doesn't get them mixed up. It could be quite confusing.

Last night a windstorm blew into town and has blown practically everything from its natural direction. One of the things it blew down is the power lines leading into my house. This merely means that the meat is rotting in the deep freeze, I am unable to see Mama Weiss and Spade Cooley on the TV set, I have to go to a barbershop to get shaved and I don't know what time it is. It's not too bad today, but last night leaving the house in Stygian darkness was a little eerie. Have you ever tried reading Shakespeare's sonnets by the light of a plumber's candle?

Our new cook, Gertrude, seems very nice but last night was the first night she spent there. There were all kinds of strange noises on the roof, probably from loose tiles and stray branches. This morning she asked me if the house was haunted.

Other than this, the show wends its way slowly toward its thirty-ninth week.

I am leaving on Tuesday for Las Vegas. Eden has developed a system that she claims will break all the gambling houses. I am equipping her with ten dollars each night. She says this is all she needs. Well, if it wasn't for the Edens Las Vegas would fold up and the whole state would become a giant dust bowl.

Don't feel obliged to write. I would like to hear from you, but not if it's a chore.

We all send our love—and don't worry about anything.

Padre

My drinking had finally gotten so bad that I had been admitted to the Menninger Clinic in Topeka, Kansas. A good friend of mine had recommended it. Eden was Eden Hartford, who eventually became Groucho's third wife.

[Hotel Sahara, Las Vegas, February, 1953]

Dear Mir;

As you will see by the stationery, I am sequestered at the above hostelry, and it's very pleasant. It's one of the newer gambling halls, and it's beautifully done in modern motif.

All these places look alike in regards to the gambling equipment. They all have faro roulette, crap and twenty-one tables, and they all have four or five owners, who prowl around tirelessly watching each other in addition to the customers. The players are a nondescript looking lot, ranging from well dressed to early Arkansas, and most of them sit expressionless as their chips gradually disappear and veer over to the dealer.

[Gambling is] a fascination that fortunately I have never acquired

191

or been afflicted with, and I am rather happy about it. Gambling too is a sickness, and people like Chico and Zeppo have to remain away from these places, lest they get ruined. Unfortunately, as far as Chico is concerned, it's too late, the boat's gone, and all they could now get from him would be his trousers.

I drove up from Beverly and among other things brought two bathing trunks. I would have been much smarter if I had brought two overcoats and earmuffs. It's really not that bad but it's not the weather for water sports.

There are seven major hotels and each one has a vast dining room and floor show. This is the come-on for the gambling. The floor shows this week probably house some of the most distasteful talent in the history of show business. I have a particular allergy to French singers, and at the moment there is in Las Vegas Hildegarde, Edith Piaf and to top it all one place has nine Frenchmen who sing with unified motions most of the songs that Piaf and Hildegarde are murdering at the other joints. Another place has a singer who resembles Bill Perlberg. His name is Alan Dale, nice voice but insists on singing "Laugh Clown Laugh" in a high treble that makes the filet mignons shake on the dinner table. Another club has Dorothy Lamour who does an act lauding Hawaii and the South Seas; for this she wears a short abbreviated costume that displays the thickest set of thighs this side of the giant sequoias in upper California.

This sounds as though I was having a miserable time. As a matter of fact I am enjoying it. Each night I take Eden to one of the night clubs. So far I've seen Alan Dale, Edith Piaf and Hildegarde, and I'm going to see all of them and then I'll never have to see one of these goddamned acts again. Well, it's a change from the regular routine and that's important.

I have avoided asking you any questions about your life in Topeka, not that I'm not interested in it, but that's your job. I tell you about Las Vegas and you tell me about Menninger. I hope you are faring well and not too unhappy. Eden sends regards and I my love.

Yours,
Padre XXXXXXXX

February 19, 1953

Dear Mir:

Thanks for the Valentine card. I thought that was it and today your letter came and it was cheerful, ebullient and optimistic—fine name for a vaudeville act. The trouble with these acts is that one of the trio is usually good and the other two are lousy, so if you ever get a chance to join up with an act of this kind run for your life.

I am sending you a group of books—not for their high literary value, but mostly because they are paperback and cheaper to ship that way. But seriously, folks, it's quite difficult to send books to one undergoing psychiatric treatment because there's no telling what story might hit you the wrong way and do you untold damage.

When you complete this batch, return them and I will send you some Benchley, Perelman and Lardner. I am surprised that you are surprised at Benchley's ability to amuse you. Benchley was one of the great ones. He musn't be read too steadily—no one must who writes in that particular style. This goes for Perelman, Don Stewart or any of the others. Lardner is something else again because a good deal of his comedy is savage attacks on the American scene. So read Benchley in short doses and I am sure you will get a big kick out of him.

I had a surprisingly good time in Las Vegas. To begin with, it was practically all free which always helps. I went to seven night-clubs in seven nights—a world's record. However, these were night-clubs where I would arrive at seven o'clock for dinner, the show would start at 8:30, run an hour, and at 9:30 I would leave. Eden would then go to the roulette table and I would go to my room. I equipped her with ten dollars a day. This was the whole purpose of the trip. She had a scheme, she told me, that was surefire. It was pretty involved and I am sure she didn't understand it herself. However, to keep you at the gaming table they supply you with free drinks. So in a very short time Eden would be half loaded and this intricate, involved scheme to bankrupt Las Vegas would become even more involved and by 10:30 she would be in my room flush with failure. On the trip back she finally confessed that perhaps her plan needed some revising. She lost seventy bucks on the trip but she had a hell of a time.

However, the trip wasn't all fun, for on succeeding nights I had to watch Ethel Waters, Edith Piaf, Hildegarde and many others who unquestionably have talent but not the kind I want to watch. However, the food was good and the air was clean, and so was most of the crowd by the end of the week. These places [casinos] are fantastic. They cost four and five million dollars apiece. There are eight of them, each one

193

more lavish than the other, and I was told on fairly good authority that in three years most of these places bring back their original investment.

Eden's sister finally hooked Howard Hawkes and they are getting married Friday, which is why I had to return to Beverly. Eden is the bridesmaid and I am staying over on one side. Melinda put in a bid to be the flower girl but I don't think it's going to be that kind of lavish affair. However, I will submit her name and see whether they are interested.

Well—I think this gives you a fairly comprehensive picture of my journey to the home of the schnook. As always, I was glad to get back home. I brought Melinda a pair of blue pants, some marbles and a small doll which she immediately ripped to shreds. I caught her in the bathroom clipping some of the hair off. She said it was all the style now—short hair.

All the people at the Guedel office send their love to you and hope to see you soon again, and so does the man who wrote this letter—your ever loving Padre,

Julius H. Marx.

March 10, 1953

Dear Mir:

I don't write you often for the same reason you don't write me. They are arduous jobs and there is very little to relate that you are not familiar with.

This is a busy week for me. A show last night—which included the sister of Pedro Gonzales and she was quite cute. Tonight is the Screenwriters' Guild affair. This is the only one of the shindigs that I attend. The actors usually have one and the directors have one, but they are usually dull and that goes for most dinners, including the dinner. The Writers' Guild usually has good sketches, including the one I did with Krasna and Wald two years ago. Time sure does fly, as your mother's mother used to say.

I am going to Phoenix on the twenty-third of March. By an odd coincidence the New York Giants will be there. I plan on staying a week, or until the Giants win a game. I am gradually easing my way into baseball. Bob Cobb, president of the Hollywood Stars, called me the other night, heard I was going to Phoenix, heard too I was a friend of Durocher's (whom, incidentally, I know only casually) and said they are in desperate need of a shortstop and catcher and would I try and wangle these from Durocher. From here it's just a step to owning the Giants and then, who knows, the Yankees. If I did own them it would be the only case on record of an owner rooting for his team to lose.

In addition to the letter you sent me, I also read your letter to Arthur and Irene and from what we gather, you seem to be coming along.

I won't write more as I have a 1:30 appointment and it's now 12:30.

Love and kisses.

Hope you are enjoying the wilds of Kansas.

Yours,
Padre

March 21, 1953

Dear Miriam:

Your well-written and comprehensive letter was received a few days ago, and I would have answered sooner had I not been laid up with a cold. As a matter of fact, this letter is being dictated while in bed.

I also had a long letter from Dr. Fleming. I don't know whether he showed it to you, but it was quite clear what he thinks should be done. It is quite a program. If I didn't care about you, I would say the hell with the whole thing and let you shift for yourself, but plus my affection for you, I sincerely believe you are worth rehabilitating. And therefore am willing to go along with the suggestions that have been presented.

As you say, this is an enormously expensive adventure, and I can only add that I hope it will be done as economically as possible, considering the circumstances.

To be specific, Dr. Fleming recommends that you remain in the hospital for five or six months, receiving during this time whatever analytical treatment is necessary. After that, he suggests you get accommodations in town, and perhaps a job. As you say, it's not particularly pleasant contemplating two years in Topeka. Many years ago I once played there for three days, and by the end of the third day I was ready to concede that life in New York or Paris could be more satisfying. I also don't relish the idea of not seeing you for such long stretches, but I'll manage to get to Topeka during that time, one way or another.

I have to regard your absence with the same sort of objectivity as though I were a parent whose child had been sent to Korea. This, too, is a kind of war, and the results are just as important to me.

You further say that I don't think much of analysis. Frankly, if I were to base my appraisal of analysis on the results that have been achieved by you and my ex-wife, I would not only have not sent you to Menninger's, but I wouldn't even send you to Glendale. But I know too many people who have been helped by the couch and confession, and I have every confidence that Menninger's in time will do as much for you.

In the near future there are certain questions that will have to be answered. For example, what do you want done with your furniture down at Sandy's? And what disposition are you going to make of your agreement with Sandy about the house itself? Perhaps your furniture should be sent to Bekins or some other warehouse until you return.

Shufro, who is at my house at present, suggests that you sell your car and set aside the money. Allowing the car to rust for two years would make it worthless. At the moment, I'm not up to writing two letters, so you might show this letter to Dr. Fleming. We all miss you and love you, and one of these days we'll all be back together again in the billiard room, shooting an extremely bad game of pool.

I don't know whether it is feasible in your present state of mind, but you write so well that perhaps you should try a story or an article or something.

One other thing and I'll quit. You seem to have some sort of guilt complex about having been in my employ under the sheltering wing of nepotism. This is far from the truth. Your job is an important one, as evidenced by the fact that since you left we have had to engage someone else for it.

I will be at the Arizona Manor in Phoenix from the twenty-third of March until the thirtieth, health permitting. I am going there principally to try to whip the Giants into shape for Durocher. If Willie Mays doesn't return, there is some talk of me being used in center field.

Tell Dr. Fleming I will try to write him next week, but you can warn him that what he receives will be more or less a replica of this letter, except of course, without the love and kisses from,

Padre

April 14, 1953

Dear Mir:

I just returned from Palm Springs with Eden and Melinda. The weather was nice and for the first time in many years I was back on a horse. Both Eden and Melinda also rode. Eden's horsemanship resembles your mother's in the old days — she does it, but she's pretty scared and can't wait until the whole thing is over. I stopped at Harpo's house and was so tired swatting flies in the living room that I had no strength left for golf, which is just as well the way I play.

We'll skip the car problem. I have it under a canvas and it can stay there until you need it.

Melinda liked the Easter bags very much and took the red one to Palm Springs with her. She had quite a time down there. Since I had no baby-sitter and Eden wanted to see Harry Richman, who is re-telling a series of old songs and older jokes at the Chi Chi, I took her along with us. This was her first visit to a night-club and I must say that despite my fears that she would get sleepy around ten, she was more wide awake at 11:30 than I was. She likes the night life and I may take her with me whenever I go out in the evening. Her mother is just as daffy as ever and awakened me the other morning at six to reveal the startling news that she had had a quarrel with her current boyfriend. It seems that when she is out with these various Romeos she talks about me (something she rarely did when we were married). She says that the boyfriends resent this and don't take her out again. So I said, "Kay, why do you bother me with this at six in the morning?" Her answer will live for quite some time. She said, "Well, it concerned you and I thought you ought to know."

It's true what you write about me seeming insincere in the commercials. Actually I am, but they feel that it has an extra value over Fenneman's mouthing this drivel so I am obliged to do it. I do it willingly but badly and, as you say, I guess it's pretty evident on the screen.

All of your paraphernalia and belongings are now stashed away in my garage and from the amount of space that it occupies you apparently have more possessions than you realize. This is not always an asset because possessions can become quite burdensome, but it's not nearly as annoying as having to buy them over again.

It was nice of Ruby to write you and I trust you will answer him within a reasonable length of time. He's a very busy man — I don't mean that he's working, but the Copper Room is closed down for repairs and he spends a good deal of time pacing up and down waiting for it to reopen.

197

Mr. Krasna, an ex-boyfriend of yours, assisted his wife and a brace of expensive obstetricians in foisting a new child on this world one day last week. Her name is Bess Krasna — by an odd coincidence the name of the horse I rode in Palm Springs.

I hope you are well and improving those shining hours in Topeka. Don't feel obliged to write any more often than you get the urge.

We all send our love and one of these days I'll see you.

Padre

Fenneman was George Fenneman, the announcer and straight man on "You Bet Your Life." The commercials were for DeSoto, who sponsored the show.

April 30, 1953

Dear Mir:

Received your letter and enclosures, and note what you say about Kay. Your analysis was very accurate. There was nothing wrong with me. She probably got soused and decided she ought to call someone. I once received a letter from Dr. Fleming in which he said that each one [Menninger patient] was charged according to their own income. Perhaps you could explain to them what Kay's income is and how much of it she could safely spend for medical treatment, and perhaps they would be willing to accept her on that basis. I haven't discussed this with her and wouldn't until I heard from you. Another thing: I am not sure that you and Kay are good for each other, but that is something we could discuss at a later date. I certainly agree with you that she is in a worse state now than she was five years ago. She still goes with that broken down actor. He too at present is going to an analyst, one time I believe because I don't think he has more than four dollars in the world. Every other day she phones me and tells me that they are through, but I am convinced that Kay doesn't know what the hell she is talking about anymore. As you point out, it's not a particularly healthy climate for Melinda and don't think I haven't given this much thought.

The DeSoto people have picked up the show for the coming year. This will also include thirteen reruns of old shows for the summer. The last part isn't definite yet for there is some difference of opinion involving the money. However, I do think this will be straightened out. The fact of the matter is that we have outgrown the DeSoto company just as we did the Elgin-American Company. They are not big enough to accommodate the increased sales that we are responsible

198

for, and though we have found them very cooperative and pleasant to work for, we were hoping that they would drop the show and let us go for Lucky Strike. I never thought I would arrive at the time when I would be rooting to get away from a sponsor, but strange things are happening in the amusement world.

There is a likelihood that I will go to New York at the conclusion of my season. If this eventuates, I will stop off a day in Topeka.

From the brochure you sent me you evidently are having gay times in the wards. I will think about the taping of those ancient ditties. Speaking of music, Dick Comen was over last week and absconded with a good many of your recordings. This, I presume, was with your permission. According to Dick, the girl he was about to marry has now departed from his life and like the rest of the world he is now going to an analyst. You may have to marry him eventually, if only to get your records back.

Krasna is now a father — this time by his own efforts. The baby is very pretty, which convinces me that there must have been another man involved. Erle is bent on having a whole slew of them now, and this lone wolf who preyed on the town with considerable success may wind up with a family as large as Eddie Foy, Sr.'s.

I can't write more as I am late for an appointment.

Love from me and all the rest and don't take so long in answering. And I may see you in a month or so.

Padre

P.S. I will send on the books you requested as soon as you return the ones I sent you.

He says Krasna became a father "by his own efforts" because Krasna already had two adopted children from his previous marriage. Eddie Foy, Sr., had a vaudeville act in the early 1900s called "Eddie Foy and the Seven Little Foys" starring himself and his seven children.

May 7, 1953

Dear Miriam:
I wrote you last week and haven't heard from you since.

I will arrive in Topeka on the eighteenth of May at 5:45 P.M. . . . and I plan on spending the balance of that day, and the nineteenth, and will leave for New York at 1:30 P.M. on the twentieth. I am finishing up the season next week and must say that the year certainly flew.

199

I haven't discussed anything with Kay about her future destiny. I wanted to hear what the Institute had to say about it first. I am not sure whether she would even be willing to consider such a move but, as I wrote you before, unless some financial arrangement could be made that would be practical for her there wouldn't be any point in bringing it up.

The weather got real hot this week and I have been using the swimming pool. I had no idea I swam so badly. My strokes resemble my golf strokes. Sorry you are not able to use it, but the pool will be there for a long time—unless we have a drought.

Tell Dr. Fleming I received his report on you and I found it quite encouraging.

I won't write any more for I have so many letters to answer. Love and kisses and at least we will spend your birthday together.

Padre

[Hampshire House, New York City, May 22, 1953]

Dear Miriam,
As you can see, I arrived safe and sound, although weary. I was much encouraged by your appearance and behavior, and I feel confident that you are going to emerge from there a real woman, able to cope with the world.

As I told you, I was much impressed with the place, Dr. Fleming and the woman who was present at our interview, I forget her name. I was glad I made the trip, arduous though it was. It was good to see your smiling face, and also the Topeka ball club.

I damn near threw up from the french fried potatoes in the little plane—it was bumpy and hot. But after taking fourteen Tums (all they had in the Kansas City Airport), I finally recovered, and arrived in New York sound in limb.

Write me to the Hampshire House. Eden sends regards.
Love,
Padre XXXXXXXX

[June 7, 1953]

Dear Mir;
This will be a hash of misspelling and errors. I haven't written a letter in months and I am as rusty as the St. Louis Browns, whatever that

200

means. At any rate it's Sunday morning June seventh or thereabouts, and raining, and this is unheard of this late in the season, and it just goes to prove that the whole world is mixed up, and the baseball season is no exception.

We arrived home a few days ago, exhausted. It's a strenuous schedule for a man of my years, a show every night, and frequently a ball game in the afternoon. Plus lunch and dinner dates almost every day. I had a good time, but it would be far more enjoyable if I could have had it in smaller doses. Saw a lot of Goody. He now hates [Milton] Berle with the same fervor that he expended last year on Tallulah [Bankhead], and next year if he works for Dennis Day, his hatred will veer in that direction. He carefully wrote down your address and promised that he would write you, and I am sure that's the last you will ever hear about it. Jane is just as jerky as ever. Her conversation is now a steady whine, usually about her troubles with her chauffeur—these men last about a week apiece. If in addition to this the Yankees lose a game, all hell breaks loose. She hasn't the faintest idea of baseball, but it's all she has, she hasn't got Goody, or the dog (he died last year), she has no housework, no occupation, just the Yankees. Actually I like her, although she frequently irritates me, however, if I were married to her I would murder her some night, probably with a baseball bat.

Kay, if you don't know, has moved again, somewhere on Wilshire Boulevard, a new apartment, a novelty that will soon wear off, but for the moment something to occupy her. I never mentioned the idea of her going to Menninger's, first because I don't think it would be good for you, and then whether it could be worked out with the income she has. As far as going to a place out here, I don't know of any that are worth a damn, so she still goes to Spira. I don't know whether she is drinking or not. I have many other problems, and I divorced Kay so that I could get away from her and the complications that were constantly arising.

I am sending you some books that were lying around the house. Some of them are good, some are worthless. I like the Hellinger book very much, and I think you too will get a kick out of it. When you are through with them, donate them to the Menninger library, and also the other books you have of mine.

I am going to the Cedars of Lebanon [Cedars-Sinai Hospital] Tuesday for an operation that is almost inevitable when a man arrives at my age. It is known as polyps on the prostatic gland (sounds like an

English watering resort). It isn't serious, but necessary, and I will hole up there for about five days. I wasn't going to tell you at all, but you might find out some other way, and this will keep you from worrying.

I hope you are well and happy. As I wrote you, I thought they had done a great job on you up to now, and if the improvement continues, I think you will soon be well along the way to complete recovery.

Love from all, and write when you feel in the mood.

Padre XXXX

June 25, 1953

Dear Mir:

I won't write much for I am not up to any great literary effort.

I read the weather reports in the middle west and you certainly have my sympathy. It's really the frying pan of America. And even when I was there, although it was only around eighty or eighty-five, I was dragging my feet. Well, you're young and I suppose it doesn't bother you too much.

I am recovering slowly and I presume in time I will be up to my old self (a ghastly prospect to look forward to).

I must say the show that most impressed me in New York was *Porgy and Bess* so I decided to go whole hog and send you the recordings. They are just great. It may be necessary, at first, to listen to them and read the libretto simultaneously. Until you are familiar with it I don't think it will make much sense.

I am also enclosing a discouraging column, for me that is, by Al Wolf of the *Los Angeles Times*. Even though you are rooting for the Yankees, the biggest trust since U.S. Steel, I hope you have enough decency to root for the Milwaukee Braves, who may eventually turn out to be the new whiz kids.

Tomorrow Andy is two years old. I discussed it with him. He didn't seem to be much interested in it one way or another. He certainly takes the added years with good grace. Well, some people are philosophical and some are not.

I am enclosing a column from the *New York Tribune*. No particular reason except that I like the subject matter and the way this man writes.

I won't write any more for I got a lot of mail while in the hospital, mostly from stangers, but they all have to be acknowledged. That's the kind of a guy I am.

202

Love from all, and write when you are in the mood.

Padre

Andy was Arthur and Irene's second child.

August 10, 1953

Dear Miriam:

The reason you haven't heard from me is because I have been too damned angry to write. The day I wrote a check for sixteen hundred and some dollars to Menninger's, which I have been doing for six months, I also received word that you were drinking again. As I wrote Dr. Fleming, it costs $20,000 a year to send you to this clinic. In my tax bracket this is approximately what remains after a year's work, and I have no intention of continuing this unless there is a drastic change not only in your behavior, but, what is more important, in your attitude toward this entire treatment.

You are not a novice anymore at the business of analysis. You have had approximately five years of it and you must realize that I cannot continue this indefinitely. As I wrote Dr. Fleming, I have many other obligations and anxieties. I remember Bennington and the various Katzenjammers you were involved in up there. I wasn't too disturbed then for after all that was college, and though you were whooping it up and having a hell of a time, I always thought you would eventually snap out of it.

I also notice in your letter, I quote, "I have been learning for the past six months and will be learning for the next two years how to live again." I hope you are not under the delusion that I contemplate keeping you there for an additional two years.

I am talking straight from the shoulder, bluntly and with anger. I hope this clarifies my attitude and the infrequency of my letters.

You say there aren't enough words to tell me how you appreciate what I have done for you. Words are very easy and in most cases mean nothing. I can only be convinced by your behavior.

And, Miriam, in the future when you are disturbed about something in our relationship, I certainly have no objection to your calling your mother, but it seems to me you should also communicate with me.

Kay's birthday is August twenty-ninth, and Melinda's is August fourteenth.

Thanks for the pictures.

Love from all,
Padre

August 27, 1953

Dear Miriam:

Your letter of August twenty-second received. I will get right to the point and try to explain some things that may not be quite clear to you.

At the rate we are going, I am spending around $20,000 a year at Menninger's. In my tax bracket this is about what I net. I think I have written you this before. I only re-emphasize it to acquaint you with the facts.

As I wrote you before, this present setup cannot continue. The fact that you might get a job in town for $40 or $50 a week, or $200 a month, would not make much of a dent in what I am paying. The $750 a month hospital fee is the item that must be eliminated in the near future. With this accomplished, and your having a job in town, the burden will be light enough to enable me to pay the cost of your analysis and what other slight expenses there might be. But the present bill is prohibitive and cannot be maintained much longer.

I realize that you have many problems. So do the boys in Korea who have had parts of their bodies shot away. I also realize that alcoholism is a sickness, a sickness that will require all your self-determination and willpower to conquer. But, as I wrote you before, I will not tolerate any Bennington attitude. If the drinking continues I will discontinue sending you any money and you will have to work out your own solution.

I have many other problems, in addition to yours. Despite the fact that Kay is divorced from me, she is still a problem because of Melinda. Melinda, too, has many problems that I have to absorb. There is also Chico, and my professional business. It's a nerve-wracking profession at best. I sleep badly because I am invariably tense and on edge from the many demands that are made upon my nervous system.

In a way, I presume this is a duplication of a previous letter I wrote you, and I only repeat these things to make you realize the importance you must assume in straightening yourself out.

I just got through reading excerpts of the Kinsey report and the only

204

conclusion I have come to is that men are imbecilic and women live forever. It was quite disheartening to read that men's sex urge is on the downgrade at the age of twenty, whereas one woman was still indulging in a love life at the age of ninety-one.

Santa Barbara society is giving a grand ball tomorrow night in which all the males are coming as Groucho Marx and all the women as Carmen Miranda. After considerable persuasion and pressure from many sources I finally consented to be a surprise guest, and later in the evening, when most of the participants are stewed, I will make an entrance and probably be lynched. The principal reason I am going is because they volunteered to give me a bungalow at the Miramar (I turned down their suggestion to live at the home of one of the socially elite) so Melinda will have a good time swimming and I will spend most of my time hiding.

Best from Eden and love from Melinda and me, and write soon.

Padre

P.S. Thanks for the ashtray. A real professional job.

September 22, 1953

Dear Mir:

By this time you should know me well enough to know that if Max Falkenstein, who apparently is a Jew, should confront me about your past or your future, I doubt very much whether I would disclose the fact that you are partial to the red-eye.

I am glad that you are so happy working at the station. What a fine name for a station—WREN—that means female. Well, there are all kinds of tubes in a television set so it's fairly appropriate.

I am up to my ears in letters, correspondence, commitments, etc., etc., and I am just unable to answer the barrage of mail that keeps coming in.

I did receive a letter from Menninger's that you were now under a different analyst and you can tell them that this is all right with me.

As I told you over the phone, Eden is in France, and from her letter yesterday, she may remain away for five or six months. This I don't like and frankly I don't know just what I can do about it. I have been going with her for two years now and what with Melinda back at her mother's for the school semester and Eden overseas, it's goddamned lonely around the house. The only sounds now discernable are the soft patter of two [maids] as they glide around the house.

I am going to Detroit on the thirtieth of this month and will be there at the Sheraton-Cadillac until the third of October. I am going there to make a speech for the DeSoto-Chrysler crowd, and then I am going to St. Louis, where Krasna's play *Kind Sir* opens on the fifth of October. I will stay a couple of days with him, perhaps three, and then fly back to the coast. I will remain in Beverly for two weeks and then go to New York. I have contracted to do a show with Caesar and Coca. However, if I don't like the material I don't have to do it. I am not going to experience another Tallulah fiasco.

This is all I have time for.

Love from all.

Padre

Dear Miriam:

Just a reminder from me that your father has a birthday on October second. You probably would have remembered, but I know that he would feel hurt if you forgot so I thought it best to add this P.S.

Your job sounds wonderful, interesting and exciting. I'm sure you'll do yourself proud. Lots of luck.

Love,

Sara

Max Falkenstein (who was not Jewish) was my boss at the radio station WREN in Topeka, where I worked while at Menninger. The show with Caesar and Coca was "Your Show of Shows," hosted by Sid Caesar and Imogene Coca.

[Sheraton-Cadillac Hotel, Detroit, October 4, 1953]

Dear Mir;

Sunday noon in Detroit, raining. Luckily I leave here at 4:15 for St. Louis. Just a line mainly to enclose this piece by Dr. Menninger, with whom I'm in complete accord on this subject.

I hate writing longhand, but the subject of the World Series has to be mentioned. I have had my eyes glued to the set the past two days and yesterday I went to the church and prayed for Brooklyn. As I left I stole three dollars from the collector's plate.

You sounded so happy over the phone and I will try to expedite the delivery of the DeSoto as much as I can. I am happy over your improvement and can only hope it continues. You have too much on the ball to allow yourself to go to hell.

All my love to you and write soon.

Padre XXXX

October 23, 1953

Dear Schmir:

I saw the DeSoto 6 hardtop today at the preview at the Ambassador Hotel and it's a mighty engaging looking vehicle. I am having installed a heater and a radio. This means if you want to get warm you can turn on the radio and get hot music. If you are bored with music, you can kill it and turn on the heating apparatus. Your car will also have power steering and I think you will be crazy about it. . . .

I am flying to New York November first and am not sure just how long I will be there. I will probably stop off a day with you in Kansas City on the way back, providing you can swing it. By that time you will have your car, I hope, and perhaps you can drive up there. It hasn't been confirmed yet, but at the moment I believe I will be living at the Hampshire House. Sara will let you know definitely.

I am going to the opening of the Krasna show on November fourth, and the opening of the Kaufman show (Max Gordon producer) titled *Solid Gold Cadillac* on November fifth. I don't know how long I will be in New York after that. I have turned down a number of guest shots and panel shows. It's silly for me to get myself worked up and then discover at the conclusion that the government has taken most of the swag away.

It'll be strange being in New York without a girl and not too much fun. However, like an invading army, I expect to live off the land.

Eden, as you know, is in Egypt. She's playing Gregory Ratoff's wife, not a big part, and after that I believe she's going into a picture that her brother-in-law is shooting, also in the same territory. I don't know when she will be back, if ever. Our correspondence is becoming increasingly sporadic and brief and I wouldn't be surprised if she found someone over the ocean that she prefers. I looked in the mirror this morning very carefully and if this is the case I think there's some justification for Eden's behavior.

Kay and her boyfriend have cracked up. They had a big fight and he's gone. Other than wearing pants it seemed to me that he wasn't much of a bargain. As usual, she supported him, and then eventually came the customary eruption. I feel very sorry for her, plus my concern because of the fact that Melinda is always involved, even if only from a distance.

I can't write more, for I have so many letters to write.

I hope you are well and that you will soon be leaving the jute mill for a private home.

Love and kisses, and write soon.

Padre

He refers to me "leaving the jute mill" because I was about to become an outpatient at Menninger, and move in with a local family.

October 30, 1953

Dear Mir:

I told you you would hear from me. There's nothing to tell you that I haven't told you over the phone.

I am leaving Sunday morning for New York, which you know. I will be at the Savoy-Plaza, which you didn't know. I am going to do a show with Arthur Murray, which I don't remember if you knew.

There has been a slight hitch in the Murray setup. They have two writers, named Foster and Green, who did a show for me last year when I was on that Tallulah show, flopping all over the stage. I told them I wanted Nat Haiken, who I think is the best (don't tell Goody). He agreed to get Haiken and just phoned now that he is not available. I then suggested Goody. If it comes down to Foster and Green I will bow out. I don't intend to make another national spectacle of myself if it can be avoided.

I am not sure just when I will be coming back to the coast; perhaps earlier than I had planned. I had some vague notion of perhaps going over to Paris to see Eden, but have decided against it. It's too arduous and is a kind of tacit admission that life without her is intolerable. This may be true but I am not willing yet to concede it.

Briefly about the clinic—as I told you before I want you to move out for two reasons. One, to cut down those god-awful expenses and, secondly, if you do move out I can only assume that you have moved a long step along the path toward regaining your full health. . . .

This is all I have time for. I have to meet your brother in twenty minutes and I am a long way from where he is.

All my love and kisses and take care of yourself.

Padre

The show with Arthur Murray was "The Arthur Murray Party," a musical variety show.

208

November 24, 1953

Dear Mir:
I showed your picture (at the typewriter) to all the people you knew at the club, and all admired it and thought you looked great.

I am exhausted. I haven't slept in two or three weeks properly and I guess I am overtired. I went to Palm Springs when I got back, which was a mistake because I can't rest in a strange bed, or with a strange dame.

I dropped your mother a note when I returned and told her how well you looked and how happy you were. Incidentally, if you have a couple of more pictures of yourself, similar to the one you gave me sitting at the typewriter, in a studious pose, you might send them on.

You now have something to tell your children—meeting Truman. He comes over as a nice warm guy, plenty of moxie and courage, but I do think he's a very ordinary man intellectually, and I guess that's one of the penalties we pay for having a democracy. The best men are not elected to the proper offices and I am sure, with rare exceptions, never will be.

I hope your car is running smoothly. Incidentally, I forgot to ask you about your boyfriend. What does he do? Is he a professional man, a working man or just a rich man's son? He's very nice looking and if his other qualifications equal his looks he might turn out to be just the boy for you.

I am on a merry-go-round today, so this will be brief.

Love from all and write when you get around to it.

Padre

My father and I had visited with Harry Truman while we were staying at the same hotel in Kansas City. The boyfriend he refers to was my future husband, Gordon Allen, also an outpatient at Menninger.

December 11, 1953

Dear Mir:
I sent you some pajamas from Saks Fifth Avenue—New York, that is—and I never received an acknowledgment from you. I also sent you a blouse and skirt from a shop in Beverly Hills, which either hasn't been received or you are too lazy to write.

There's not much to tell you. This is just to give you an opportunity to have something in your letterbox when the postman rings twice.

I don't know if I wrote you, but Kay is going to Korea next week.

She is full of all kinds of medical shots at the moment, and also of love for a gent named Lenny Sherman who beat hell out of her three or four weeks ago. She came over to my house and it looked like she had just gone through ten rounds with Rocky Marciano. I was shocked at her appearance. She vowed that she would never see him again and when I called her apartment a few days ago he answered the phone. So I say to hell with it. To each his own. There are many women who flourish on a diet of mistreatment and neglect and apparently she is one of them. He is also a comedian of sorts. He is what is known in night-club circles as a "stand-up comic." To the best of my knowledge he has never had a job. This should give you an idea of what a desirable catch he is.

From your description your boyfriend sounds like pretty hot stuff and I hope this isn't just a temporary infatuation. Why I say this I really don't know, for if it doesn't work out it would be silly to continue.

These last two paragraphs make very little sense, but as you know, that's my stock in trade.

I received a badly written letter from Eden a few days ago, in which she told me that she might return pretty soon. I hope she does. I have been out with a lot of dames since she left for Europe, but I must say that I haven't found anything that I prefer.

If you contemplate purchasing a Christmas present for your old gray-haired father (which only isn't gray because of a steady application of some cheap hair dye that a barber friend of mine sneaks in from Bombay), I am badly in the need for a silk scarf for those occasions when I don a dinner jacket. It's a kind of item that Noel Coward affects and carries off very well, and there is a likelihood that someone may carry me off. At any rate, that's what I want.

I could write more but I have a luncheon appointment and I have to get the lead out, as they say in the armed forces.

Love and kisses, and write soon.

Padre

Miriam—I guess the above answers your query about the gift for your father. I am sure you can get the scarf in Topeka, but if you prefer that I get it for you here, let me know. Will write you at length one of these days.

Sara

December 18, 1953

Dear Schmir:
Apparently our letters crossed in mid-air.

I note what you say about my saying you were engaged. I never told anybody this. In the first place, it's a kind of old fashioned word that I haven't used in years. Plus this, I don't discuss your private affairs. I told Sheekman, who is getting increasingly jerky as the years wear on, that you were going with a nice fellow in Topeka. So forget it.

Glad you liked the skirt and blouse. I bought you some flannel pajamas in Saks while I was in New York. Apparently you never received them, and I am not sure whether you still wear that sort of habiliment.

This is that week before Christmas. Probably the ghouliest week of the year. This afternoon I have to get one of those goddamned Christmas trees again that nobody looks at once it is in the living room; and the remnants of this tree, in the shape of needles, linger on for many weeks in the furniture, carpets and drapes.

Melinda asked about a set of aluminum dishes and I told her Santa would bring them. She said, "Don't you think I know there's no Santa Claus? I know it's you. I knew it when I was four years old, but I didn't want to hurt your feelings."

Miss Hartford breezes in Sunday from Paris, according to her telegram, full of cold germs and the customary assortment of basic French words which will come in mighty handy if we ever eat at LaRue's or she winds up in a cathouse.

I am sending you a Christmas check for $150, which you can use for whatever purpose you see fit, including sending it back.

I have been having quite a joust with the dentist. This is a new one. The first day I walked in I opened my trap. He cased it carefully and said, "I am afraid, Mr. Marx, we (they always use the editorial 'we') are going to have to do over your whole mouth." Boy, was he a prophet.

I hope this letter finds you in as good shape as you were when last I saw you.

Love from all, and a Merry Christmas.

Padre

December 30, 1953

Dear Mir:

At long last, as Churchill would put it, snapshots. This is as good as I can do. As a rule nothing shows up on the film.

I am doing a show tonight and leaving for Palm Springs in the morning. What with packing, etc., this will have to do until I return. I hadn't planned on writing you at all. This is merely an excuse to send you the pictures.

Hope you are well and enjoying your work.

Love from all,
Padre

P.S. Thanks for the scarf (it's beautiful) and the tobacco.

January 14, 1954

Dear Mir:

As a little girl in California you always yearned for the snows of the east. From what I read in the papers here you are getting your wish, in spades, as they say at Hillcrest.

I am over at my office opening a two-week supply of mail. One letter is from a clergyman in New Jersey telling me how important humor is from the pulpit, and could I send him some jokes about Senator McCarthy. Another letter is from some dame in Chicago who is giving a party where everyone comes dressed as Groucho Marx. She would like, in addition to many things, two or three dozen large sized photographs of myself. This letter reached the waste basket before I finished reading it. Another is from a widow whose husband had been a chain cigar smoker, and she would appreciate it if I would blow some smoke rings on the show—for this, she said, would bring her even closer to her husband than when he was alive. He must have been quite a fellow. There are dozens of letters here asking for contributions for everything ranging all the way from a synogague in North Attleboro, Mass., which only wants me to send them enough money to build a $20,000 church. A DeSoto dealer in Oregon wants me to rush up there and make a speech for the Kiwanis club. Practically every letter has a request for my services or for my money. I don't know which is the most ghastly.

We finally got some rain here. Just in the nick of time, as half the state was on fire for the past few weeks. The flames were only a half-mile from Mount Wilson and had they not been stopped, they would have burned up all the instruments and professors that are being used in probing the outer spaces. The day the rains came was a dilly. We had thunder and lightning, and then to top it off, just as I was about to take a nap a neat little earthquake lumbered along and shook my fifteen-room mansion like it was a hammock on the prairie.

I have foolishly consented to do a four minute spot with Cantor on the thirty-first. This is subject to my approval of the material. Harpo was on the Spike Jones show last week. I don't know whether you saw it.

Your sister Melinda is going on my show next Wednesday. She is going to sing a song from *The King and I*. She has all the gestures coached by Miss Virginia Semon. My chief reason for having Melinda on the show is not that her talent is so extraordinary, but my character on the show (which, I might add, isn't completely unlike my character off the show) is that of an elder roue, always on the make and quick to make a pass; and since this can be a fairly disgusting character I think the injection of a wholesome thing in the form of a small innocent girl bleating the lyrics of Oscar Hammerstein may be helpful in letting the onlookers know that there is another side to this nauseating character . . . the father and stern parent, head of the household, bulwark of the American home, ready at a moment's notice to fight for Old Glory and the land he loves.

On this patriotic note I will sign off, hoping you are the same.

Love and kisses,
Padre

January 28, 1954

Dear Schmir:
Yours of January eighteenth received and this is the twenty-eighth and I am answering what is for me almost immediately.

I am glad you liked the dress. Eden picked it out; also the caviar — which I picked out.

I am doing a short bit on the Cantor show this Sunday. Just as an introduction of Cantor — and the only thing that might interest you on the show is the fact that his daughter Marilyn is also appearing. I understand she isn't too good but I will try to remain in my dressing room and not see this. He's an amazing guy, this Cantor. He does a radio show weekly, a television show once a month, he's on all kinds of guest appearances plugging his picture, and last week Guedel told me

213

he went to see him about the possibility of doing a quiz show. I think everything he does is a device to get away from Ida. I can't blame him too much. I think if I was Eddie I would skip the whole thing and go to the Zambesi River in Africa. There at least he might run into Ernest Hemingway.

I went to Vegas last week and won fifty cents in the nickel slot machines. This is the only time I ever gambled there. I took the fifty cents and bought a box of foot salve because this venture involved standing on my feet for over an hour. I must say I am not much of a bargain to the Vegas crowd. I had a suite of rooms, gratis, and all the checks for my meals were lifted by the various night-clubs. I don't know how welcome I will be if I ever return. My guess is that they had me confused with Chico or Zeppo and concluded I would take a beating at the crap tables. I had invited Arthur and Irene along but Steve came down with the German measles (Hitler's influence still continues) so they couldn't go.

I had a good time down there. Like it better than Palm Springs. As Solly Violinsky once remarked about Hollywood, "No matter how warm it is in the daytime, there's no place to go at night." This goes for Palm Springs too. When I go to Vegas I fly in an hour and a half. When I go to Palm Springs it's a four-hour drive.

Hope you are well, and except for the epidemic of colds that strikes this town every winter, we are all in good shape.

Love and kisses,
Padre

P.S. I am sending you some snaps in various poses, showing how I spend my days. How I spend my nights couldn't be sent through the mails.

Solly Violinsky was a screenwriter.

February 26, 1954

Dear Mir:

I can't write you any kind of a letter now because I am leaving town for a couple of days and I am not packed and I have so many other things to do and take care of.

I am doing a show Monday and I have a meeting Tuesday, and another show on Wednesday. Last night I M Ceed the Screenwriters' Guild dinner. Big success, so they say. Anyway, it was a lot of work and the only satisfaction you get is when a few people whose judgment you respect tell you you were good. Speaking of performance, I am enclosing a slight clipping from Hedda Hopper's column that you might enjoy.

Eden and I are still hitting it off. What the end will be, God only knows.

Melinda will be on the show in about three weeks.

Krasna had a baby girl last night—that is, Erle did. And he now has, to the best of my knowledge, two of each. For a fellow who plays a lot of golf and writes a lot of material, he seems to spend a lot of time in the hay.

It was nice talking to you and next week, perhaps the end of next week, I'll call you again.

Am glad you are going to see Arthur and Irene. It was unfortunate that he was laid low with the German measles in New York. I blame it on Hitler.

Love and kisses and a happy March fifteenth.

Yours,
Padre

March 12, 1954

Dear Mir:

Another brief note. Your letter sounds real good. I know it's hard to hear a letter, but that's the way it sounds.

I relayed your complaint about your DeSoto to Mr. Langridge and the enclosed letter I trust is self-explanatory, even though it probably won't do any good.

I think it was a good notion on your part to take up bridge. It replaces conversation, and to my mind there are very few people who are equipped for conversation, other than the casual.

I am on my way to Hillcrest where an obnoxious photographer named Gene Lester, who at the moment is employed by the S[aturday] E[vening] Post to take pictures of me for Arthur's serialized biography, awaits me. I read the book twice and on the whole thought it was quite good, but objected to many personal things which I requested be removed. At first Arthur was quite difficult about this, but he finally acceded to my request and we are now back on speaking terms.

On the twenty-eighth of March I will be on the Hammerstein and Rodgers cavalcade sponsored by General Foods. I will do a brief bit and since it is going to be televised on both major networks simultaneously it will be very difficult for you to avoid seeing it.

Kay is embarking on a USO tour beginning this Sunday, as far east as New York, and it will do her good to get out of the apartment on Wilshire Boulevard and see what is happening to the rest of the country.

I have just finished signing checks for my income tax and I have come to the conclusion that this is no longer a free country. A free country is where a man would be allowed to keep the money he earns, but not when they grab ninety-one percent. The Boston Tea Party was staged for much less reason. Unfortunately, everyone has grown so accustomed to working for the government that there's practically no protesting anymore. In Russia they take your cattle and crops; here they do it simpler—they just take your bankroll and when you die if you are lucky enough to have anything left, they grab a good hunk of that.

Well, enough griping. It's just a method of letting off steam. I am sure complaining to you about the income tax is not going to solve the problem. I don't know how important you are down in Washington, but I don't think you are big enough to solve this problem.

I am sending you a $100 check for St. Patrick's Day. He's the patron saint of Pat O'Brien and I know this will make him very happy.

Love from all and write when you are in the mood.

Padre

Arthur's book, Life With Groucho, *was published in 1954. Pat O'Brien was an actor best known for his portrayals of hard-boiled Irishmen.*

March 19, 1954

Dear Mir:

Received your letter and will answer you briefly. I am leaving for New York Tuesday, the twenty-third, and am doing a show on Monday, the twenty-second. I am taking photographs for the *Saturday Evening Post* for Arthur's book, and running a house and worrying about Melinda while her mother is away, and it leaves very little time for anything.

I will be on television Sunday night, the twenty-eighth, contributing a small part to the Rodgers and Hammerstein festival. On April ninth I am doing a "Person to Person" show with Ed Murrow. He is putting two or three hundred cameras in my house along with all the

216

other necessary electrical equipment and I am afraid it will take some time before the joint will look the same again.

Speaking of joints, I have done over the whole bar room. Threw out the old poverty-stricken gift from Lester Cowan which, incidentally, is the only pay that I got for the pathetic contribution I made to *Love Happy*. It now has carpets and drapes, and by comparison the living room looks pretty shabby.

Speaking of bar rooms, I am certainly happy that you can now be around booze and still abstain from using it. Have you any notion how long you will still be under analysis? I am not trying to hurry you particularly, but just curious. How long do you think before there will be a decrease in the number of visits you have to make?

The Sheekmans went to Europe—ostensibly for a pleasure trip; actually because his option wasn't renewed at Twentieth Century. This does not mean that he failed over there, but only that they don't keep any writers on contract anymore unless they have an immediate assignment for them. As you probably have read, the lush days are over in the movies. It's been whittled down to a hard core and personally I think they are in a much healthier financial condition. Anyway, the Sheekmans will have fun. No one has the joy of living to a greater degree than Gloria and she will have fun wherever she goes.

Melinda is getting so she can write a little now. She still requires help but if the words are small she can stumble through a fairly incoherent story.

I can't write more because I am too damned tired. The reason I am writing is because I will be in New York and I know I won't have either the time nor the inclination for correspondence.

If you see High Tax Harry give him my regards.

Love from all, and I'll be at the Hampshire House if you feel in the mood.

Sorry about the hundred, but at least you have a tax deduction.

Padre

High Tax Harry was President Harry Truman.

April 5, 1954

Dear Mir:
The postcard you requested I presume has arrived. This will be followed by this short letter.

I have just returned from the wars. I don't know if you saw the

217

show. Except for the *Times* and *Tribune,* all the New York papers and all of the people seemed to like it. The comedy spots had the life hacked out of them, for thirty minutes before the show we were still twelve minutes over. I had a seven-minute spot which was cut to four.

However, the trip was fun. I saw a lot of shows. General Foods paid for the whole thing and I did my usual bang-up job in insulting practically everyone I met. If you see the current *Time* magazine, there's a piece about quiz shows, also my photo, and it's quite flattering. There's also a review of the Rodgers and Hammerstein show.

As you know, April fourteenth is the anniversary of the assassination of Abraham Lincoln. This was a momentous and tragic day in our history. I think the whole world grieved as much as we did. Therefore I think it fitting that I should send you a hundred-dollar check to ease your way through this tragic month.

Goody told me that he had phoned you, and also that he had written you. He's a strange character and it's quite a feat getting him to write a letter. He hardly writes me at all, which I don't mind because it means that I don't have to answer. I am getting more reluctant all the time to write letters. My flair for correspondence is decreasing with the years, but I've done a lot of it in my time and I guess I am just tired of writing.

I am enclosing a letter from Langridge and one from the DeSoto people. If your car still doesn't give better mileage I suggest that you take these letters and shove them in the gas tank — or you might try the new Texaco gas. Their advertisement sounds like their fuel is a combination of Mumm's champagne and Ponce de Leon's elixir of life. Anyway, try it. I think it's the same price as the other fuels. This paragraph will give you an idea of how naive I still am.

Are your plans still to come to California in August? And how is your love life?

Kay has returned from the wars. I don't see her often but we talk on the phone from time to time. She is planning on moving again. She claims that the garbage disposal backed up and dumped all the debris she had dropped in back in the living room. I guess this is what they call "moderne."

That is all for now.

Hope you are well, and love from all,

Padre

April 23, 1954

Dear Schmir:

The night I called you on the phone and gave the receiver to Bob Dwan, I had no idea he was going to be schlemiel enough to hang up. In the future I'll phone you from the Owl Drug Store's phone booth where there will be no danger of outside interruption.

I am glad you are keeping your weight down. One hundred fifteen seems a little thin for a girl of your height and I don't advise you to remove any more. Slimness, too, can be overdone.

Eden is now taking French lessons. I'll give you one guess who is paying for them. However, I don't mind. I would rather have her sitting in a Berlitz office mouthing French words that she will probably never get a chance to use, than have her hanging over a bar or falling into some other kind of mischief. She tried to hook me into this adventure but I've become pretty cagey and stepped nimbly to one side.

Palm Springs was a huge success. I returned with a cold. Melinda came back with 100 temperature. Gummo caught a cold, and two of Harpo's kids came down with a cold and ear infection. Next time I go away for a vacation I think I will spend a week at Cedars of Lebanon. It's not much fun, but it's much safer—unless you run into a young surgeon who needs a big fee so he can get married.

It's been quite cold here the last week, which kept me from the ball park. I plan on going Saturday and Sunday afternoon, but the night games are a little too frigid for my low blood pressure.

I won't discuss the American League race nor Senator McCarthy. I am trying to avoid anything distasteful and I find both these subjects fit this category very nicely.

The automobile business is ghastly, except for Ford. They have certainly grabbed off the cream of the sales this year. It's a very sporty looking car and apparently that is what the public is going for. They have passed Chevrolet. The only one of the Chrysler products that is doing any good is the DeSoto branch, which I must attribute to my show. The auto dealers are real panicky and anybody with any money in his pocket today can practically make his own deal.

I have so many letters to write that I will bring this to a close.

I am sending you a picture of me in one of my rare appearances in a night-club. This was a party after the preview of the new Danny

Kaye picture, *Knock on Wood,* written by Panama and Frank, and certainly, in my opinion, the best picture he has had.

Love and kisses,
Padre

Bob Dwan co-directed "You Bet Your Life."

April 30, 1954

Dear Miriam:

At your request I have sent you the paraphernalia you desire. How's that for a business letter opening? It was sent collect because it was picked up at the house, and the drayman, having no scale with him, was unable to estimate the cost.

I am going to Europe May fourteenth for a month. No particular reason, except that too many of my friends are dying recently, and I have decided that before I knock off I'd better take another look at what the Old World looks like. This is an arduous journey and I have mixed emotions about making it. But I will fly both ways so that I won't consume too much time. I am also leaving early so that I will be back by the time Melinda gets out of school and also when you come from Topeka.

I will go to England, France and Italy. In these three countries I will see George Kaufman, Max Gordon (God help me), Harry Kurnitz and the Sheekmans. The Sheekmans are now starving in Italy. He has gone there to write the great American play. Secretly I think he's gone there because he was out of work. This doesn't necessarily mean that everyone who is at liberty goes to Italy, but it is easy to hide in those hills around Rome. Caesar did it, so why not Sheekman?

I note what you say about your job being extremely difficult. I think it might be a good idea for you to have a talk with Max Falkenstein and explain to him precisely what you explain to me in this letter. For fifty dollars a week I don't think you should be obliged to do transcribed commercial announcements, in addition to your regular chores. I think they have a pretty cheap buy in you and are taking advantage of it. I would rather you took another job that was less of a mental strain, even though the salary was less. It seems rather absurd for me to be paying seven or eight hundred dollars a month to bring you back to health and jeopardize this for two hundred a month.

I spoke to Goody the other night—that is, he called me—and he will be here on Monday, the tenth. I am looking forward to spending time with him.

I am busy as hell and if it was you you wouldn't write at all. I have a show this Monday and a show on Wednesday and with the meetings and preparations and passports and inoculations I'll just about make it.

Love to you and hope the package arrives.

Will call you if you will let me know just when you will be there.

Padre

May 13, 1954

Dear Schmir:

I am calling you tonight at six, and I am leaving tomorrow morning at seven.

Goody told me all about you, how well you looked and what a good time he had, and from his attitude apparently there was no untoward incident.

I hope your car is running and you are riding again. I don't know how fast you were going, but go slower. I am glad you were able to resist temptation to attempt to solve the problem by hitting the bottle, but I have a hunch you are through with this sort of thing.

I am sending you a $200-check for your birthday and I want you to feel free to purchase anything with this money that your little heart desires. That is, anything except a General Motors product.

I am dead tired. So many "thank you" notes to write and phone calls to make. I only hope this trip doesn't take too much out of me. There's always a tendency to overextend yourself physically on this kind of expedition but I will try to regiment my vitality. The Schlaes, who live next door, are adding a new room. They are putting this addition under my window—at least it seems that way—and between that and the McCarthy hearings I feel about as rested as Secretary Stevens.

I won't write more. I will speak to you tonight.

Love and kisses and take care of yourself.

Padre

[Hotel Hassler-Roma, Trinita Dei Monti, June 12, 1954]

Dear Mir,
This is Rome. It's an exciting and history laden city. I will see some of it, but not too much, for the strain of travelling is beginning to show, and I am beginning to think more and more of the backyard and the pool, etc.

I hope you can come home this summer, and if you answer this, air mail, to the Savoy Hotel, London, I will know what your plans are.

We have had considerable rain in Europe, but the showers are sporadic, and eventually the sun comes out. I bought you a sexy nightgown and a Borsalino beret that I hope you like. I would buy you more, but the problem of carting the stuff around becomes gigantic.

I won't write more. I seem to spend all my time here writing postcards and eating spaghetti.

Next year, if you are through at Menninger's, I would finance a European trip for you. All my love and kisses and try and come home.

One of these days Eden and I may get married. I would like to know how you and Arthur feel about it?

XXXX Padre

July 13, 1954

Dear Mir:
I was delighted with your letter and to read that you are back in the groove and unlikely to depart from it soon.

I spoke to Mr. Brown, the head mechanic at the DeSoto station locally, and I explained to him your carburetor trouble and he promised to write something out that I could send to you that you could show to this giant mind who fouls up the cars locally in Topeka.

I note that you drove 400 miles to Wichita. I only hope that you drove more leisurely than you did when I was in your car. Many people are unaware how swiftly they drive—even after they hit something. So don't place such a heavy foot on the throttle. You will find you get there almost as quickly and it will save your nerves, the car and perhaps someday your life.

This is Tuesday afternoon and I am leaving Thursday morning by train for Sun Valley.

The rumor that Melinda is going to appear in a movie at Paramount is just some more of that inaccurate information that spews out of the radio and news columns most of the day. There was some talk of her doing a weekly TV show. Although the offer wasn't definite, I would still reject it. She can be an actress if she desires when she grows up, but there's going to be no repulsive stage moppet in my family at the age of eight.

Speaking of age, Melinda's birthday is August fourteenth, and Kay's is August twenty-ninth.

I am sure the air conditioner will help your spirits.

I am enclosing a check for $100 because July fourteenth is Bastille Day in Paris. This is the day they struck for liberty and it is very difficult to have any freedom without money.

I am reading the Ben Hecht book and one of these days, when we have all read it, I will send it on to you. I do think that sending you the Lillian Roth book was a mistake. In the future I will only send you books about teetotalers.

All my love.

Eden is glad you like the paraphernalia.

I'll drop you a line from Sun Valley.

Padre

The Ben Hecht book was Hecht's autobiography, A Child of the Century. *The Lillian Roth book was* I'll Cry Tomorrow, *about her comeback from alcoholism. On July 18, 1954, Groucho sent me a telegram from Sun Valley that read: "You now have a mother named Eden. Love from both—Padre." Eden was twenty years old. I was twenty-seven.*

August 3, 1954

Dear Mir:

Yes, I did receive your wire, and thanks.

About Gordon—I really don't know what to tell you. It seems kind of foolish to pay all this money to the clinic and then act contrary to their wishes. On the other hand, I used to be single and know what it was to be in love. Again, there's a reason why you are both there and if you have no confidence in their orders then it seems to me you shouldn't be there. I don't think any advice I give you is going to make much difference. It's a very confusing situation and I have so many other problems that I can't give it as much time and vitality as I would like. Well, as you say, the hell with all this.

I am glad you got the air conditioner in time to save you from frying. We, too, have had hot weather but as a rule a breeze blows in from the Pacific.

Please don't send us a wedding present. Your good wishes are enough. I know you can't afford it and neither can I.

While I am on the subject of money, I want you to get the hell out of Topeka and have a decent vacation so I am sending you a check for $200. With this you can either fly to a cooler spot or buy a small piece of acreage in Kansas and build a motel.

I have just finished the Hecht book and it impressed me tremendously. Needlessly vulgar at times, but the overall is so great. As you know, it's a long, thick book but I read it swiftly. Couldn't read anything else until I finished it. Ben is a big talent and also has courage, something very few of us have.

It doesn't seem possible, but in two weeks I'll be doing my first show. Those thirteen weeks certainly flew.

Tonight the Krasnas are throwing a party for fifty people for me. Eden too, I presume. It's nice of them to do this, but frankly I'd rather have dinner alone with them and go to a movie. All the unfunny jokes and cracks. I've heard them for years. They never vary and they get staler with each marriage. I'll just have to quit getting married. Wonderful line I read, I don't know where: "With old age you are free from the tyranny of sex." At the moment I assume this seems fairly academic to you, but don't worry, you'll get older. Just be patient.

I can't write more. I have too many other letters that have piled up. All my love. Eden's too.

Padre

This was a response to a letter I had written about marrying Gordon against the Clinic's wishes.

September 8, 1954

Dear Miriam:

Perhaps your trip home may have done some good, despite the harm it did create, and perhaps my last speech to you may have a salutory effect on your future behavior. I wrote a strong letter to Dr. Miller. In essence it contained just about what I said to you before you left so there's no point in rehashing this whole thing.

That was a very nice letter you wrote Melinda and she seemed quite pleased with it. I agree with you. Despite the fact that I am her father and you are her sister, I think she's quite a kid. I only hope nothing happens to her on her way toward maturity. I certainly get a big bang out of her, and at night when I put her to bed she has on this little silk

224

nightgown and she gets down on her knees and prays. That's worth all the nuisance value she contributes during the day and I must say I am a pretty lucky fellow. Yesterday I took her and Cindy Gordean, who is also a pretty cute trick, to the Farmer's Market. I don't get there very often but they love it. It's almost like a fair grounds to them. It gets increasingly crowded and it's practically impossible to get a table. I had quite a time juggling three trays and trying to guard a table and hollering for somebody to remove the dirty dishes. While this was going on they had quite a squabble on how to divide the french fries.

I am leaving tomorrow morning for Detroit. I will be back on Sunday the twelfth. They want me to see the new car and drive it around thinking this will increase my enthusiasm in the commercials. They haven't said this but I presume this is the purpose. We are going stag—Gummo, Bernie Smith and Bob Dwan. There may be some loose dames in Detroit who are eager to meet four charming fellows.

Regarding the bathrobe. Apparently when you went east you took two bathrobes. There was a terry robe that I bought in Paris that I imagine is in your possession since I can't find it in the house. I received one bathrobe from you and I would like you to return the other one. At no time have I been under the impression that you had deliberately taken either of these robes, and I am surprised that you should even think so. The terry robe I would like returned for sentimental reasons. It's the only thing I bought in Europe for myself, and I would like to retain a memento of my weeks on the Continent.

I have so much to do I can't write more.

Your letter was a very nice one and I only hope that you can live up to some of its resolutions.

Love and kisses from all and as soon as Kay learns to write, Melinda will answer your letter.

Padre

Bernie Smith was co-director of "You Bet Your Life."

September 16, 1954

Dear Miriam:
This is the last time you will hear from me for two weeks for Sara is leaving for New York—Roberts, that is—and I have built up an animosity toward the typewriter—the machine, that is—that can only be explained by Brill, Jung and Freud combined.

Your friend will have tickets for the show for September twenty-second. I will leave them downstairs and she can come and get them. If Eden isn't present, I will invite her in. If Eden should happen to be there, she can wait outside and I will shove the tickets under the door.

Your letter seems much more optimistic and sensible and the shambles that took place a few weeks ago at my dwelling may turn out to be all for the best. I am sure the Clinic would have been much quicker to allow you to move into an apartment had it not been for your trip to California. I sympathize with you, trapped in that small room. As you say, the people you are living with seem to be real nice but it's tough conversing with people where there are no common interests.

All the bathrobes have now arrived. This is a special kind of thief — who steals them in numbers. Over the years, in vaudeville, I encountered a good many bathrobe thieves, but none of them, even the top crooks, ever stole more than one robe at a time. To blithely fly away with two bathrobes is a record that will live long in the annals of thievery.

About Gordon — I think you are making a wise decision. I know it is difficult. If you really love each other I am sure you will ultimately get together again.

The snapshots were real nice and you look very cool.

Melinda is back in school and I now spend a good deal of my afternoons phoning to Kay to be sure that Melinda (a) has her eyes examined; (b) goes to Dick Comen and has her fangs gone over; and (c) a few other odd jobs that Kay will quickly promise and never fulfill. I know that eventually I will wind up doing them, but she's worth it.

Speaking of brothers and sisters, I presume you have the first installment of the *Saturday Evening Post* with its story of a certain lecherous, miserly conniver who unfortunately happens to be your Padre. Frankly, I am not crazy about the whole thing. This doesn't mean that I don't think Arthur did a good job, but my private life is a subject that I would have preferred isn't written up in a national magazine, despite all the elisions I insisted upon. It will do a lot for Arthur professionally, and for his sake I am glad he was able to sell it.

A year ago I was single, living not too lonely a life in my little fifteen-room cottage. I now have a wife, a cat and three weeks ago I became the reluctant owner of a black French poodle named DeSoto (what an actor won't do to mollify the sponsor). When we got him he was three weeks old and his mother, like most modern mothers, was unable to supply him with as much milk as he required. I forgot to mention that there were four other puppies who were also futilely nibbling at this dried up well. So he is bottle-fed. He lies on his back and with his front paws he holds the bottle exactly like an infant. One of these days I will send you pictures of him.

We all send love and I will try to get Melinda to sit down and write you a letter.

Love and kisses,
Padre

October 8, 1954

Dear Schmir:

Thanks for the sox. They came in mighty handy.

I didn't tell you, but I won $100 on the Giants. Some fellow laid me $100 to $50 that Cleveland would win. So I had $100, $50 of which I gave to Eden with the stipulation that she had to watch the Series. After the first game she offered me the money back if I wouldn't insist on this. So I wound up with $50, and I sent you a bathrobe for $40, which I hope you have received by this time. So I made $10. This is $2.50 a game, and because of the strain of watching the Series, my hair is snow white and I am going to have to spend a fortune buying hair dye.

I note what you say about your job. I would hate to see you lose this job for I am sure that whatever else you may get in Topeka would be duller. At least this way you are remotely connected with show business and literature. So put in forty-four hours like you have agreed to do because winter is coming on and the winds blow real cold when you are out of work.

You certainly are going to be busy with night school, photography and auto mechanics. I think it's admirable of you to want to work that hard, but you are made of good stuff and it's just a question of utilizing and coordinating your talents.

Eden left at 8:30 this morning with Ann Frank. They drove down to the General Hospital and Eden is going to work all day in the psychiatric ward where they rehabilitate, or attempt to rehabilitate, sick people, mostly veterans of the last war. Ann Frank has been doing this for quite some time and I hope Eden likes it because we both know that everyone must have an occupation. Just having fun doesn't suffice.

The dog is real cute. He's gradually ruining all the carpets in the house and to watch him and Suki play together — if filmed and shown in a movie theatre, it would be a laughing riot.

227

They also say about California that you never can tell where one season ends and the next one begins. This is ridiculous. I can tell. This is the week when I stow away the furniture around the pool, the barbeque which was used twice all summer, and start looking for the phone number of the roofer which will be necessary because he will eventually appear and plug up three new holes in the roof.

Love from the dog, and the cat, and Melinda, and Eden, and me. I'll call you—probably tomorrow.

Padre

Ann Frank and her husband, producer Melvin Frank, were friends of my father's.

October 11, 1954

Dear Schmir:

This is not a letter—just an excuse to send you $150 to buy some clothes. Jack Frost will soon be whistling around your tiny bedroom window and I am sure that with some new clothes (and you damned well better spend the money on this) you will be fortified when you leave the house in the morning and probably whistle all the way on your way to work, assuming that you haven't been bounced by that time.

Love,
Padre

October 23, 1954

Dear Schmir:

Yours of the sixteenth to hand. I don't know quite what that means, but that's the way they talk in the business world.

As a matter of fact, this is the twenty-third and was my father's birthday. Thursday was Gummo's birthday. He is hibernating in Palm Springs and I wired him: "Dear Gummo: Come off it. At your age Woodrow Wilson was president of the United States."

We had dinner for Durocher Wednesday night. Among those on the dais were Fred Haney, Charlie Dressen, me, Tony Martin, Benny, Jessel (that goes without saying), Danny Kaye, Danny Thomas,

228

George Burns, Harpo and his golden harp. I was foolish enough to make a comparatively clean speech despite the fact that it was a stag audience. I got some laughs but not the kind of yoks that the other boys got. However, I have some kind of a block that doesn't allow me to publicly shout the customary four-letter words. I will solve this in the future by not appearing at any stags. I am not amused by the dirty words, nor do I admire those who use them. It's a little disheartening when one realizes what a small field there is for cleverness, particularly in the world of humor. This goes for Lardner, Perelman, Benchley, Fred Allen and all the great ones, with the exception of Allen, who is lucky enough to be in show business; the rest of them had an extremely difficult time making a living. When I say a living, I mean comparable to those in other walks of literature of the same stature.

A few months ago I became an uncle, courtesy of Maxine Marx, or Culhane. This morning I again became an uncle. A small ginny was born in Rome. The father, I presume, is Howard Hawks. The mother, via Caesarean, is Eden's sister, whom we used to call "Icy Knockers" in the days when we were making the sailor picture at RKO. It's an eight-pound boy and it apparently is already eating spaghetti.

Speaking of the sailor picture, the one I did with Bendix, I tried running it the other night for Melinda. After two reels I had to shut it off. I couldn't watch it and Melinda had left the room. There's an old saying, "Let the dead past bury its dead," and I am a firm believer in never looking backward. There are too many horrifying things lurking there.

I am sending you some unfunny napkins with smart cracks written by a couple of boys on the show. Apparently there's a market for this sort of backyard humor, and since everyone else is cashing in on it I thought I might just as well.

I must go. Your sister is going to be on my show in about ten weeks. This time she is going to be a contestant and I have to meet Howard Harris today for he has to interview her and find out something about her private life. This I would surmise is a fairly meager subject.

So glad you like the money and the robe. I don't mean the picture—I mean the one you wear after emerging from the shower.

Love and kisses and one of these nights I'll call you.

Padre

P.S. I am sending you a very interesting and necessary piece of advice written by Henry McLemore. I am sure this will do no good but it might be wise to ponder over it. You are still young and it seems rather foolish to tempt fate the way you do with your foot on the throttle.

November 30, 1954

Dear Mir:
I received your long letter of November twentieth and will answer with a short letter on November thirtieth.

I'm happy that you will see the Yankees next summer, and with the purchase of Turley from the Baltimore Orioles, they should have a good chance of regaining the top. They seem to be able to buy anything they need—like General Motors and Ford. Well, I'm not going to worry about it anymore.

. . . About the Gordon situation, I cannot advise you anymore. You will just have to work it out between you, the analyst and the city of Topeka.

This is a jumpy week for me. Arrived back from the Springs yesterday, had a meeting today, a show tomorrow and I have to fly to Frisco Thursday for the weekend to do some more commercials for DeSoto.

The other DeSoto looks very nice. He just got clipped. I got clipped. From him they took hair and from me lucre. He's a real cute dog. Even the cat likes him. I suppose I like cats better than dogs because they're more female—regardless of their sex. When finally you weary of them and throw them out, you don't have to pay them alimony for X number of years.

Irwin Allen is getting daffier all the time. He was just tossed out by a gal and got nicked to the tune of $11,000. God knows this could be catastrophic enough but the blow to his pride must have been something—really something. She left him for a seventy-year-old horseplayer in Florida. He has a large wide streak of masochism that enjoys being bludgeoned. He has the $11,000 itemized and pulls it out at the slightest provocation. Long as his affairs can be the center of the conversation, he seems perfectly happy.

I hope you're well again—and except for a few major illnesses, we're all in fine shape.

Love and kisses,
Padre

Irwin Allen was a screenwriter, director and producer whose films included The Story of Mankind *(1957).*

December 1, 1954

Dear Mir:
I don't know whether you noticed it, but I wasn't in a particularly amiable mood while talking to you last night on the phone. The fact of the matter is I was rather angry—and I still am.

As you know, I've been separated from your mother more than ten years and although I deeply sympathize with her condition, I resent your calling me about her to complain about Arthur. As you further know, I'm not a young man anymore nor am I a middle-aged one and many shocks and disturbances that leave a young man comparatively free make a deep impression on an older one.

You may not be aware of it but there are other people also with problems. There is Kay, for example. Her problem is largely because she is Melinda's mother and is completely unaware of the fact that this involves certain responsibilities. Fortunately for her, I'm deeply attached to Melinda so I do enjoy the many things that I have to do for her. Nevertheless, there are many more than one in my position should have to do.

I spoke to Arthur this morning and he, too, was pretty angry. He said you constantly call up your mother and tell her all kinds of things that disturb her. This I have no control over, but it seems to me that since you go to an analyst you should relate these problems to him and not to your mother. She, as you fully well know, cannot even solve her own problems. I also am married to a young woman who, too, has a family—and this involves many responsibilities. Then there is Art and his family, Chico, who is out of work and will probably never work again, and lastly my own job which requires a cool head and steady nerves.

To sum this up, it would be very helpful to all of us if you would tell your problems to your analyst. You're not a child anymore and I know there are things that bother you, otherwise you would not be in Topeka. But you also have to pitch in.
                                        Love,
                                        Padre

[December, 1954]

Dear Mir,
This won't be much of a letter, for I am typing this at home. I haven't been to the office in quite some time, principally because I have had

231

a virus, and still have remnants of it, but I find out that after a while you GET USED TO IT AND IGNORE IT. The capital letters that were just printed were a mistake and had no connection with anything. My typing is a little rusty. I wanted to write you a short letter, since I received a short gloomy one from you this morning.

I am sorry I wrote you such an angry letter last week, but I have a lot of things to contend with. I won't enumerate them; I believe I did that in my previous letter. However, when you are angry at Arthur, for example, don't write me about it, write Arthur; this is what I mean, and what I wrote you.

I was too ill to do a show last week, and I am hopeful that I will be able to do one Wednesday the fifteenth.

I am sorry you lost your job, but I am sure that you will be able to get another one. I do hope you can get one that is connected, even if remotely, with show business, for you know what Irving Berlin keeps saying, and every time he says it, it costs some studio a veritable fortune: "There's no business like show business."

I'm getting pretty discouraged with the looks of this letter and I may as well abandon it. This is a pretty shabby job, and the only reason I attempted it was because I didn't want you to think I was angry at you, for you know I love you, and that I think of you every day, and to prove it I am sending you a Xmas check. Best from Melinda and Eden too and write soon.

Your Padre

December 23, 1954

Dear Mir:

I received your short novel this morning and in return will write you a short note. It's just thirty-six hours before Christmas, so I don't know if this check for $200 will reach you in time to hold off your creditors. It's true, I promised you $500, but since you are not very cagey with a buck, my plan was to send you the $300 and then send you the balance about a month later. I realize now this plan was all right for me but not for you. I'm delighted that you have a new job even though the salary is minute. It will give you a chance to go along with a growing concern rather than with a stagnant one, and I'm sure you'll make good on the job. . . .

Kay went and bought Melinda a springer spaniel for Christmas and a parakeet. They are calling the dog Groucho. I'm sure there's a resemblance. I have never seen this animal but I look like almost all dogs. To further complicate things, Kay purchased a parakeet and the whole layout sounds like a nice place not to live in.

I won't write you any more as I have too many things to do—too many places to go—too many people to see—and besides that, my feet are cold.

A Very Merry Christmas and All My Love,
Padre

April 29, 1955

Dear Mir and Gordon:
These infrequent letters are going to be even more infrequent now that I have to write Mir and Gordon as compared to the good old days when I just had to write Dear Mir. I'm not implying that I disapprove of the marriage, but writing two names involves considerably more labor on my part, and I may have to ask for overtime, a guaranteed annual wage and fringe benefits.

But seriously, folks (ah there, Milton Berle), I'm very happy over this alliance and only hope that it's more permanent than some of mine have been. I don't know how it got around, but it was picked up by most of the papers throughout the United States, and I can only attribute this to the fact that Gordon sells automobiles.

As you know, I received a wire from the hospital notifying me of your departure and it said "letter follows" and was signed by a gent named Mr. Wood. So far I haven't received any letter so I assume that the whole thing has been worked out between you two and Menninger.

This has been a busy time for me. I've been doubling up on shows so that I can get away. Monday I throw my swan song for the season; Tuesday I'll be packing, mostly Eden's effects that she is unable to stuff into her suitcase; and Wednesday morning I'll by flying high, wide and handsome—or as handsome as one can with a kisser like mine.

I've had many surprises in my long and eccentric career, but I must say that one of the greatest was receiving $100 from Mr. Gordon Allen. It isn't that I distrusted him, but it's so unusual for anyone related to me to return money that I was shocked virtually beyond repair. To begin with, I didn't expect this money back. I'm so suspicious of it now that I have it that I hesitate to cash the check.

Speaking of checks, I'm enclosing one for you and your hubby

233

which will enable you to buy some aluminum pots and pans. These are the ones I always see advertised on TV. These frying pans, for example, fry square eggs. Why a square should taste any better than a round one is beyond my comprehension. But that's the selling point that this aluminum company uses. As I get older I seem to become more out of tune with the world at large and the things that are taking place. The songs baffle me. The cars are now getting so complex that one needs a navigator to watch over the equipment on the dashboard—and now square eggs . . . This is the last straw.

Everyone seems to be delighted at the news of your marriage and I wouldn't be surprised if someone sends you a present. My love to you both—also from Eden, who on Thursdays is very busy playing ping-pong with some psychotics at the County Hospital.

I will be at the Savoy Plaza in New York May fourth, and on May tenth I'm going to make a national idiot of myself by appearing on "Who Said That." I appeared on the program once before with considerable success but at that time I was younger and brighter. Now I'm getting like Shakespeare's King Lear—old and full of sleep.

Love,
Padre

Gordon and I had gotten married on April 22, 1955 in Santa Fe, New Mexico, by a justice of the peace (who had formerly run a gas station around the corner from Beverly Hills High School). Afterward, we phoned Padre with the news and to ask him for a one-hundred-dollar loan. He was terribly impressed when Gordon paid it back. We were married against the Menninger Clinic's wishes, but they did take us back as outpatients.

May 24, 1955

Dear Mir:

Hope you had a nice birthday and that you didn't feel any older than you did last month. I have just flown in from Chicago where Horace Heidt and I botched up the airwaves for thirty minutes. I don't know whether you saw the show or not. Luckily, I haven't met anybody yet who has. However, the sponsor and the agency both liked it and since they were the ones who had to shell out the lucre, that was all that was necessary.

Having just returned from three weeks in the east, the mail has stacked up pretty high. I saw a few games in the east and those damn Yankees continue winning. Well, you can see them for yourself now in Kansas City, so I won't write any more about them.

I am happy that you are finally going to quit Topeka and move, even though it's only Connecticut. At least there you will be within hailing distance of civilization. Do you plan on working or are you going to retire on your laurels and sit back and watch the world go by? Maybe now you will tackle the most arduous job of all, which is writing. I think you have a talent for it. If I didn't think so, I certainly wouldn't urge you. Whether you feel up to it psychologically is something else again. This is something you will have to decide for yourself. Sometimes there is just as much therapeutic value in writing as there is in analysis. I wouldn't say this would apply to everyone, but in your case it might. Anyway, it's something to think about.

I'm doing a show from Hollywood called "Remember" June nineteenth. They are taking one year—1938—and reliving it: all the unusual things that occurred that year like Wrong Way Corrigan, Johnnie Vandermeer pitching two no-hitters with the Cincinnati Reds, five minutes of Ethel Barrymore in White Oaks, Oscar Levant playing Gershwin's piano concerto as he did that year at the Lewissohn Stadium—and many other things will be dredged up out of the past.

I am glad you are coming west for a few weeks. Helen Perrin called this morning and wanted to know where she could send you a wedding gift. I told her you were coming out this summer and she could deliver it personally—so you see, on your trip here you may be showered with silver, French perfumes and other things that rock the room.

I won't write more because I'm too damn tired. Tell Gordon he can call me anything he wants to as long as he calls me early for dinner. This is a joke that your grandmother used to tell when I was married to your mother and for all I know may have contributed substantially to our divorce.

Love and kisses,
Padre

Horace Heidt was a bandleader who had a radio show called "The Horace Heidt Show," among others, from the 1930s to the 1950s. Gordon and I did move to Connecticut, where his parents lived, that fall.

July 6, 1955

Dear Mir:
It was nice talking to you and I'm sorry you are having so much trouble, but I hope this is the bleakest part and that from here on in it's going to be all comparatively smooth sailing. I'm sending you a check to help out.

I was at Art's house the other night on the Fourth of July and we had a good time with the kids. Art bought some harmless fireworks and they were real excited (not the fireworks—I mean the children). No one was injured except that I ate too many barbequed frankfurters.

I'm taking Melinda and Art and his family to Coronado for a week. I wish you could join us, but from what you say perhaps it's better if you wait until your recovery is more certain before psychologically endangering yourself. It seems a shame that you will come so near and that we still shouldn't see each other, but I did see you a few months ago in Kansas City, so it's not too bad. Perhaps in a few months after you have lived in Connecticut in comparatively good shape you can fly out and spend a few weeks with us. It seems to me that would be more sensible than attempting it now.

I can't write any more as I have to rush off to a business meeting and then to a few other odd places.

All my love to you and best to Gordon—and on those occasions that you can't write, please see that Gordon does.

> Much Love,
> Padre

[Hotel Del Coronado, Coronado, California, July 17, 1955]

Dear Mir and Gordon,
Sorry your trip ended so disastrously, but I have a hunch that you are coming over the summit and that things will be a little more pleasant in the near future.

> Love from all to you both,
> Padre XXXXX

I ended up at Stormont Vail Hospital in Topeka with a disease called neuropathy after Gordon and I had started a trip west. I had been taking a drug to keep me from drinking, which caused the neuropathy. I had to stop taking it, and began drinking again when I got out of the hospital.

July 26, 1955

Dear Mir:
You certainly have had your share of misfortune, but I must say your letter was considerably more encouraging than the one from Dr. Miller three days earlier—but perhaps there was marked improvement at

that time. I know it is going to be expensive but don't worry about it. It's better than dying or being permanently off your rocker. If you can get a copy of the current *Reader's Digest* with a story by [Jim] Piersall, center fielder for the Boston Red Sox, read it. It's a wonderful saga of courage.

I have just returned from Coronado with wife, child and grandchildren and must admit that I am pretty beat. I will be glad to go back to work again to get some rest. August tenth we go to bat. The vacations always seem so short and the thirty-nine weeks so long. However, I am not complaining. I'm glad I'm working. Many of my contemporaries are permanently washed up. I went sailing on a small skiff in Coronado and must admit found it rather restful. Art was the skipper. We were doing great, skimming along the top of the waves like the USS *Constitution*. At this point of the voyage I had decided to buy a sailboat and spend the rest of my years drinking rum and frequently breaking into a hornpipe. Just as I had arrived at these conclusions, Art, with a masterpiece of seamanship reminiscent of the captain of the *Titanic,* who insisted there were no icebergs within a radius of five hundred miles of his ship, maneuvered us onto a sandbar where we hung for two hours until two small boys aged ten and twelve arrived with an outboard motor and towed us ignominiously into port.

I ordered a portable typewriter for you and it should arrive in the next ten days or so. In the meantime, don't worry, take it easy, my best to Gordon and if the mood strikes you, please write.

Much Love,
Padre

[August 6, 1955]

Dear Mir, and Gordon,

Your letter was quite encouraging, and it was doubly welcome since it was typewritten instead of your childish scrawl. I keep reading the weather reports from the rest of the country and I must say you kids are not be be envied. It's been warm here too, but as you know at night it cools off, enough in my case to even use the electric blanket. Of course this wouldn't apply to everyone, but I am known as No Blood Marx. Nothing courses through my veins except venom and a low grade cellophane.

We are both quite puzzled at your firm refusal to accept the nightgowns and bed jackets. Is it because you are allergic to things frilly? Or is it because you feel sorry for an old broken down quizmaster and therefore assume that he is unable to afford both nightgowns, bed jackets and Bermuda shorts? These things that were sent you are not necessarily used only in a hospital. I understand there are tootsies and disciples of Jelke all over Manhattan Isle and the Gold Coast of Chicago who spend hours on end lolling around chaise lounges, hacking away at their profession. Apparently you don't realize it, but it is possible for you to have not only the frilly things but the Bermuda shorts without putting your old man in the bankruptcy courts. So by return mail if you will let us know what your wishes are, we will be only too happy to comply.

I am sorry that I neglected to tell about your sister's appearance on the Johnny Carson show. Before she appeared, it was described to me as the briefest of bits and it didn't seem worthwhile to notify anyone.

Next Wednesday night I will be at the Brown Derby at 6:45, and at 8:00 I will have a makeup man with halitosis (this is a must in their profession) poring over me with all kinds of grease and cosmetics, trying vainly to make me look as though I were Gregory Peck's younger brother instead of Charles Coburn's grandfather. This will be my ninth year at this racket and I am beginning to wonder which is the most arduous, the sameness of the menu Wednesday night at the Derby or the actual show itself.

Eden is becoming very handy around the house. She bakes bread, she types and dyes my hair with an expertness that formerly one could only get at Elizabeth Arden's or one of the other expensive beauty parlors. She has many other admirable qualities and characteristics, some of which I don't think it is safe to discuss through the United States mails. We are as happy as two bird dogs and I hasten to assure you that the resemblance does not end there.

Tempus fugit department—your sister Melinda will be nine years old on the fourteenth of August. That afternoon there will be ten miserably spoiled brats from surrounding homes, each of whom will be mollified with an uncommonly bad hamburger and a badly made birthday cake, and then whisked off to a second rate movie while her father goes back to sleep. This about covers the present situation and so we say farewell to the typewriter until another day. Love and Kisses, I'm glad you seem to be on the Road to Recovery.

Padre

[August 24, 1955]

Sunday noon.

A warm day in August, and for the first time in weeks I am going to the ball park with Nunnally Johnson. Melinda has just gotten over a cold and Kay is laid up with a bum leg and crutches, and oh, I could write you a lot of cheery news along those lines, but I imagine you have plenty of similar information that you could relate, so I will quit it and go on to something else.

Took Melinda to the studio last night and she saw *A Day at the Races* for the first time, and she laughed long and loud. It may have been just imagination, but she seemed to look at me with more respect than she formerly had. Up till then she had never seen me in a good picture, but just a few of the bad ones I had made in the twilight of my career, but I wouldn't be surprised if she now has me mentally in the same class as [Dean] Martin and [Jerry] Lewis and the other current comics.

I am taking her and Arthur and Irene to see the D'Oyly Carte Company open at the Biltmore tomorrow night in the *Mikado*, and the following week I'll take her to see *Pinafore*. She seems to like them, and I am only sorry that you can't be here to see them with us. . . .

I read today about the floods, tornadoes and other visitations of nature that seem to take particular delight in wreaking their vengeance all through the East, and it's so nice to live west of the Rockies, where men are men, and nothing seems to descend on us except a little smog and a few inches of delicate rain.

It's too bad you aren't well enough to occasionally journey to Kansas City and watch the Yankees lose the Pennant. This is just wishful thinking on my part, but I am hopeful that one of the other teams may squeeze through. But I don't trust those bastards—they have disappointed me too many times by coming through at the last moment.

This isn't much of a letter, but as you know this is being done at home and is purely a labor of love. I wouldn't do this for anyone else. They get the dictated letters; they may be better typed, but they aren't composed of blood, sweat and tears. This is.

Love and kisses, best to Gordon and write soon.

Padre

September 9, 1955

Dear Miriam and Gordon:

Received your letter and it's too damned hot to write. It's too damned hot for practically anything, but I don't want the hospital to sue you so am sending them the check you requested. Am also sending you $100—only because I'm crazed by the heat and don't know what I'm doing.

I think it would be a good idea if you did get a job—even if only a part-time one.

Getting back to the weather, I went to Vegas over the weekend to get away from the heat in Beverly Hills. It doesn't seem to make much sense to go to the desert to escape the heat, but it was 110 in Los Angeles and a mere 105 in Vegas.

I took Melinda with me and she saw three night-club shows. Last night I took her to see *It's Always Fair Weather*, a Comden and Green opus, with Dan Dailey, Michael Kidd and your old baseball chum, Gene Kelly . . . Also Cyd Charisse. It's a real hep picture and when it comes to Kansas I suggest you see it.

Eden's sister has arrived from Denmark with her one-year-old child, out of Howard Hawks, Sr. Before they left Denmark, the Danish nurse (who must have been a fine piece of pastry) dropped the kid and it arrived here with a black eye. It looks a midget that had slugged it out in a waterfront saloon. He is a cute kid, and Dee, who was quite a playgirl in her time, has turned into quite a mother. Melinda is delighted with the whole setup. She helps take care of the baby and is having a hell of a time rushing around with wet diapers and dirty milk bottles.

I am doing a show October eighth—a "Cavalcade of Show Business," based on the Joe Laurie–Abel Green book. As usual I will be lousy. I don't know why I keep accepting these jobs. The government takes most of the money and I never come off too well. I'm beginning to suspect I'm just a bigger ham than I thought I was.

Because of my age, the heat and the time element, I can't write anymore. Love and kisses—and best to Gordon.

                  Padre

October 3, 1955

Dear Mir,
I am sending you a check for $600 instead of $500. This should cover your requirements until you arrive—assuming that you do. The way you drive, I wouldn't bet on it.

We had dinner at Hillcrest last night and I had forgotten to order a cake. They rarely taste any good, but everyone seems to think there should be one. However, I thought I solved the problem rather neatly. I stuck a knife in a glass of water, put a piece of pumpernickel on top of the glass, and then stuck a lighted match into the pumpernickel. Everyone seemed very happy with this substitute. They all sang "Happy Birthday" off key—and I saved six dollars. If pumpernickel holds out in America, I predict that, in time, the orthodox birthday cake will become a thing of the past.

I won't write any more. This is a hard week for me. First I watched Brooklyn lose the game in the first three minutes due to Alston's stupidity in keeping Spooner in when it was obvious to everyone but him that the only thing Spooner had on the ball was his two hands. Well, at least I learned how to shave the Gillette way. Then I went over the script that I am doing next Sunday and a cold chill went down my spine.

Love and kisses. My best to Gordon.

                                        Padre

Gordon and I lived in Connecticut until 1959, when we broke up. The letters my father wrote during that time are, unfortunately, lost. I then moved back to California, where I remained, which is why my father's correspondence more or less stopped.

May 26, 1967

Dear Miriam:
Happy Birthday!!! Sorry that I missed it but you must realize that I have a case of galloping senility and can barely remember my name.

If you have another one, let me know in advance.

                                        Love,
                                        Your Father

From 1967 to 1977 I was in and out of various hospitals and clinics being treated for alcoholism. I got sober in June of 1977; I was fifty years old. My father died on August 19, 1977 at the age of eighty-six.